Zombifying a Nation

Contributions to Zombie Studies

White Zombie: Anatomy of a Horror Film. Gary D. Rhodes. 2001

The Zombie Movie Encyclopedia. Peter Dendle. 2001

American Zombie Gothic: The Rise and Fall (and Rise) of the Walking Dead in Popular Culture. Kyle William Bishop. 2010

Back from the Dead: Remakes of the Romero Zombie Films as Markers of Their Times. Kevin J. Wetmore, Jr. 2011

Generation Zombie: Essays on the Living Dead in Modern Culture. Edited by Stephanie Boluk and Wylie Lenz. 2011

Race, Oppression and the Zombie: Essays on Cross-Cultural Appropriations of the Caribbean Tradition. Edited by Christopher M. Moreman and Cory James Rushton. 2011

Zombies Are Us: Essays on the Humanity of the Walking Dead. Edited by Christopher M. Moreman and Cory James Rushton. 2011

The Zombie Movie Encyclopedia, Volume 2: 2000–2010. Peter Dendle. 2012

Great Zombies in History. Edited by Joe Sergi. 2013 (graphic novel)

Unraveling Resident Evil: *Essays on the Complex Universe of the Games and Films.* Edited by Nadine Farghaly. 2014

"We're All Infected": Essays on AMC's The Walking Dead *and the Fate of the Human.* Edited by Dawn Keetley. 2014

Zombies and Sexuality: Essays on Desire and the Walking Dead. Edited by Shaka McGlotten and Steve Jones. 2014

…But If a Zombie Apocalypse Did *Occur: Essays on Medical, Military, Governmental, Ethical, Economic and Other Implications.* Edited by Amy L. Thompson and Antonio S. Thompson. 2015

How Zombies Conquered Popular Culture: The Multifarious Walking Dead in the 21st Century. Kyle William Bishop. 2015

Zombifying a Nation: Race, Gender and the Haitian Loas *on Screen.* Toni Pressley-Sanon. 2016

Zombifying a Nation
Race, Gender and the Haitian *Loas* on Screen

Toni Pressley-Sanon

Contributions to Zombie Studies

McFarland & Company, Inc., Publishers
Jefferson, North Carolina

LIBRARY OF CONGRESS CATALOGUING-IN-PUBLICATION DATA

Names: Pressley-Sanon, Toni, author.
Title: Zombifying a nation : race, gender and the Haitian loas on screen / Toni Pressley-Sanon.
Description: Jefferson, North Carolina : McFarland & Company, Inc., Publishers, 2016. | Series: Contributions to zombie studies | Includes bibliographical references and index.
Identifiers: LCCN 2016025524 | ISBN 9780786494248 (softcover : acid free paper) ∞
Subjects: LCSH: Zombie films—History and criticism. | Haiti—In motion pictures. | Race in motion pictures. | Imperialism in motion pictures.
Classification: LCC PN1995.9.Z63 P74 2016 | DDC 791.43/675—dc23
LC record available at https://lccn.loc.gov/2016025524

BRITISH LIBRARY CATALOGUING DATA ARE AVAILABLE

ISBN (print) 978-0-7864-9424-8
ISBN (ebook) 978-1-4766-2584-3

© 2016 Antoinette Pressley-Sanon. All rights reserved

No part of this book may be reproduced or transmitted in any form or by any means, electronic or mechanical, including photocopying or recording, or by any information storage and retrieval system, without permission in writing from the publisher.

Front cover image © 2016 iStock

Printed in the United States of America

McFarland & Company, Inc., Publishers
Box 611, Jefferson, North Carolina 28640
www.mcfarlandpub.com

For Louko, who made his film debut in *Zombi candidat*.
Rest in peace, *frè mwen*.

It's never *just* a movie.
—Chris Rock, *Top Five*

Table of Contents

A Note on Spelling   1
Preface: Zombis/Zombies and Me   3
Introduction: Of History, Neocolonialism, Vodou/Voodoo and the Zombi/Zombie   7
One. *White Zombie* and *I Walked with a Zombie*: The Haitian Revolution and White Southern Fears   25
Two. *The Love Wanga*: The American Occupation and Miscegenation   64
Three. *Heading South* and Zombification or "Haiti is open for business"   89
Four. *The Serpent and the Rainbow* and the 1986 Revolution   119
Five. *Zombi candidat à la présidence ... ou les amours d'un zombi* and the Resurgence of *La politique de doublure*   141

Conclusion: Tasting Salt   162
Chapter Notes   167
Works Cited   179
Index   187

A Note on Spelling

The reader will note that the term for the syncretic spiritual tradition of Haiti is spelled "Vodou." This is the spelling that has been promulgated by KOSANBA, the Association for the Academic Study of Vodou headquartered at the University of California Santa Barbara and which has been accepted by the Library of Congress.

Throughout the text I distinguish "Vodou" from "voodoo," the term that one finds most frequently associated with the spiritual tradition in popular literature and film, newspapers, and unfortunately, scholarly writings. As the editors of *Race, Oppression and the Zombie* (2011) note, however, "voodoo" "has come to encompass every ignorance of the true religion."[1] It invokes the tradition that is often misunderstood at best and vilified at worst, summoning racist images of "a devil-worshipping, black-magic wielding, and uncivilized tradition imagined by Western popular culture."[2]

Thus, when I use the term "Vodou," I refer to the spiritual tradition of Haiti proper. When I use the term "voodoo" I refer to outsiders' misreading of it, both in film and in literature. When I quote others', including scholars', words or titles of texts, I retain the spelling of the word as they use it.

Throughout the text I use the French spelling for the Vodou spirits called *loas* as well as their proper names, rather than the spellings that are used in Haitian Kreyòl, the language of the Haitian majority.

I also use two spellings of the term that, in the American tradition, is written as "zombie." When I am discussing films that emerge from the American film tradition (aka Hollywood), I use that spelling. However, when I discuss the films that come out of the French tradition, *Heading South* by Laurent Cantet and the Haitian tradition, *Zombi candidat à la présidence* by Arnold Antonin, I use the French spelling of the term,

1

A Note on Spelling

"zombi." Although Jacques Tourneur, director of *I Walked with a Zombie*, was French, he produced the film for a North American audience and deployed many of the same stereotypical images around black culture that the directors of *White Zombie*, *The Love Wanga* and *The Serpent and the Rainbow* deployed. Thus, I use the spelling "zombie" for his film as well. In the introduction and conclusion of the text I use both spellings as they provide an overview and address both iterations of the figure.

Preface: Zombis/Zombies and Me

Dolly back to 1991 when, with a suitcase of clothing and a box of novels, I went to live in Haiti for two years. President Jean-Bertrand Aristide had just been elected and there was a profound sense of hope about the country. One late afternoon while taking a break from getting lost while trying to make my way around Port-au-Prince I sat in a small restaurant on the main thoroughfare of Grand Rue. A young man, tall and lanky, walked in and struck up a conversation. After about an hour of pleasant exchange he asked me if I believed in zombis. I cannot recall my answer, but whatever it was, within a half hour I found myself following him down a pretty deserted road heading toward a nearby cemetery in search of one. It suddenly occurred to me that it was getting dark, I had no idea how to get home, and the zombi that he wanted to show me could very well be me. I politely excused myself and found my way to a nearby corner to catch a taptap.

Flash forward to 2006–2008 when I was writing my dissertation on manifestations of memory of the transatlantic slave trade and slavery for my Ph.D. In what I thought the unlikeliest of places, the zombi resurfaced (I discuss the phenomenon extensively in a forthcoming book project). This material manifestation of memory in the figure of the zombi in West Africa and the Caribbean prompted me to seek out other representations of it in an American context. The zombie films from the early days of American cinema I subsequently sought out were not only edifying, they were fun. One thing led to another until my (mostly) pleasurable research turned into the book that you hold in your hands.

My work is much indebted to Peter Dendle's essay, "The Zombie as Barometer of Cultural Anxiety," Kevin Boon's article, "Ontological Anxiety Made Flesh: The Zombie in Literature, Film and Culture," Tony Williams'

Preface

"White Zombie Haitian Horror," Kyle Bishop's article "The Sub-Subaltern Monster: Imperialist Hegemony and the Cinematic Voodoo Zombie," and several articles within Christopher Moreman and Cory James Rushton's edited volume, *Race, Oppression and the Zombie: Essays on Cross-Cultural Appropriations of the Caribbean Tradition*, which helped me to understand that I was on to something in wanting to read the treatment of race, gender, and sexuality in what are considered more traditional zombie films. Stephanie Boluk and Wylie Lenz's excellent edited volume, *Generation Zombie: Essays on the Living Dead in Modern Culture* (2011), and in particular two essays, one by Chris Vials and the other by Gyllian Phillips, have been critical to my conceptualization of the zombi/zombie. Seeing how these scholars have pushed the reading of the zombie as a tool in the imperialist project also helped me to push my own readings of the figure further to consider the role of international tourism in the disfranchisement or, as it read it, attempted zombification of the Haitian poor. Bishop is correct in stating in his preface of *American Zombie Gothic* that his "book and its predecessors demonstrate that the zombie phenomenon has yet to be plumbed to its depths in academic and literary markets." The present work is further evidence of the richness of themes that zombi/zombie films tackle.

Like many of the other texts on the subject, I begin my analysis with the classics, *White Zombie* and *I Walked with a Zombie*. However, my study digresses in its exploration of a less-discussed film from the early twentieth century: *The Love Wanga*. I also discuss a film from the late twentieth century, *The Serpent and the Rainbow*, which, although not a B-movie, recalls the zombie films of the 1930s and 1940s. I have never been much for gore, which accounts, at least in part, for my digression from other volumes that continue with the zombie's trajectory to its contemporary recognizable incarnation as the flesh-eating monster that got off the ground with George Romero's *Dead* series. My drive to keep the zombi/zombie in the Caribbean in general and Haiti in particular took care of that problem. But my focus is also an outgrowth of my area of scholarly interest, which is West African, Caribbean, and African American cultural production. As such, I am always looking for ways that the "empire talks back" and the subaltern speaks in ways that we can hear. Fortunately for me, in 2009, *Zombi candidat à la présidence … ou les amours d'un zombi*, by Haitian filmmaker Arnold Antonin, was released. Antonin not only returned the zombi to Haiti, but he actually gave him a memory and voice with which to express his disfranchised and degraded state. Finally, as a scholar, part of my job is to advance understandings of whatever topic I add my voice to. My text, then, not only reads the traditional zombi/zombie as part of the Haitian cultural tradition along with its uses by Hollywood, but it also re-excavates understandings of the zombi/zombie as a being whose labor is consumed by its master. Thus, another way that my reading of the zombi/zombie figure digresses from previous readings is in my relating the phenomenon to female sex tourism and Northern white women's consumption of the Caribbean black male's sexual labor to zombification.

Since I argue that the phenomenon offers a lens into the unequal relationship between the Global North and the Global South, unlike Bishop and perhaps other scholars who wish to see a continuation of the zombi/zombie figure, it is my hope that the sociopolitical and economic conditions that give birth to the zombi/zombie over and over again will come to an end. At that point it is my hope that we will all have tasted the salt that would free our collective consciousness and, like the zombi/zombie, be released from our own liminal states.

Introduction: Of History, Neocolonialism, Vodou/Voodoo and the Zombi/Zombie

The anthropologist Sidney Mintz highlighted the inextricable relationship between Haiti's sociopolitical history and its indigenous belief system called Vodou when he wrote in the introduction to Alfred Métraux's English translation of *Le Vaudou haïtien* (Voodoo in Haiti) (1972) that "*vaudou* ... played a critical role in the creation of viable armed resistance by the slaves against the master classes—and against the armies of other powers besides France that were interested in resubjugating the once immensely profitable colony."[1] Furthermore, the ethnographer and medical doctor, Jean Price-Mars'[2] writing that, "*1804 est issu du Vodou*" also reflects the impossibility of disentangling Vodou from the country's sociopolitical history.[3] Finally, the spiritual underpinnings of Haiti's history and destiny are also made clear in Vodou scholar and *asogwe*[4] Patrick Bellegarde-Smith's assertion that "The engagement of Vodou in Haitian temporal affairs and history has been constant. The many revolts of the enslaved were efforts toward freedom and liberation writ large, from within an ethos that, at the outset had incorporated similar elements from diverse African ethnicities."[5]

In the years following its revolution Haiti was made to pay dearly for having the audacity of spirit to declare itself free while all of the nations around her remained gripped by slavery. The American president Thomas Jefferson referred to Haiti as a pestilence, and several U.S. publications depicted the nation as a spectacle of barbarism. The island quickly became associated with the most base behavior as reports of insurgents impaling white babies on pikes were circulated. Later, Spencer St. John's *Hayti: Or,*

Introduction

The Black Republic, published in 1889, which depicted child sacrifices and cannibalization, was taken as fact. The practices that he attributed to the subjects of his text have endured in the foreign imagination.

By 1915 Haiti was invaded, not by France as Haiti's second leader, King Henri Christophe, had feared, but by the United States in the form of Marines who saw it as their Christian duty to save Haiti from itself. With the invasion, the idea that Haitians were children in need of fatherly guidance was promoted. As historian Mary Renda notes, "Paternalist discourse was one of the primary cultural mechanisms by which the occupation conscripted men into the project of carrying out U.S. rule."[6] Sociologist Laënnec Hurbon surmises that the U.S. became interested in dominating Haiti politically and militarily with a long-held ideology toward Vodou that interpreted it as evidence of barbarism from which the people of Haiti "must be delivered."[7] The Marines remained in place for 19 years, thus marking the longest uninterrupted occupation during the period of the U.S occupation of numerous Caribbean and Latin American nations.[8] They brought in their wake an amended constitution that allowed foreigners to own land and the reintroduction of monocrops and plantation labor, which the poor—many of whom were disfranchised as a result—recognized as a new form of slavery. Where during the period of slavery the monocrop was sugarcane, in this new world of foreign-owned business, it was bananas and later, rubber.[9]

The American Marine occupation and the opening up of the country to American monocrop business also made way for an influx of American tourists, anthropologists, artists, and journalists who found inspiration in what many of them viewed as a primitive land inhabited by primitive people. One of the more notable visitors to the island nation during those years was the journalist William Seabrook.

Where from the time of the revolution, in the foreign imagination, Haiti and Vodou were associated with cannibalism and human and animal sacrifice that were depicted in works such as St. John's, the publication of Seabrook's *The Magic Island* in 1929 shifted the focus to zombies. Anthropologist Franck Degoul calls Seabrook's text "quasi-anthropological literature,"[10] suggesting that the way that it was presented made it seem like a credible work of scholarship. The fact that Seabrook had spent a year living with a Vodou priestess added to his credibility as a source for the "truth" about Haiti. However, Charles Najman argues that Seabrook's text was a fantasy that stimulated and reinforced the old prejudices of slavery: "black, despotic and cannibalistic." As the myth of the living-dead grew, it took on the function of justifying the "civilizing mission" of the United States in Haiti. Indeed, as Najman postulates, with the publication of *The Magic Island* "the living dead became, sadly, celebrated across the United States and Europe."[11] Degoul correctly concludes in "We are the mirror of your fears" that, as a result of such writings about Haiti, in the foreign mind, the following link was made: "Haiti: it is Vaudou; Vaudou: witchcraft; and witchcraft ... zombification."[12]

The goal of this text is four-fold. It explores how three films, *White Zombie*, *I Walked with a Zombie*, and *The Serpent and the Rainbow* that emerged from the foreign white male imagination acted as cathartic expressions or mirrors of their fear of a black nation ruled by black people in the context of Haiti's two revolutionary moments and their aftermaths (1804 and 1986). Secondly, it discusses *The Love Wanga* as a working through of the United States' "Negro problem" during the Jim Crow Era, which corresponded with and continued beyond the Marine occupation. Thirdly, through a close reading of a film about 1970s Haiti, *Heading South*, I extend my understanding of, or rather, reconnect the figure of the zombi/zombie to the history of slavery. To that end I explore what I read as a late twentieth century representation of the zombi/zombie in the context of Duvalierism and the opening up of the country to sex tourism. Finally, to unpack *Zombi candidat à la présidence ... ou les amours d'un zombi*,[13] a contemporary film written by a Haitian writer and directed by a Haitian filmmaker, I engage with Degoul's theorization that zombification has been re-appropriated by the Haitian people to serve as a form of empowerment as the Haitian poor continue to be a source of disfranchised and exploited labor. I also read the film as an exploration of *la politique de doublure*, a practice that dates back to the nineteenth century and that has been revived in the twenty-first century.

All of the films that I discuss comment on critical moments in Haitian history. As such, I contextualize the films in relation to five pivotal moments: The Haitian Revolutionary War from 1791 to 1804, the first American Occupation from 1915 to 1934, the introduction of widespread international tourism in the early 1970s, the exile of Jean-Claude "Baby Doc" Duvalier in 1986, and the current crisis of a U.S.-led multinational military occupation that began in the early 1990s.

Introduction

I posit that the filmmakers that I discuss here also draw, whether deliberately or accidentally, on Vodou spirits or *loas* to get their messages around taboos, fears, and aspirations across to their audiences. Thus, in my reading, the *loas* "work" as much as the worldly characters who are portrayed in the films, performing ideological labor. Therefore, following an overview of several of the *loas* that I identify in the different films from within the spiritual tradition, I discuss how they are read and represented through the filmmakers' divergent lenses.

My discussion is situated within the genre known as zombie studies, and largely, limits itself to films that would be traditionally recognized as belonging to the zombi/zombie film genre. However, as part of my larger project of exploring the figure of the Haitian poor as disfranchised and silenced—a principle feature of the zombi/zombie—I include the film, *Heading South*, by French filmmaker, Laurent Cantet, that would not be immediately recognizable as a "zombi/zombie" film in my study. As I argue, not only does the naming of the film's protagonist, Legba, mark it as one that invokes Vodou as a source of inspiration, but also, the depiction of Legba as well as the other Haitian men in relation to the foreign white women visiting Haiti as sex tourists, comments on internal as well as external attempts to zombify the Haitian poor sociopolitically and economically.[14] My reading of the films references and draws on the work of scholars who have written about zombification in terms of the history of slavery and the exploitation of the enslaved person's body until physical death releases him or her from his or her tortured state.

Zombi/Zombie Origins

Najman avers that Seabrook represents Haiti as a country that "breathes the spirit of the old, faraway Africa with its myths, terrors, superstitions and its terrified adoration of the forces of nature."[15] In fact, the term "zombi/zombie" which refers to a person who is believed to have died and been brought back to life without speech or free will, can be etymologically traced to Africa as Hans Ackerman and Jeanine Gauthier explain in "The Ways and Nature of the Zombi."[16] For example the word, *fúmbi*, meaning spirit, has been recorded in Cuba, but according to the authors, probably originated from the Yorùbá or Congo, the two principal

Of History, Neocolonialism, Vodou/Voodoo and the Zombi/Zombie

African languages spoken in Cuba. *Mvumbi* (cataleptic individual or invisible part of man), *nsumbi* (devil), *nvumbi* (body without a soul), *nzambi* (spirit of a dead person), and *zumbi* (fetish), all originate from the Congo region, while *zan bibi* or *zan bii*, meaning night bogey, is from the Ghana, Togo, Bénin area.[17] As literary scholar Doris Garraway espouses in her book, *The Libertine Colony: Creolization in the Early French Caribbean* (2005), "The idea that through sorcery souls may be captured and humans reduced to slavery exists throughout West and Central Africa, the latter notion occurring frequently in the context of real or imagined labor exploitation suggestive of European influence, slavery, or colonialism."[18] Moreover, several scholars of Vodou have proposed that zombification is punishment for social misbehavior meted out by the Haitian *Bizango* secret society.[19]

The consumption of one's life force constitutes zombification. That is, the victim is made into a "living-dead." Zombis/zombies can be either, *zombi cadavre*, corpses that a *bokor* (sorcerer) has extracted from their tombs and raised to be made to work or they may be spirits without a body, *zombi astral*. I limit my discussion to *zombis cadavres* as they are the ones that are represented in the films I discuss. Such zombis/zombies are not quite alive as the spark of life that sorcerers wake in the corpse does not wholly give the dead person back his or her place in the land of living. Rather, he or she remains in the misty zone that divides life from death, in a liminal zone. Zombis/zombies eat, move, hear what is said to them, and even sometimes, speak. However, they are socially dead because they are simply beasts of burden that their master exploits without mercy, making them work on plantations, weighing them down with labor, whipping them freely and feeding them meager tasteless food.[20] Their master consumes their labor until physical death releases them from their liminal state.

Zora Neale Hurston recounts her own investigation into the zombi/zombie in Haiti in her work, *Tell My Horse* (1937). In her reading, zombis/zombies are "aware of everything happening but do not have available the means to act."[21] A true living dead, they have listless eyes, a stiff walk and a nasal voice, all of which mark them as being of the "other world."[22] While many scholars claim that zombis/zombies have no memory of their pasts, according to Hurbon, based on the stories of zombification that he collected and recounts in his text, *Le Barbare imaginaire* (1988) "*les zombis recontent tout ce qu'ils avaient vécu. Car ils n'étaient pas morts pour de vrai*" (zombis remember everything they've lived through because they are not really dead).[23] In *Zombi candidat*, Antonin depicts just such a zombi who remembers his life before his zombification.

Several scholars have written about zombification as a reflection of and comment on the history of colonization and enslavement. For example, in "Necropolitics" (2003) philosopher and political scientist, Achille Mbembe, discusses slavery as zombification, although he does not use the term. As he says, "First, in the context of the plantation, the humanity of the slave appears to be the perfect figure of a shadow. Indeed, the slave condition results from a triple loss: loss of home, loss of rights over his or her body, and loss of political status. This triple loss is identical with absolute domination, natal alienation, and social death (expulsion from humanity altogether)."[24] He concludes that, "slave life, in many ways, is a form of life-in-death."[25] The enslaved person, with his or her existence appearing as a "perfect figure of a shadow," is like a "thing" possessed by another person.[26] Similarly, anthropologist Karen McCarthy Brown has claimed that in Haiti, the zombi is a memory of the loss of control over the self suffered during slavery.[27] Furthermore, as Joan Dayan remarks, "Born out of the experience of slavery, the sea passage from Africa to the New World, and the revolution on the soil of Saint-Domingue, the zombi is the story of colonization."[28]

The zombi's/zombie's physical consumption signifies its spiritual consumption. Indeed, the idea of consumption, or the self being taken over (eaten, consumed) by the other in the Caribbean, has its origins in the colonial experience when the Spanish first arrived on the island that they named Hispaniola. After consuming the indigenous population's labor to the point of near-extinction, they began importing African people to also consume their labor until the point of death. According to Michel-René Hilliard d'Auberteuil, a French observer, the working life of an average plantation worker who was born on the colony was little more than fifteen years.[29]

Echoing writers and scholars who discuss Haiti's lack of sociopolitical and economic development, René Depestre, the ethnologist and writer, has argued that, "It is not by chance that there exists in Haiti the myth of the zombi that is, of the living dead, the man whose mind and soul have been stolen and who has been left only with the ability to work.... The history of colonization is the process of man's zombification."[30] While Depestre views the zombi as a Haitian myth, he sees it as a way to understand slavery and colonialism via-à-vis a Marxist paradigm.

The Zombi's/Zombie's Legacy

Depestre's comment speaks to both the physical state of enslavement as well as the psychic and spiritual hold that slavery and colonialism continues to have on Haiti. Like Métraux, Mbembe, Depestre, and McCarthy Brown see a zombi's/zombie's life in terms that echo the harsh existence of an enslaved person in Saint-Domingue. As such, turning someone into a zombi/zombie is the worst thing that someone can do to someone else. Robbing the victim of free will and severing his or her kinship ties is perceived as a reinstatement of slavery.[31]

The interpretation of exploited labor as a form of zombification is not a thing of the past. The trope of the living dead as mindless, soulless workers persists contemporarily as Haiti continues on a path of political, economic, and ecological impoverishment and violence perpetuated both from within and from outside the country. This can be seen, for example, in its being under the shadow of a multinational military force (MINUSTAH)[32] while first, President René Préval and then Michel Martelly, pitched the slogan, "Haiti is open for business," to the international community, selling the country as the perfect environment for cheap factory labor and beach resort vacations.[33]

This twenty-first century military occupation and the concomitant initiative to sell the country to an international audience echo the various forms of institutional oppression that the Haitian majority has suffered throughout their colonial and postcolonial history as well as contemporarily under neocolonialism. As literary scholar Kaiama L. Glover avers "The creature's victimhood, mutism, social disenfranchisement, and infinite capacity for suffering, make it a fitting metaphor for the postcolonial Haitian in particular and the alienated individual in general."[34]

Processes of Zombification and Respite

Several scholars have offered explanations of how a zombi/zombie is made. According to Hurbon, a powder placed in the path of an intended victim kills him or her. After the victim is buried a *bokor* or sorcerer raises him or her from the grave and then, through a series of rituals, which include calling the victim's name three times, forcing him or her to walk before him, and whipping him or her, turns the person into a zombi/zombie. For Hurbon, the zombified person is not alive nor dead, but has been brainwashed or is in a sleep-state.[35] In *Passage of Darkness* Wade Davis echoes Hurbon in his theorization of the use of a poison powder, but suggests that the powder is fed to the intended victim. According to Hurston, zombification also involves a ritual in which[36]

> The victim is surrounded by the Bocor's associates and the march to the hounfort (Voodoo temples and its surrounding) begins. He is hustled along in the middle of the crowd. Thus he is screened from prying eyes to a great degree and in his half-waking state he is unable to reorient himself. But the victim is not carried directly to the hounfort. First, he is carried past the house where he lived. This is always done. Must be. If the victim were not taken past his former house, later on he would recognize it and return. But once he is taken past, it is gone from his consciousness forever. It is as if it never existed for him. He is then taken to the hounfort and given a drop of liquid, the formula for which is most secret. After that the victim is a Zombie. He will work ferociously and tirelessly without consciousness of his surroundings and conditions and without memory of his former state.[37]

The one thing that the three descriptions about the process of zombification have in common is that the victim is released from his or her torture in death.

Consumption Reciprocated

The physical and spiritual consumption of the black body as signified by zombification is not unidirectional. While the mostly white male colonists feminized and consumed the indigenous population and then continued with their consumption of the African body as well as the land, both in Africa and in the New World, they too were consumed by the corruptive system of enslavement and exploitation on which the West fed. My reading of the films foregrounds the motif of ingestion or consumption that began with colonialism and extends it into the contemporary moment (late twentieth century). But, as I argue for all of these earlier films, the "island natives" are not the only ones who are consumed. Rather, the Westerners, in their contact with the Caribbean, are also consumed or rather, possessed by it. I also argue that whites' possession of and by the island continues in female sex tourism as a new form of colonialism and zombification of not just the "nouveau slaves," but also the "nouveau mistresses."[38]

Of History, Neocolonialism, Vodou/Voodoo and the Zombi/Zombie

The Politics of Disavowal

The 1915 occupation carried out on behalf of American businessmen vis-à-vis military intervention enlisted the media as part and parcel of the military operation. As Renda argues, the American propaganda machine was paramount to its success. As such, almost as soon as the operation began, reports and books emerged from the military personnel stationed there. For example, there was Brigade Commander John H. Russell's nephew, J. Dryden Kuser, who published his travelogue, *Haiti: Its Dawn of Progress After Years in a Night of Revolution* (1921) in defense of the occupation. Seabrook's book was followed in quick succession by a number of writers who titillated the American imagination with tales of Haiti, many of which included stories of zombies. For example, John Houston Craige's *Black Bagdad* (1933), which is tellingly subtitled "The Arabian Nights of Adventures of a Marine Captain in Haiti" was published in 1934. Lieutenant Faustin Wirkus, a Marine, wrote of being crowned king on one of the small islands off the coast of Haiti, La Gonâve.[39] According to Chris Vials, *The Magic Island* is based on reports from Lieutenant Wirkus, which Seabrook relates as if he witnessed the events first-hand.[40]

As Vials argues, the zombie and the accounts that featured them "played a central role in creating imperial discourses of the Caribbean."[41] Also, "much like imperialism itself, which ingests another country without allowing it to become a valid part of national culture, exoticism injected Haiti into American culture while maintaining its foreignness and presumed inferiority."[42] Vials' use of the word "ingests" here is particularly relevant for my purposes as it speaks to the work of consumption that is also closely linked to Othering and the politics of disavowal that began with the colonization of the Caribbean. It is precisely because the Caribbean in general and Haiti in particular, is Othered that the illusion of "absolute difference" and "inferiority" can be maintained. It is this disavowal of the inhabitants' humanity that facilitated and continues to facilitate the Global North's attempts to contain and consume them. As Lizabeth Paravisini-Gebert argues in "The Representation of Woman as Zombie" (1997), "the ideology of Haiti as the land of 'Voodoo' … has sustained American indifference to the fate of the island and its people" and has been critical to the work of disavowal and subsequent consumption.[43]

Introduction

This disavowal is even more meaningful when looked at historically. As the site of the first successful slave revolt, Haiti posed a threat to those who were still profiting from the colonial system. That threat had to be contained. Consequently, the international community sanctioned Haiti diplomatically and drew a cordon sanitaire around news of the revolution. The sociopolitical and economic threat that the revolutionary nation posed was transferred to the zombi/zombie, which, as Todd K. Platts argues, "engenders terror because of ingrained phobia of infectious contagion, loss of personal autonomy and death."[44] The fear that imperialist leaders harbored about their own loss of, not only their own autonomy, but also their power over others—in other words, their death as world powers—via their relationship with revolutionary blacks, was embodied in the zombi/zombie. According to Vials, Seabrook's book

> reveals the persistence of the fear of Haiti's revolutionary spirit as a contagion and a psychological need to contain the subversive potential of this memory by presenting Haiti as the site of the world's last and only docile slaves. In effect, the figure of the zombie functions symbolically to put Haitians back in chains, not as the singing, carefree objects of the paternalistic imagination, but as emasculated objects of pity.[45]

Thus, the U.S. government with the support of its military arm, found a way to control the contagion that Haiti represented. Hollywood was also enlisted in the project of control and containment through its portrayal of Haiti as the source and home of the zombi/zombie.

U.S. Expansionism and the Trope of the Zombie

Michael Richardson rightly insists on contextualizing the "birth" of the zombie as a popular phenomenon in the American imagination as part and parcel of the U.S. Marines' 1915 invasion and subsequent occupation of the country. Hollywood's representations of the zombie emerged against a backdrop of, not just the American occupation of Haiti, but also its other imperialist aggressions that began just before the turn of the century.[46] These military aggressions were all carried out as part of a larger U.S. project that was predicated on the docile native allowing himself or herself to be invaded and consumed by American businessmen and tourists.

However, when the Marines arrived in Haiti they did not find what they expected. Rather than deference and fear that dominated white interactions with subordinated blacks in the southern United States from which many of the Marines were drawn, the enlistees encountered a people who did not have the same understanding of race, color, or class and who were proud of their revolutionary history. As Richardson remarks, "The experience of serving in Haiti appears to have represented for many of the marines a genuine encounter with otherness, an encounter with which they were psychologically entirely unprepared, and which affected them in unpredictable ways. In particular, coming in contact with an environment in which black people were masters did not fit in their view of the world."[47] Their solution was to change reality by depicting the exact opposite of what they found. For them the country's inhabitants were their wards, recalcitrant children in need of paternalistic guidance. As historian Hans Schmidt observes, the United States saw itself as the self-appointed trustee of civilization in the Caribbean. It was thus obliged to safeguard its definition of standards of decency and morality.[48] The enforcement of those standards that were steeped in paternalistic racism meant that gross human rights violations, sexual violence, and impropriety as well as armed resistance to their presence, most notably from the peasant population, marked the Marines' tenure.[49]

The zombie, the epitome of the docile native with no control over his or her own person, went a long way towards upholding the image of the white "savior" civilizing the "natives." The alternative was for the white person to be corrupted by the barbarous "natives," which we also see depicted in the earliest films about the zombie. Both of these depictions held cultural and political currency well beyond Haiti's borders.

The battle to contain Haiti continues to be waged on the ground contemporarily. Not only is the battle still being waged militarily, in for example, Haiti being occupied since 2004 by a UN military force, but also in Haiti's former President Martelly, advocating for turning the country into a haven for foreign-owned textile companies as well as a major tourist destination. Again, this text explores how these battles over black bodies were waged onscreen in several films from the mid- to late twentieth century. It also argues for a claiming of the narrative voice by filmmakers who see Haiti through the lenses of memory; the very faculty a zombi/zombie is supposed to lack, allowing him or her to speak for him or herself. Unlike the unsexed automatons that Vials argues populated the B-horror movies, the oversexed mulatto woman in *The Love Wanga*, the monstrous *bokor* in

The Serpent and the Rainbow, or the voiceless beach boys of *Heading South,* Haitian filmmaker, Arnold Antonin's 2009 zombi of *Zombi candidat* grants news interviews and talks of remembering orgasms with the woman that he remembers and still loves.

Filmic Trajectories and the Monstrous Haitian

Houngan (Vodou priest) and biochemist Max Beauvoir[50] has commented on how Hollywood has been conscripted to Other Haiti and Haitian people throughout history when, during an interview, he stated, "In fact, the United States developed an organization called Hollywood that started to make movies—large quantities—and those movies were largely against Haitians and Vodou."[51] Echoing Beauvoir, but in a larger context, Gwenda Young writes that, "racism was endemic to the Hollywood system."[52] As the ultimate representation of blackness, Haiti was particularly targeted and Hollywood found the perfect foil in Vodou, a religion that was saturated with Africanisms and rebellion. As a way of robbing it of its power in the American imagination it became inextricably linked with zombies, which were in turn appropriated and ingested by the American public.

Monstrosities

Indeed, the zombie is now a filmic icon in Western culture. Though it has transformed over the years, attributable largely to filmmaker George Romero's reconceptualization, it remains at its base, an example of the monstrous that works as a barometer of cultural anxiety.[53] Both Kevin Alexander Boon and Peter Dendle consider the meaning of the term, "monstrous," from a cultural standpoint and delineate the way that the figure has been deployed over time. Boon begins by considering the etymological origins of the term "monster," which sets a boundary space between human and non-human, being and non-being, presence and absence. He argues:

> That which is defined as monstrous (and the definition of monstrous is an exclusively human enterprise) was not supposed to happen; that is, it is unnatural and as such a malformation of some universal design. Furthermore, that which is defined as "monstrous" threatens the purity of the human form as that form is intended by whomever

is responsible for that universal design. To articulate the bias another way—human beings are, by divine mandate, supreme in the universe and anything that threatens human form or status is monstrous.[54]

In a historical context the very nation of Haiti is monstrous, something that "was not supposed to happen." The revolution that gave rise to the nation, waged by enslaved workers in the French colony of Saint-Domingue was an "unthinkable history," in the words of anthropologist Michel-Rolph Trouillot. It was not supposed to be successful. The monstrous Haiti was punished shortly thereafter when the international community imposed diplomatic sanctions on the fledgling nation until 1825, twenty years after independence, when then-president Jean Pierre Boyer agreed to pay France the huge sum of 150 million francs in indemnity.[55] The U.S. would not recognize Haiti until much later, in 1862.

Though in a Haitian cultural context, the zombi is not someone to be feared, but rather, pitied because of his loss of control over his mind, his labor, his soul, and his fate, he is a monster in Boon's sense of the word as a "malformation" which "threatens the human form" as a thinking, feeling, souled being who has (at least the illusion of) control over his labor. Once someone dies, he or she is supposed to be able to "rest in peace"; a repose that is denied the zombi who is made to work in a state that hovers between life and death.

Taken in its most basic sense, this idea of the monstrous is dependent upon some defined normative standard against which the monstrous can be measured. Because in a white male heterosexual society, it is he who stands as the standard against which all else is compared, then anyone who deviates from him—a woman, black, homosexual, person with disabilities, the elderly and so on—is potentially monstrous.[56] Therefore, by very definition, women, mulattoes, and blacks, both American and foreign, are monstrous creatures. Thus, looked at racially, the black body is monstrous, an aberration that is a malformation of the pure, white body.[57]

The understanding of the black body as monstrous in its opposition to the white body can be seen in eighteenth and nineteenth century depictions of the Caribbean in travel writing. For example, in an excerpt that sociologist Mimi Sheller includes in *Consuming the Caribbean* (2003), a British tourist writes of black women whom he saw going to market: "Their faces are always repulsive, the thick lips and wide nostrils being fatal to European ideals of beauty...."[58] Such comparisons were useful to the work of disavowal that feminist scholar Sara Ahmed says allowed the white traveler to gauge his or her own whiteness and fix in place the difference between the "strange," and I would add, monstrous Others as the European moved through the tropics and viewed the objectified bodies of various exotics, making comparisons amongst different Others.

Gendered Monstrosities

Monstrosity was also gendered, with the female body being seen as monstrous and threatening to the male. Not only is the female seen as a deviation from the male, but she is seen as deviant. Her very sex is seen as monstrous and a potential contaminant. As Barbara Creed has argued in *The Monstrous Feminine* (1993), *Dracula*, starring Bela Lugosi (also in *White Zombie*) is a meditation on the threat that the vagina holds for the unsuspecting man who gets caught in her lustful web. The black male and the white female must be tamed, therefore, lest they threaten the survival of the "universal design" that is embodied in the white male and his survival through his own conceived embodiment of the nation, the white woman. Where Vials argues that in tale after tale from the 1930s and 1940s, "the environment rich with jungle drums and unbridled passions of the Other threaten to turn the white woman, the pinnacle of Western civilization, into a de-feminized automaton rendering her sterile and unable to reproduce either her race or her nation,"[59] I would argue that the real fear is that she will forsake the white man for the Caribbean man, thus producing another "monster," the mulatto. The mingling of the black and white body gives rise to this new monster as it presents the possibility of producing an offspring that is evidence of the "pure" mixing with the "impure." It also threatens the continuation of the white male heterosexual bloodline and with it, the hierarchies that have set him up as normative. Put simply, miscegenation left unchecked, would mean the extinction of whiteness and its privileges; a cause for great anxiety amongst those invested in it.

Black feminist scholar Michele Wallace notes that for Thomas Dixon, the author whose novel inspired *Birth of a Nation*, the fear was that mixed-race blacks who in his mind, "combined the immorality of the black race with the ingenuity of whiteness, could tip the balance in a negative fashion if not exterminated."[60] Both "Dixon and Griffith were afraid that racial impurity would lead to cultural degeneration and ultimately, white invisibility."[61] They were, of course, not the only ones who felt this way. In fact, the widely-held white fear of interracial mixing and the hope that evidence of it would not be produced is reflected in the word, "mulatto," the term for mixed-race people with etymological origins in Spanish and Portuguese for a mule; an animal produced by a sexual union between a horse and a donkey and unable to reproduce itself. The thought of these "repulsive," "wide nostrils," and "thick lips," or "bullet-headed, jet-black, with a nose like a squashed tomato"[62] as another European writer described his black servant—in other words, monstrous men and women—of the British tourist imagination mixing their blood with that of whites was the stuff of nightmares. Therefore, if, as Gyllian Phillips suggests, *White Zombie*'s Murder Legendre, the sorcerer, is racially ambiguous, then his potentially mixed heritage reflects that fear which is projected onto him as the source of his villainy.[63] Not only is he a threat because he owns both factory and government agents (in the form of the zombie gang), but he also presents an even more primal source of horror related to miscegenation; that of infection or contamination of the white race.[64] In *The Love Wanga* the ambiguity about the antagonist's origins is gone as not only is Cleeli, the *mambo* (voodoo priestess), monstrous as a sexually liberated woman, but also as a product of miscegenation. We also have Jessica and Carrefour from *I Walked with a Zombie* who are monsters for different reasons. Whereas Jessica is monstrous because she is a corrupted and corrupting woman, Carrefour is monstrous because of his black masculinity. Although he is rendered harmless or rather, impotent, through zombification, his very existence is monstrous. As such, they are both transgressive. However, Jessica, in some ways, is *more* transgressive because, as a white woman, she represents the potential continuation of the white nuclear family structure, seen as her divine mandate. Her behavior with Wesley, for whom she wants to leave her husband, threatens societal norms.

The Chapters

I begin my study with a comparative discussion of *White Zombie* (1932) and *I Walked with a Zombie* (1943). Both are well-known and pop-

Introduction

ular B-horror movies that were directed by the Halpern brothers and Jacques Tourneur respectively. Many scholars have written about both of these films, with *White Zombie* even having a whole book devoted to it. It was in these two films that the struggle over the perceived danger of and to the white woman in the Caribbean was waged. As Paravisini-Gebert notes, both films have had lasting effects as the power of the images evoked of slavery and zombification. Moreover, the invocation of black/white sexuality as the repository of the erotic has endured over the years.[65] I read the films as calls for a return to the time of colonialism and slavery as a kind of natural order. In addition, I consider the diverse depictions of women in both films, proposing that they reflect the American white male desire to return her to her subjugated place in a U.S. context.

Following my reading of those two films I discuss *The Love Wanga* (originally *Ouanga*), directed by George Terwilliger. *The Love Wanga* is not so well known partly because, after filming was completed, Paramount Pictures refused to release it in the U.S., perhaps because it dealt with the subject of miscegenation. It digresses significantly from the other films from the era in a number of ways, including its use of a black woman in a starring role and in her depiction as a perpetrator as well as a victim. There are several lessons contained in the film, one of the most important of which seems to be, "stick with your own kind" as Cleeli, the female mulatto plantation owner and *mambo,* is warned to do several times.

Chapter Three takes as its cue, a line from Cantet's *Heading South*, about sex tourism in Haiti: cash has replaced the guns that kept Haitian people subjugated during the early half of the twentieth century. In the chapter, I argue that the face of Haitian zombification has changed. As such, I return to the original definition of the zombi as the exploited, alienated, and voiceless black body to guide my reading of the film. My discussion explores the Caribbean as a site of hedonism and the availability of the Caribbean landscape and its black inhabitants (as part of the packaging of all-inclusive resorts) as a continuation of the plantation system of yesteryear and the consumptive practices that were integral to it. I argue that contemporarily, sex is a form of zombified labor whereby the sex worker has little or no control over his or her body, desire has little or nothing to do with the act and in the unequal political and economic relationship between the tourist and the beach boy or girl, he or she is an object to be consumed—silent and acquiescent—for the pleasure of the sex tourist. Where in the past this domain was controlled by men, in more recent years, women have increasingly participated.

As my discussion of *Heading South* demonstrates, the tools of the colonizers/sorcerers are no longer whips and guns or powders and charms, but sex and "the American dollar," as a character from the film says. Following the metaphor, I invoke the language of cannibalism that has also been associated with the Caribbean vis-à-vis tourism.[66] As the zombi's soul is consumed by the sorcerer, so too is Haiti consumed by this new form of zombification.

The films I discuss in the early part of my study also speak to the way that zombie (as well as vampire or mummy) films are used as outlets for American sociopolitical anxiety. As Annalee Newitz shows in her investigation into the correlation between U.S. and European releases of horror films since 1910, there have been spikes during years of major historical events involving war or social upheaval (2008). Indeed, scholars in the emerging field of zombie studies suggest that the monster can be "read as tracking a wide range of cultural, political, and economic anxieties of American society."[67] With this in mind, in Chapter Four, I turn to the 1988 horror film, *The Serpent and the Rainbow*, directed by Wes Craven. *The Serpent and the Rainbow* was inspired by ethnobotanist Wade Davis's study by the same name. As Vials argues, Davis's book "re-popularized the image of the Haitian zombie—along with its larger narrative of Haiti as a haunted land of primitive superstition—at the precise moment when Haitians were making enormous sacrifices to destroy the Duvalierist state."[68] This is no coincidence. 1986—two years before *The Serpent and the Rainbow* was released—marked a second revolutionary moment for Haiti when a popular uprising forced the dictator, Jean-Claude "Baby Doc" Duvalier, out of the country. Given colonial countries' fear of the revolutionary black nation in the early nineteenth century it is no wonder that the film industry, as part of the U.S. imperialist machine, would again be deployed to further its agenda. As I argue, in much the same way that Vials argues that radio and film were used in the 1930s and 1940s to facilitate the Othering and subsequent ingestion of Haiti, *The Serpent and the Rainbow* again took up the task. Indeed, as Vials states, *The Serpent and the Rainbow* illustrates the long reach of the zombie narrative first crafted in those early years.[69]

In Chapter Five, my analysis shifts to a reclaiming of the zombi through a discussion of Antonin's *Zombi candidat*. The film is based on a screenplay by Gary Victor, a Haitian writer and master of the macabre about a man who is turned into a zombi and then comes back to life to tell his story, reunite with the love of his life, and run for president of the country. I argue that, unlike the films of the mid-twentieth century *Zombi candidat* is a satire that posits the zombi as a potentially liberatory figure given Haiti's current political crisis. At the same time it is unclear if liberation is open to all subjugated peoples or just men, as the roles of women in the speaking masses' potential new society is left ambiguous at the film's end.

Finally, in the Conclusion I summarize the major arguments I have made throughout the text and remind the reader of the prescient nature of the zombi/zombie, not just a metaphor, but as a reality. This reality is evidenced by news reports that surfaced in the weeks following the outbreak of cholera, a disease that Haiti had never seen before, of people in different areas of Haiti murdering those who they believed were spreading the illness in order to zombify others.

I read all of the films as text, which allows me to explore the sociopolitical issues that surround them as well as the *loas* who are represented in the characters. In line with Deutsch who argues, "…representations are not objects at all, but social relations, themselves productive of meaning and subjectivity,"[70] I take the films as extant examples of social constructions of the zombified body and the struggle for control of the island nation at several critical moments in the nation's history; one of which is currently underway in the contemporary international military occupation in collaboration with various political and economic actors both internal and external to the country.

CHAPTER ONE

White Zombie and *I Walked with a Zombie*
The Haitian Revolution and White Southern Fears

A good deal of scholarship exists on Victor and Edward Halpern's *White Zombie* (1932) as well as Jacques Tourneur's *I Walked with a Zombie* (1943).[1] This chapter does a comparative reading of the two films to suggest a rethinking of the films through the lens of white male imperialist longing for a return to the colonial period.[2] As part of the work of situating traditional zombie films in relation to pivotal moments in Haitian history, I posit that the films, produced as they were during and after the American military occupation that lasted from 1915 to 1934, call for a return to the time of colonialism and slavery as a kind of natural order. Relatedly, as I discuss in the introduction, Vodou is integral to Haiti's political history as well as its contemporary reality. It also greatly impacted filmmakers' imaginings about the nation. Thus, I also discuss the Vodou *loas* who I propose are represented in several characters in the films. Finally, I consider the diverse depictions of women, proposing that the two films reflect the American white male desire to return her to her subjugated place in a U.S. context.

William Seabrook's *The Magic Island* was the first major English-language text to conjoin the concept of the zombie and the term, both of which had been written about but not connected explicitly before then.[3] Since that time, as anthropologist Franck Degoul argues, zombification has been "tacked on to the Haitian reality as if it were intrinsically linked to the Haitian."[4] Thus, we have the formulation: "Haiti: it is Vaudou; Vaudou: witchcraft; and witchcraft ... zombification."[5] But we should remember that the zombi precedes the U.S.'s early twentieth century invasion.

As Kyle Bishop rightly argues, the zombie is "a cultural artifact" that was "born of slavery, oppression, and capitalist hegemony."[6] As such, it is "a manifestation of collective unconscious fears and taboos."[7] This chapter, thus, discusses these films that were conceptualized and produced during and after the U.S.'s imperial invasion as a working through of white male aspirations, fears, and taboos that were born of the colonial era.

The Films

The Halpern brothers' *White Zombie*, which starred Bela Lugosi of *Dracula* fame as the zombie master, Murder Legendre,[8] is about a young American couple, Neil Parker and Madeline Short, who travel to the mansion of Charles Beaumont, a plantation owner in Haiti, to get married. Just after the nuptials, the young bride dies and her body is later exhumed and zombified by Beaumont and Legendre. In the end she is saved from her zombification when the native zombies as well as Beaumont and Legendre perish. The young couple is presumably able to return to the United States and live happily ever after.

Jacques Tourneur's *I Walked with a Zombie* is about a young, single Canadian nurse named Betsy Connell who leaves the cold and snowy Canadian winter to travel to the balmy Caribbean island of Saint Sebastien[9] to care for Jessica, the wife of a plantation owner named Paul Holland.[10] Jessica suffers from a kind of mental paralysis presumably as a result of "a mysterious fever." Betsy falls in love with Paul and in an act of self-sacrifice, tries to cure Jessica of her illness using voodoo. During the course of the film the audience learns that Jessica had sowed disharmony in the family by falling in love with Paul's half brother, Wesley Rand, and trying to leave her husband. Accordingly, Paul and Wesley's mother, Mrs. Rand, the wife of a deceased missionary, had her zombified in order to punish her. Whereas in *White Zombie*, the lone female character, Madeline, is voiceless for much of the film, *I Walked with a Zombie* features several women: Betsy, the female protagonist who interprets much of the film for the audience, Mrs. Rand, the matriarch, and Jessica, the beautiful woman who is zombified. All of the women represent different sides of the feminine and feminized, and relatedly, the nation (both the U.S. and Haiti).

One. White Zombie and I Walked with a Zombie

The Specter of the Haitian Revolution in the Atlantic World

Under French colonial rule, which lasted from 1659 to 1791, Saint-Domingue became the most profitable colony in the world. Historian Laurent Dubois notes that "By the late eighteenth century, it was the world's largest producer of sugar, exporting more of it than the colonies of Jamaica, Cuba, and Brazil combined."[11] The colony "also grew fully half of the world's coffee although it covered only about 10,600 square miles—about the size of Massachusetts."[12] Saint-Domingue was, in fact, "more valuable to France than all the thirteen colonies of North America were to England."[13] The French were able to extract so much labor from the enslaved population because of the cruelty with which they ran the system. Historian Carolyn Fick has documented the French's usage of enslaved workers, delineating their day that began at five in the morning when they were awakened by the sound of the *commandeur's* whistle or by the crack of his whip or, on large plantations of over a hundred slaves, by a huge bell.[14] After working for several hours, they had a two-hour lunch break from noon until two after which they would continue working until sundown. On many plantations, after working in the fields all day, they had to feed the animals, traveling a sizable distance from the plantation in order to do so. Finally, according to Fick, the workers had to gather firewood for their dinners of beans, manioc, occasional potatoes and very rarely, if ever, meat or fish. During the harvesting and grinding season the workers' days were even longer.[15]

In August 1791 about 200 enslaved workers are believed to have gathered in a wooded area called Bois Caïman, beyond the reach of the plantations and their owners. There, under the guidance of a *houngan* named Boukman Dutty and a *mambo* named Cécile Fatiman, those in attendance took a blood oath to secure their liberty or die trying. The ceremony marked the commencement of the armed struggle that was successful, in part, because the enslaved workers joined forces with the colony's "free people of color"[16] against their mutual enemy. Following 12 years, 4 months, 1 week, and 4 days of revolutionary war, on January 1, 1804, Emperor Jean-Jacques Dessalines, the nascent nation's first leader, renamed the land the Republic of Hayti in memory of the island's original inhabitants who had been practically exterminated by the Spanish.

The people the colonizer had consumed as part of the slave system: the indigenous population, Africans from different parts of the continent as well as the creole population,[17] took their spiritual systems, combined it with their military prowess[18] and their natural resources, and orchestrated a revolution. Their act, according to Dubois, was a profound and irreversible transformation[19] that upended the status quo. Indeed, "by defeating the French forces, [the revolutionaries] created a space where former slaves could exercise cultural and social autonomy to a degree unknown anywhere else in the Americas."[20] Historian Alyssa Goldstein Sepinwall states the situation more strongly averring that, "after 300 years of African slavery in the Americas, the revolution in colonial Saint-Domingue sent shock waves throughout the New World and back to the European metropoles. For slave-owners and their allies, the world was turned upside down; the very words Saint-Domingue conjured up a terrifying alternative universe in which whites could lose their power, their fortunes, and even their lives."[21]

Indeed, the revolution sent shock waves through the Atlantic world. Thus, it is an understatement to say that the French regretted the loss of its enormously profitable colony. Another colonial power, the British, feared that the Haitian Revolution would affect its hold on Jamaica and her other slave colonies. Spain had lost her colony of Santo Domingo, next door to Saint-Domingue, and feared the spread of her influence to Puerto Rico and Cuba. The U.S. had a particularly difficult time with the revolution, perhaps because of its close proximity. According to historian Tim Matthewson, American southern slave-holders feared that Haiti's success would lead to the spread of rebellion. As the years progressed the pro-slavery factions in the south stepped up their attacks against Haiti, calling its revolution proof that "Haitian violence arose from the character of Afro-Americans, not out of slavery itself."[22] In these slave-owners' minds, blacks' inherent violence was evidenced by accounts such as that by an ex-slave which told of people who "hung up men with heads downward, drowned them in sacks, crucified them on planks, buried them alive, crushed them in mortars…, forced them to eat shit … cast them alive to be devoured by worms, or onto anthills, or lashed them to stakes in the swamp to be devoured by mosquitos, … threw them into boiling cauldrons of cane syrup" and "[flayed] them with the lash."[23] The irony of southern slave owners' accusation of Haitian's inherent violence should not be overlooked.

Rather, we should remember that the cruel behavior that was attributed to the newly liberated people of Haiti was taught to them by the colonizers. Therefore, if violence was inherent to anyone it would have been the slave-owner and pro-slavery agents; not those who had been enslaved.

This post-revolutionary period of time was read very differently by the liberated population who saw it as a "flicker of inspiration and hope" that enabled them to imagine "a world in which the scourge of slavery could be eradicated."[24] If read through the lens of zombification, the success of the revolution meant a release from the lifeless existence that slavery represented for enslaved people. The violence that followed may then be understood as their awakened consciousness, for as Alfred Métraux reminds us, once awakened, the zombies' realization of their degraded state "rouses in them a vast rage and an ungovernable desire for vengeance. They hurl themselves on their master, kill him [and] destroy his property."[25] It is perhaps this violent awakening that "refugees"[26] from Saint-Domingue/Haiti related in their writings about the revolution and its aftermath. But, again, like the accusations of barbarism that were leveled at the insurgents by slave-owners, the writings from "refugees" should also be read with a keen eye towards understanding the motivation behind the publication of such accounts. I would argue that ultimately, these verbal and written indictments were tools to be used in the imperialist battle to return Haiti to its "rightful" role as a colony populated by laborers whose bodies could again be consumed by their masters; in other words, rezombified.

For its transgression, Haiti suffered prolonged diplomatic isolation. Its flag was repeatedly disrespected[27] and France extorted its economic resources by demanding huge reparations[28] as a precondition for entry into the global market. Although France, along with Britain finally recognized Haiti's independence in 1833, it was not until 1862 that the United States capitulated.[29] Nonetheless, despite its recognition on paper, the international community never forgave Haiti for the sin of taking its independence, according to philosopher and sociopolitical activist Noam Chomsky.

Reestablishing Order

With the abolition of slavery and the birth of the women's suffragist movement, both in the late 1800s, white American men lost their assurance of their supreme position in the family as well as in relation to formerly colonized populations. Where in the eighteenth and early nineteenth centuries, they had unrestricted access to feminized bodies, both female and male, the upturned world of the late nineteenth and early twentieth centuries presented them with the challenge of reestablishing their power. They found opportunity beyond the U.S.'s borders and embarked on a quest to penetrate, subjugate, and consume less powerful nations. In the process they established themselves as the husbands, fathers, and sons of a major world power who would protect their nation from the threat that the specter of liberated blackness posed both within and outside its borders. The ensuing expansionist project on which the U.S. embarked also reflects its desire to engage in the work of conquest that it had witnessed other European nations like Portugal, France, England, Spain, Italy, and Belgium engage in during the colonial era. As Bishop suggests regarding the appeal of the zombie to Hollywood filmmakers, the expansionist project allowed the U.S. to "vicariously sample the pleasures of colonization and imperialist exploitation that, as a nation, it had essentially been denied."[30] Concomitantly, the "zombie fantasies" that circulated in the United States during the American Occupation of Haiti were "both an admission and denial that U.S. policy in Haiti resurrected a colonial, *even slave economy*"[31] (emphasis added), according to Jennifer Fay.

The work of conquest commenced just before the turn of the century when the U.S. annexed Puerto Rico (1898) and began occupying Cuba (1898–1902). It then created the country of Panama in order to build a canal there (1903–1914); it occupied Honduras in 1911 and then sent troops to Mexico in 1914. After beginning its occupation of Haiti in 1915 it continued with the Dominican Republic in 1916. That same year the U.S. sent troops to Mexico again. In 1917 the U.S. purchased the Virgin Islands from the Danish and finally, in 1926, began occupying Nicaragua.[32]

Haiti, in particular, seemed to be a favorite site of invasion, with U.S. navy ships entering Haitian waters 24 times between 1849 and 1913 to "protect American lives and property."[33] As Hans Schmidt remarked, "Haiti's independence was hardly given token recognition"[34] and there was little consideration given to the rights of the people. To the U.S. they were an inferior people who were "unable to maintain the degree of civilization left to them by the French or to develop any capacity for self-government entitling them to international respect and confidence,"[35] wrote Assistant Secretary of State William Phillips, when he recommended the policy of invasion to then U.S. President Woodrow Wilson who in turn, acted on his recommendation. The military invasion and subsequent occupation of Haiti opened the country up to be consumed by U.S. businessmen like J.P. MacDonald who owned a railroad and banana plantations as well as journalists like Seabrook and tourists in search of a "good time."

From Cannibal to Zombie

The tradition of making the Caribbean available for white consumption goes back several centuries as sociologists Mimi Sheller (2003) and Ian Gregory Strachan (2002) demonstrate. In writings about the Caribbean region from the sixteenth and seventeenth centuries the Caribbean was presented as a traveler's dream; a land of tropical fecundity and excessive fruitfulness.[36] Later, in travel literature that was produced in the late nineteenth century, writers wrote about the islands and their people with "a sense of proprietorship" and of "being at home as [they] moved through the landscape."[37] These writings made Europeans and Americans who read these narratives eager to grasp the paradise that was presented and "make it their own."[38] Sheller posits that the image of fecundity and fruitfulness of the land went hand-in-hand with that of the islands' inhabitants. As fruits could be plucked from the trees and consumed, so too could the people. However, Haiti, from the time of the revolution, resisted these narratives of accessibility that were spread about much of the Caribbean. This was so, not only because of its revolutionary history, but also the political upheaval that followed.[39] In effect, Haiti was uncontainable and thus, uncontrollable.

Even if they could not contain it, the international community found a way to label it. In *White Zombie: Anatomy of a Horror Film* (2001) Gary D. Rhodes argues that tales of Haitian cannibalism abounded from the late 1800s with the publication of "nonfiction" by writers like American Spenser St. John (1884) and Englishman James Anthony Froude (1888). It continued as late as 1921 with an issue of the *New York American* which featured an article titled "Why the Black Cannibals of Hayti Mutilated Our Soldiers" and later in the text by John Houston Craige titled *Cannibal*

Cousins (1934). These depictions of Haitian cannibals echo the writings of Christopher Columbus who over three centuries prior described the original inhabitants whom he called Caribs as barbarians who dismembered and ate their enemies. Columbus proposed that colonization and enslavement would help the indigenous people cease this practice. But as Lola Young argues, this attribution of savagery to "the Caribs" not only served as justification for the indigenous population's enslavement, it also acted as a screen to guard against European guilt about their own savagery; in other words, their own consumptive practices.[40] The cannibal was laid to rest when, according to Sheller, Hollywood zombie movies, of which *White Zombie* was the first, brought "the ethnological sensationalism of travel in Haiti to the big screen and the zombie entered North American and European culture as a creature more terrifying than even the cannibal"[41] had been. As such, "cannibalism began to fade out of the discourse surrounding Voodoo in favor of zombies,"[42] according to Chera Kee.

Literary and later filmic representations of the zombie were also the means by which whites sought to exercise control over a belief system that not only exceeded their understanding, but could be used against them. Although Europeans did not understand the spiritual system called Vodou that emerged from the colony, they knew that it was a powerful force in the insurgents' lives. They also knew that the population of Haiti continued serving the spirits who had inspired their revolutionary fervor. As such, these spirits or *loas*, represented dangerous forces that, through representation both in written texts and later in film, could be corrupted and deemed monstrous, rendered as impotent, and thus, controlled and contained, at least in the minds of foreigners. By appropriating the *loas* and their agents, *houngans*, as well as *bokors* who are believed to be responsible for zombification under the auspices of the *loa* Baron Samedi, filmmakers, as agents of American imperialism, found a way to allow their compatriots to, not only control and contain Vodou, but also consume it and its adherents from a safe distance.

Gendered Race

Both the Halpern brothers and Tourneur had to tackle the issue of race in their films. It would seem that Tourneur did a much better job of it in *I Walked with a Zombie* than the Halperns did in *White Zombie*. The Othering of Haiti begins immediately with the Halperns' imagining of a Haitian traditional chant by several black people gathered in the road. The chant was apparently inspired by those that had been depicted in earlier portrayals of voodoo such as in the play, *Voodoo* (1914) by Henry Francis Downing set in Barbados and England from 1688 to 1689.[43] At the helm of the carriage carrying Neil and Madeline sits a slack-jawed, wide-eyed Negro of the American racist imagination. Although Rhodes argues that the driver "does not appear part of any 'Uncle Tom' tradition" the character is clearly an ethnic caricature. He is, in fact, a product of the racism that pervaded Hollywood pre–1950s, which by and large prevented any sustained engagement with black characters. As Gwenda Young argues, Hollywood attempted to deal with the endemic racism of the industry by including "safe" caricatures in the 1930s, exemplified in "Stepin' Fetchit and the maid figures of Hattie MacDaniel, Butterfly McQueen and Louise Beavers."[44] These stereotypes came under fire in the 1930s and early 1940s and Hollywood responded by simply writing "black characters out of screenplays rather than face criticism from the liberal wing of American society."[45] According to Michele Wallace, on the whole, those characters that were written into scripts suffered a kind of symbolic death that was "marked by stereotypes, representational stagnation, chaos, or structural absence. Meanwhile, the realities of the lives of blacks were kept in the shadows, where they continued to be viewed by most of the American public as largely irrelevant to the course of American events and sensibilities."[46]

Not only is the carriage driver, played by Clarence Muse, an African American composer and actor, depicted visually as a stereotype with his wide, bulging eyes and mouth slightly open as if his lips are too heavy to close, but his irrelevance is conveyed in his not being named in the film. In addition, when he asks Legendre, in a racist projection of Black English, "You know where is the house of Monsieur Beaumont?" Legendre does not respond to him, but simply walks over to the door of the carriage and looks in at the white couple. Later, when he spots zombies on the horizon, the carriage driver's superstitious nature, believed to be endemic to blacks, comes through when he yells, "Zombie! Alé vite! Alé!" before driving away recklessly. Taken together, the coach driver's speech, his visage and limited and irrational dialogue, and Legendre's dismissive treatment, all fly in the face of Rhode's contention that the actor's "role suggests the production's modicum of sympathy to the situation of serious black actors."[47] Although Rhodes tries to attribute some dignity to Muse's character, the fact is that the actor was up against profound American racism that was responsible for a characterization that belies the portrait of "knowledge" and "credibility" that Rhodes insists he conveys.[48]

In *White Zombie*, white womanhood is to be protected. One of the film's "Catchlines" suggested by United Artists for theatre use in 1932 was "They knew that this was taking place among the blacks, but when this fiend practiced it on a white girl ... all hell broke loose."[49] Also, as Bishop notes, Dr. Bruner, the white missionary in the film tells the zombified woman's husband that he had been trying to challenge Legendre's power for years, but it is only when a white woman is turned into a zombie does he act.[50] Indeed, the exploitation of labor was fine for the blacks, but in zombifying a white woman, Legendre "appears to have crossed a greater moral line."[51] Despite these obvious invocations of race as a major theme of the film, Rhodes insists that, "*White Zombie* does not pursue a racist argument."[52] Furthermore, he almost completely dismisses the importance of race in the film stating that "although the title may well have caused at least a few viewers and critics to consider ethnicity ... it seems quite clear ... that the intended meaning of 'White Zombie' was Madeline's innocence, virginity, and most particularly her status as a bride."[53] Thus, he relegates his discussion of the "white" in the film's title to a reference to Madeline's innocence and virginal qualities, "symbolism with deep roots in literature and poetry."[54] However, he makes no mention of the fact that this symbolism came out of the Victorian era when Africa was being penetrated by Europeans and whiteness was being defined in relation to blackness as whiteness' antithesis: impurity, baseness, and savagery. Furthermore, this assertion of the purity, innocence, virginal status and worthiness for legitimate marriage that is attributed to the white female character implicitly invokes her opposite even when she is not represented: black women. As Norma Manatu argues, "[g]iven that white women were invested in the 'cult of true womanhood,' '[t]he sexually denigrated [black] woman ... [was] used as a yardstick against which ... true womanhood was measured.'"[55] Furthermore, Manatu reminds us that, from the time of slavery black women were denied the laudable attributes of fragility, delicacy, and femininity ascribed to white women. Neither her physical nor her sexual labor was hers to guard as it did not belong to her, but rather, to her master. "Unlike white women, black women have never had the benefit of being on the proverbial pedestal and allowed to be 'feminine.'"[56] In fact, black as well as mulatto women were "[e]xcluded from the feminine and confined to the world of work and sexuality."[57] Thus, even though the black and mulatto woman are not visually represented in *White Zombie*, Madeline's purity hinges on their impurity as part and parcel of the colonial and postcolonial Caribbean experience.

It is true, as Peter Dendle assesses, that unlike many of the films from that era, *I Walked with a Zombie* did not depict African Americans as incompetent and self-defeating. However, it should be noted that the vast majority of the black characters (except perhaps the carriage driver) are all obviously light-skinned, thus alleviating some of "the Negro problem" for white audiences while also marking their difference.[58] As with *White Zombie*, at the time that *I Walked with a Zombie* was made, not sure what to do with them, filmmakers were still writing blacks out of films, integrating them into white discourse, or reducing them to the status of exotic or powerless or making them into ineffectual caricatures of "Others."[59] Young writes that "It is against this socio-historical and cinematic background that Tourneur's *I Walked with a Zombie* can be read as a text which, in some ways, challenges the dominant representation of blacks and black discourse in American cinema and society."[60]

The *Loas* in Haitian Vodou

Unlike "the distorted and pejorative definitions of Vodou that are popular to the West," Patrick Bellegarde-Smith explains that Vodou is in fact, "a coherent and comprehensive belief system and worldview in which every person and every thing is sacred and must be treated accordingly."[61] According to religion scholar Leslie Desmangles, Vodou, like many other traditional religions of the world, teaches that the universe is populated "by thousands of invisible spirits who are inherent in all persons and things, and who direct the physical operations of the universe."[62] As such, the rise and decay of things, the rotation of days and of astral bodies, the cycle of seasons, and the succession of human generations are all parts of a grand cosmic scheme, which are perceived as the manifest faces or personae of the *lwas*."⁶³ Thus, the *loas* are associated with not only "the substances in which they are infused, but also the manifest changes in those substances."⁶⁴ Finally, while *serviteurs* (those who serve the *loas*) believe that they reside in all matter in the cosmos, substances (such as people) are only the "vessels or conduits through which the *lwas* can show their faces, or manifest themselves."⁶⁵ At the same time, the relationship between the *serviteurs* and the *loas* are reciprocal and inextricable. The *loas* rely on their supplicants for offerings and remembrance and in turn, watch over, guide, and offer counsel to their human charges. As anthropologist Karen McCarthy Brown puts it, the role of the *serviteur* is to feed and honor the *loas* so that they in turn will remain strong and continue to advise them, warn, and protect them.⁶⁶

Filmic Representations of the Loas

There are several *loas* who can be said to be depicted in both *White Zombie* and *I Walked with a Zombie*. They include Baron Samedi, the *loa* who governs the realm between death and rebirth, Carrefour who filmmaker and Vodou adept Maya Deren calls "The Young Man at the Crossroads" and the counterpart to Papa Legba, Master of the Crossroads, and finally, Erzulie, the goddess of love. The characteristics associated with the *loas* are not those that emanate from within Vodou culture, but rather from outside, in the foreign imagination. As such, rather than dynamic forces that offer counsel and intercede on behalf of their supplicants as they do in the Vodou tradition, the *loas* of the filmmakers' imaginations are malicious, corrupted, and corrupting on one hand, and ineffectual on the other.

READING BARON SAMEDI IN *WHITE ZOMBIE*

White Zombie conducts a sinister reading of one of Vodou's principle *loas*, Baron Samedi, guardian over the realm of death and rebirth. As a deity, Baron's symbol, a black cross, sits "at the entrance of every Vodou burial ground" to remind visitors "that they are about to enter a territory where Ginen⁶⁷ and the profane world are said to intersect each other,"⁶⁸ according to Desmangles. As a personage, Baron is depicted as wearing a frock coat and striped trousers, formal apparel once worn by government officials at funerals.[69] As Deren indicates, it is Baron Samedi "who governs the ... invisible forces of magicians. It is through him that the zombies are brought up from the grave."[70] A song to Baron Samedi illustrates this principle: "hold that man.... Don't let him go, heavenly judge, hold that man...."[71] While this side of Baron as zombie master is depicted in the film through the character of Legendre, his other side, which I discuss in relation to *Zombi candidat*, as healer, is absent.

Legendre, as zombie master, is expressed early in the film when he offers Beaumont some zombified workers, adding, "They are not worried about long hours. You could make good use of men like mine on your plantation." In context, Legendre's offer, of course, refers to slavery, when, as I have discussed, during harvest season, enslaved workers had to toil ceaselessly day and night. It also invokes the Marines' *corvée* system, which was revived from 1916 to 1918 to force peasants to build roads. If they "resisted conscription, they were forcibly taken from their homes at night and from their fields they tended during the day."[72] Fay connects the revival of this system to the memory of slavery, saying, "Chained and marched to the island's interior, and working at gunpoint, peasants of this first Black Republic experienced the occupation as slavery's uncanny return."[73] Even though it is not made explicit in the film, the viewer can infer that the zombified men shown working in Legendre's sugar mill were plucked from their families and doomed to work for him, unable to resist until their final death, also recalling the slave experience and ultimately, zombification.

In the scene, Legendre is established as not only an agent of zombification, which would make him simply a *bokor*, but the source of it. This is accomplished in the power that he exercises over the realm and process of zombification. For example, at one point in his conversation with Beaumont, Legendre gestures towards a man who towers over him and is still obviously very strong physically but reduced to a ragged, wretched cretin. His eyes stare widely, however, blankly, ahead. He has no will of his own and any threat he may have posed when he was alive is completely gone in his present form as Legendre's puppet. Afterwards, in presenting Beaumont with the powder that will turn Madeline into a zombie, he instructs, "Only a pinpoint, Mr. Beaumont, in a glass of wine, or perhaps a flower."

When Beaumont tries to return it, Legendre takes on a demonic quality both in voice and posture that also resembles that of a hypnotist.[74] "Keep it. You may change your mind.... Send me word *when* you use it" (emphasis added). Legendre's visual and verbal cues allude to the supernatural quality of his power that transcends the realm of man.

In this initial exchange with Beaumont, Legendre as Baron, is conflated with the Christian idea of the devil who makes people sin. In fact, later in the film, in a classic "the devil made me do it" move, Beaumont regrets his decision to zombify Madeline and tries to make amends. During the exchange and later when he gives Madeline the flower with the poison on it, Legendre is posited as Baron, the ultimate zombie master and Beaumont becomes the *bokor* who administers the poison to the victim, Madeline.

At the same time, if Beaumont is being posited as a foreigner (French according to Bishop, American according to Fay),[75] then his entering into an agreement with Legendre who represents the corrupting Caribbean, also makes him a victim of evil forces beyond his comprehension and control. He has momentarily fallen under Legendre's evil spell; a sense that is reinforced when the camera focuses on Beaumont's confused expression as he walks away from Legendre. He seems to regain himself momentarily as he turns at the gate that separates Legendre from the zombies in the mill and says, "I'll find another way." However, the certainty that Legendre and by extension, Haiti and its spiritual forces, will prevail is in Legendre's reply: "There is no other way."

Legendre's domain as the graveyard and his power over the dead is also depicted when, in the cemetery, by way of introduction, Legendre gives a brief history of the men who will aid him and Beaumont with their macabre task of digging up Madeline's grave: "They are my servants.... In their lifetimes they were my enemies," adding that he will take Madeline as he took them. Legendre is clear about the power that he harnesses. When Beaumont asks him what will happen if the zombies regain their souls, Legendre responds that they would tear him to pieces. However, secure in his total power over the realm of suspended life, zombification, he assures him that that "will never be." His words can be seen as voicing the confidence that was tinged with the fear of slave uprisings and reverse colonization that plagued the colonists, but also Americans who invaded Haiti, as Bishop proposes. Like the enslaved worker, the Haitian peasant always represented not only labor potential ("they are not worried about the long hours") but also the potential for violent rebellion, which the zombie also represents once given a grain of salt, according to traditional belief. While Legendre affirms that the zombies' rebellion "will never be" Beaumont's question also affirms what already *is* in the history of the Haitian Revolution and in the reality of the *Cacos*, rebellious armed forces who waged war against the Marines under the leadership of Charlemagne Péralte. Their fear seems to have been resolved in the film in the last scenes when Beaumont pushes Legendre to his death and then destroys himself, thus freeing Madeline who was held captive by first, Beaumont and then Legendre. In this instance, she represents the innocence of the U.S., which is restored with the death of the two representatives of the corrupted and dangerous Haiti.

Carrefour in *I Walked with a Zombie*

Although in many ways the *loa*, Carrefour, does not seem like a major character in the film, he was used to sell it. One of the most widely circulated examples of publicity for *I Walked with a Zombie* features him carrying a limp Jessica in his arms. In another, a frightened Betsy stands beside a zombified Jessica opposite him. Finally, there is the image of Carrefour's hulking shadow superimposed on an awakened Betsy as she lay in bed.

Indeed, as several scholars suggest, reflecting more sensitivity and a better understanding of Vodou than the Halperns, Tourneur's *loas* are more in line with the way they are understood amongst *serviteurs*. For example, Carrefour, the tall, imposing figure of *I Walked with a Zombie* is within Vodou, associated with Papa Legba, Master of the Crossroads.[76] Unlike Legba, who presents in Vodou as an old feeble man, Deren describes Carrefour as "huge and straight and vigorous, a man in the prime of his life. His arms are raised strongly in the configuration of a cross. Every muscle of the shoulders and back bulges with strength. No one whispers of smiles in his presence."[77] Deren explains, "it is Carrefour who may loose upon the world the daemons of ill chance, misfortune and deliberate, unjust destruction. No man, however carefully he may have built up a logical structure of proper and good destiny is wholly safe from such disruption."[78] Furthermore, "if Legba commands the divinities of the day, Carrefour commands the daemons of the night. The divinities of the day are fundamentally just, and if they cause a man misfortune, it is for just cause, a punishment that disciplines the recalcitrant serviteur. But the daemons of the night are dangerous, for they can be put to work by the arbitrary will of men and by the manipulations of magicians."[79] At the same time, it is Carrefour who can protect against these demons, and "it is in his name that the garde against such harm is fashioned."[80] While Tourneur demonstrates an understanding of the *loa* with the character depicting multiple aspects of the *loa*'s personality that Deren explicates, he is nonetheless zombified, and thus rendered impotent as a divine force.

The audience first sees Carrefour in the opening scene of the film walking toward the camera a few paces behind the petite Betsy on a beach in the Caribbean. In a voiceover, Betsy explains that she has walked with a zombie. In deference to her foreign (presumably American and Canadian) audience, she laughs and acknowledges that "It does seem an odd thing to say. Had anyone said that to me a year ago I'm not at all sure I would have even known what a zombie was. Oh, I might have had some notion that they were strange and frightening ... even a little funny. It all began in such an ordinary way." The visual and aural cues signal that it is Carrefour to whom she refers as "strange and frightening." However, while visually, he is strange and frightening, the threat that he poses is neutralized in his also being "a little funny."

The next time the audience sees Carrefour is after Alma, Jessica's maid, has drawn the directions to the *houmfort* using cornmeal, usually used to draw *vèvè*,[81] and gives both Betsy and Jessica a "voodoo patch" to ensure their safe passage past Carrefour. Although Alma refers to him as a god, when Betsy and Jessica encounter him, he is depicted as a zombie with "the eyes of a dead man, not blind, but staring, unfocused, unseeing" of Seabrook's description.[82] Rather than the vigorous man in the prime of his life from Deren's description, a god, Carrefour is reduced to a shell of a person, unable to speak or act on his own volition. His power is further undermined later, when a *houngan* is able to control him (rather than him being in control) and sends him to Fort Holland to fetch Jessica.

Bryan Senn comments on the poetry of the scene in which Betsy and Jessica encounter Carrefour at the crossroads, proposing that

> For the eyes, the sequence becomes a veritable feast of menacing shadows and unseen presence as the two women ... pass. Then the smooth camera motion and alternating

viewpoints ... draw the viewer into this nocturnal trial of subdued terror as Betsy comes upon such disturbing sights as a human skull in a circle of stones ... a sacrificial goat suspended from a tree, and the zombie himself—first revealed as a pair of naked feet in the tiny pool of Betsy's flashlight which then shoots frantically upwards to illuminate his unearthly, staring countenance towering above her (and us). Thanks to the clever, sensitive and evocative staging of.... Tourneur, the atmospheric lighting and fluid visuals ... and the determined-yet-uneasy playing of Francis Dee [as Betsy], this three-minute sequence becomes one of the most effective and poetically moody moments in all of voodoo cinema (or any other celluloid branch, for that matter).[83]

While I agree with Senn's comments on one level, it is important to remember that what we see is also connected to what we hear and what we *think* we know. Thus, the film served to reinforce many of the stereotypes that whites had about blacks even before they stepped into the movie theatres. It was precisely this hulk-like black figure staring blankly ahead that was the stuff of white nightmares, not just for movie-goers but for white imperialists who harbored the exact fear that is depicted on screen; that their women would be caught out in the middle of the night and contaminated in the most intimate ways by black men. Furthermore, the film, like *White Zombie*, was linked to the Catholic Church's anti-superstition campaign as they both came out around the same time, and as Hurbon asserts, "proclaimed Haiti a hotbed of magic and sorcery."[84] Thus, although *I Walked with a Zombie* is allegedly about the fictitious country of Saint Sebastien, it clearly uses Saint-Domingue/Haiti as its inspiration and reference. All of these factors go into what the audience perceived even as they may have been entranced by the poetic mood that Tourneur set.

Unlike the Vodou Carrefour, Tourneur's Carrefour, like Legendre's cretin from *White Zombie*, is presented as the ultimate zombie, who, with his formidable size and strength, is capable of profound destruction, but only at the behest of his master. Although he is huge and straight, the vigorous Carrefour of the Vodou pantheon is transformed into a speechless zombie, devoid of life. While he still guards the crossroads he does so, not of his own volition, but because he is commanded to do so. With no will of his own, he cannot command the demons of the night. Rather, he is commanded. As such, in the foreign imagination, he is rendered impotent. Through such maneuvers, Hollywood distorted the Vodou spirit's meaning and significance, making him controllable and thus, containable. Moreover, since the audience later learns that it is Mrs. Rand who controls him, his power is transferred to her as representative of the U.S. imperialist project. Although she is a woman who is, in many ways, also to be controlled and contained, her wardrobe of tailored suits renders her a sexually ambiguous figure, with power over both the physical and spiritual world of the blacks.

After invading the intimate space of Betsy and Jessica's bedroom, Carrefour is again, first presented as a shadow, invoking Haiti as specter that the revolutionary nation represented to slave-owning societies. Rather than arms raised in the configuration of a cross from Deren's description, Carrefour menacingly approaches Paul with his arms outstretched like the stereotypical zombie. The only person who is able to stop him is Mrs. Rand when she calls out his name. The scene insinuates that while Paul has control over the white world (Jessica, Betsy, and Wesley) Mrs. Rand has ventured beyond their world into that of the Other. In both cases, power over both the physical and spiritual world is not held by the indigenous populations, even their own epistemological creations, but by whites who have taken and appropriated them for their own purposes and usage.

Erzulie in *White Zombie* and *I Walked with a Zombie*

A third *loa* who manifests, although problematically in both *White Zombie* and *I Walked with a Zombie* is Erzulie, the Vodou goddess of love. Desmangles explains that Erzulie symbolizes fecundity. She is "the mother of the world who participates with the masculine forces in the creation and maintenance of the universe."[85] Because she is seen as sexually fertile, *serviteurs* "invoke her in matters related to conception and childbearing. Indeed, without her patronage a woman would not be able to conceive."[86] Furthermore, as a symbol of fecundity, Erzulie "is not identified merely with sex. Like the Virgin Mary, to whom she corresponds, she is imagined as the symbol of womanhood, the image of exquisite beauty that fills every man's dreams."[87] It is these attributes of Erzulie: fecundity and sexuality embodied in her womanhood and her association with the Virgin Mary, with which the white woman was associated and which the white man most feared in her contact with the Caribbean. Where during the colonial era, a black Caribbean man's sexual contact with a white woman would have been punishable by disfigurement, castration and ultimately, death, in post-revolutionary Haiti, white men held no authority.

One. *White Zombie* and *I Walked with a Zombie*

In *White Zombie*, white men's fear of the black Caribbean man having access to white women is alleviated by turning the white woman, Madeline, into "a de-feminized automaton"[88] in the words of Chris Vials. But while Madeline may be an automaton, she is hardly defeminized. In fact, she is highly sexualized in, for example, being shown at one point in her underwear as I discuss later, and then in what resembles a wedding dress, laying immobile on a bed in Legendre's mansion waiting to be summoned by him. But here it is a brand of feminization and sexualization that strips the white woman of autonomy and agency, as a white male fantasy. At the same time, if Vials is correct in his characterization of Madeline as an "automaton," then even if she does fall into the hands of "the natives," neither would benefit. Not only would she be unresponsive sexually, but she would also be barren, incapable of sullying white blood by birthing mulatto children, and thus, safe.

Joan Dayan remarks that in colonial historians' written representations of Erzulie, she is known as, among other things, "the Tragic Mistress" and as "a commentary on the harrowing reality of Saint-Domingue."[89] A goddess born on the soil of Haiti, Erzulie "recalls the violent yoking of decorum and lust."[90] While Dayan is referring to Erzulie as evidence of the thrusting of the white master's lust onto the black and mulatto woman under cover of darkness in colonial Saint-Domingue, that flaw of lustfulness has been transferred onto the black and mulatto woman and attributed to her. As representative of the nation, that lustfulness is also associated with, not only the indigenous population, but also, through their contact with the Caribbean, whites who are infected with its corruptive lure. In *I Walked with a Zombie*, Tourneur gives full expression to whites' corruption by depicting a zombified Jessica as also highly sexualized and reveals her to be guilty of having an extramarital affair with her husband's brother, Wesley. As such, they both threaten the white family structure. Because they are irredeemably corrupted and corruptive they must die at the end of the film.

Jessica's corruption is reinforced and the necessity of her death explained when her body is found floating in the Caribbean Ocean and what sounds like an African American minister intones a prayer:

> Oh Lord God, most holy, deliver them from the bitter pains of eternal death. The woman was a wicked woman and she was dead in her own life. Yeah Lord, dead in the selfishness of her spirit and the man followed her. Her steps led him down to evil. Her feet took

hold on death. Forgive him, oh Lord who knowest the secret of all hearts. Yeah Lord, forgive them who are dead and give peace and happiness to the living.

Jessica's "deadness" refers, not only to her zombification, but also to her social deadness after she betrayed the white family structure by having an affair with her husband's brother. The prayer contrasts the condemned Jessica and the corrupted Wesley with Betsy and Paul who have virtuously resisted their attraction to one another. They are rewarded in the end with Paul being rid of his alcoholic brother and his cheating, burdensome wife, and the two being allowed to be together in peace and happiness, "alive" in their fidelity.

Island Possession

The U.S.'s military occupation of Haiti was a claiming of the land and its people as they were before independence. This claiming is communicated in the first scene of *White Zombie* when Neil, Madeline's fiancé, comments on the spectacle of blacks in the middle of the road digging the grave, quipping "Well, that's a cheerful introduction for you to *our* West Indies" (emphasis added). While, indeed, his retort may be read as a comment on the U.S.'s occupation of the country that was taking place at the time, the setting, laden with references to the colonial era, from the coachman's archaic dress (a cape), to the colonial mansions, and even the archaic means of production that Fay notes are marked by "only the monotonous moan of creaking wood as the men labor,"[91] harken back to a "before-time." While this "before-time" did not necessarily include them (as Americans) as international colonial powers, we should remember that the imperial project was part and parcel; in effect, a continuation of the colonial project. As an American citizen, Neil's claiming the Caribbean for himself and Madeline in this imperialist era of expansionism recalls the colonial era when men who looked like him would have owned, not only the country, but also its people. Their women would have benefited personally and financially from that ownership.

The slave era is also recalled when the couple arrive at Beaumont's estate and Neil, in admonishing the coachman for driving so recklessly, learns that they had come across zombies, corpses who were made to work in the sugar mills at night. Where Fay argues in "Dead Subjectivity: White

Zombie, Black Baghdad" (2008), that Legendre's mill is modeled after the real American owned sugar mill called HASCO (Haitian-American Sugar Company) of the 1930s, I would also suggest that the mill recalls the slave era sugar mill.[92] Again, under French colonial rule, Saint-Domingue, the Pearl of the Antilles, was "the world's largest producer of sugar, exporting more of it than the colonies of Jamaica, Cuba, and Brazil combined."[93] Also, again, the slave experience resembled the practice of zombification when, as Dubois remarks, "most of the slaves toiled on sugar plantations."[94] About the process of sugar production, he explains, "Harvesting cane is backbreaking work, made risky by the razor-sharp spines of the tall stalks and the insects and snakes nested in the fields. Once cut, cane had to be processed quickly, so enslaved workers—usually women—worked day and night feeding the cane stalks into large stone mills, which it was all too easy for hands and arms to be pulled in and crushed."[95] Not only is the alienation of one from his or her labor suggested in Dubois's description, signifying zombification, but also the gendered aspect of the process in the way that it was primarily women who were charged with working ceaselessly for the master. Not only was she forced to work on the sugar planation, but also in the bed as producers of the next generation of laborers, both with other enslaved workers and as his concubine. In other words, all aspects of her bodily labor were the property of the master who owned the island and its production.

There are also clear invocations of the slave era in *I Walked with a Zombie*. For example, when Betsy arrives in Saint Sebastien her carriage driver gives her a history lesson saying, "Times gone, Fort Holland was a fort, but now no longer. The Hollands was most old family, miss. They brought the colored folks to the island; the colored folks and Ti Misery." The driver tells Betsy that Ti Misery, a slave ship figurehead, is a very old man who lives in the garden at Fort Holland. "He has arrows stuck in him and a sorrowful weeping look on his black face." The driver clarifies that Ti Misery is "just as he was in the beginning on the front side of an enormous boat." To Betsy's suggestion that he is talking about a figurehead he responds, "If you say so, miss," and then continues as if he has not been interrupted: "and the enormous boat brought the long-ago fathers and the long-ago mothers of us all, chained to the bottom of the boat." For the driver, the history is alive, just as relevant and prescient as it was in the past. The insinuation is that the conditions of those who are descended from enslaved workers who were brought to the island with Ti Misery have not much changed.

Betsy's response to his explanation of the black inhabitants' origins: "They brought you to a beautiful place, didn't they?," as she smiles and settles back into the coach, denotes a willful misreading of the place that she has come to. As Young notes, it is "as if sunshine and pleasant surrounding made the slave's lot easier!"[96] While the driver's informing Betsy about the origins of Ti Misery illustrates the past's intrusion on the present and how "long ago events contain echoes that return to haunt the present,"[97] she chooses to hide behind her ignorance, maintaining an image of the place that will be comfortable to her. The driver's enigmatic but polite reply enables him to address her ignorance, as understated as it is. His "If you say so, miss, if you say so" hints at a contempt for her ignorance and undercuts the authority over the island that she assumes in discounting the history that he relates to her.

The exchange between Betsy and the coachman also invokes the image of the "island paradise" devoid of its connection to its history that had taken root in the Western mind. As Polly Pattullo says about the Caribbean in regards to tourism, "It is the fortune, and misfortune, of the Caribbean to conjure up the idea of 'heaven on earth' or a little bit of paradise in the collective European imagination … the region, whatever the brutality of its history, kept its reputation as a Garden of Eden before the Fall."[98] As such, the scene connects the slave era when whites had supreme authority to 1930s Haiti when the country was being opened up to Americans through the military invasion. So even as the driver is telling Betsy of this terrible history of the island's inhabitants, their setting—riding through a pathway lined with tropical trees while birds are heard singing nearby—allows Betsy to ignore the violent history that produced her dream turned reality: being driven through paradise under palm trees by a black servant who, in her mind at least, can only repeat, "If you say so miss, if you say so."

Mastery over the natural, economic, and spiritual Caribbean was critical to white ownership of it. There are several times in *I Walked with a Zombie* where a presumably intimate knowledge of the Caribbean is presented as justification for ownership of it. For example, when she and Paul are on their way to Saint Sebastien by boat, Betsy naively finds her surroundings to be beautiful. Paul cuts in on her thoughts, saying insistently, "It's not beautiful" and points out her ignorance by calling her a newcomer whose thoughts are easy to read. "It seems beautiful because you don't understand. Those flying fish, they're not leaping in joy; they're jumping in terror. Bigger fish want to eat them. That luminous water; it takes its gleam from millions of tiny dead bodies. The glitter of putrescence. There's no beauty here; only death and decay." Paul continues, "Every good thing dies here. Even the stars," before walking off to leave Betsy with her thoughts. Paul's conjoining natural (luminous water) and economic elements (large fish eating smaller fish) in his commentary on the Caribbean environment, allow it to be read as a judgment passed on the island's black inhabitants as well as his family's history as slave traders and plantation owners. As such, he may be referring to that exploitative relationship between whites and blacks as "bigger fish" who devour the smaller ones— both the indigenous populations of the Caribbean and the imported Africans. His remark thus, points to the cannibalistic nature of the slave system and its relations of power that persist contemporarily. Again, the audience can surmise that these relationships are something about which Betsy knows nothing based on the later conversation that she has with the coach driver when her utter ignorance about the place is revealed.

The Holland/Rand family's authority over the spiritual world is also established later when, while Betsy is inside the house talking with Wesley, voodoo drums cut in. "The jungle drums. Mysterious, eerie," Wesley jokes. Although associated with voodoo, a belief system with practices that were supposedly feared, they are given the mundane function of signaling the end of the workday at the sugar mill. Consequently, they are rendered harmless, even banal: "Saint Sebastien's version of the factory whistle," according to Wesley. Later, while the family is having dinner, the conch shell is heard, apparently as part of a ceremony to ask the *loa* Damballah for rain. Again, just as Wesley did with the drums in the beginning of the film, he and Paul reduce the ceremony to the mundane. When Betsy remarks, "You don't seem very disturbed by it. I thought voodoo was something everyone was frightened of" Paul puts the spectacle into perspective, talking about ceremonies like one who has attended many of them: "They sing and dance and carry on and then as I understand it, one of the gods comes down and speaks through one of the people." While Senn sees this as evidence of " a truly adult approach to voodoo"[99] Young remarks that his explanation is so cynical and patronizing that the viewer begins to turn against him.[100] I do not agree with either of these assessments. Rather, for me, Paul's explanation offers a way of domesticating the seemingly uncontrollable Caribbean; a desired effect. I do however, agree with Young that Tourneur undermines Paul's "authority" by cutting to Wesley who remarks, visibly uncomfortable, that, "for some reason they always pick a night like this. This hot wind even sets me on edge," as he reaches for the whiskey decanter. In such instances of which there are several, Wesley is positioned as the one member of the family who is bothered by voodoo. As I discuss later, it is because the island has "possessed" him.

Histories from Below

The exchange between Betsy and the coachman is also an example of a history from below that is dismissed by those who do not want their idealized impression of their world infringed upon. The listener, Betsy, is representative of the hegemonic ideology of one who will return "home" to tell about his or her adventures that support the status quo; examples of which have been seen in writings by St. John and Seabrook, among others. This fact is also made clear in that it is Betsy's voice that provides the voiceover narration for the entire film. She, like St. John who never witnessed any of the macabre ceremonies he wrote about in *Hayti or the Black Republic*, is the voice of authority as well as the voice of reason as a white child of the North. However, unlike St. John whose authority was never questioned, this filmic presentation centering on Betsy and which portrays these pronouncements within a larger context, undermine the lone voice of authority that St. John enjoyed as only one of a few racists who traveled to the land of the Other in order to regale armchair tourists back home with his stories.[101]

Betsy's perspective is, in fact, repeatedly undermined by Paul. However, as a white woman, her perspective takes precedence over a black man's, at least in her own mind. Although a contemporary audience might be able to see and accept the reality about which the driver speaks, audiences from the 1930s were, like Betsy, probably not so attuned to or even interested in the history he relates, largely because of its source: a black man, as well as the fact that it demanded that they reevaluate their relationship to "their island paradise."

One. *White Zombie* and *I Walked with a Zombie*

The audience soon gets another glimpse into the immediacy of the black inhabitants' memory of the trauma of slavery in learning from Paul that when a baby is born on the island, the women weep and they rejoice when someone dies. While as an outsider, Betsy is totally ignorant of history's impact on contemporary life in the Caribbean, Paul whose family's history is deeply intertwined with that of the black inhabitants as former slave traders and owners, is very knowledgeable. He is the one who informs her of the history when he takes her outside and shows her Ti Misery/Saint Sebastien, saying, "It was once the figurehead of a slave ship. That's where *our* people came from; from the misery and pain of slavery. For generations they found life a burden. That's why they still weep when a child is born and make merry at a burial." As they both turn and watch the male servants retreat from them, Paul adds, "I told you Miss Connell. This is a sad place."

Where Betsy was able to dismiss the coachman's history of the island and Ti Misery, suddenly hearing it from the mouth of a white man—the descendant of a trader and a master—and seeing evidence of it in the literal body of a white woman, Jessica, she begins to reflect on the history. Given the context and the source as someone she respects, the history is more accessible and digestible. Nonetheless, even with her acceptance of the history, her understanding of the figurehead as Saint Sebastien appropriates it, making it accessible to the European audience.[102] As such, its meaning is wrested away from the inhabitants of the island whose history is entangled with the figure and appropriated by Europe to tell another history.

In these scenes, several different histories of the same figure resonate. There is the European's version of the history that resonates more with the film's intended audience, tied as it is to Christianity. While it would seem that Paul's explanation of the figurehead restores its meaning, he also appropriates the history by inserting himself and his family into the narrative as victims rather than as perpetrators of violence. As a more valued and trustworthy member of the human race who would have been above deck during the middle-passage crossing, his link to the figurehead supersedes that of the enslaved Africans who were chained below. But Paul's remarks can also be read in another way: his use of the possessive "our" may also allude to his sense of ownership of the island and its people. As "the Hollands was oldest family" in Saint Sebastien they would be seen as patrimonial figures; sites of origin for the current inhabitants, as it were. Again, the notion of proprietorship creeps in, in a most fundamental and foundational way. Finally, in yet another reading of the film, Paul's remarks may belie his "pure" European heritage and expose him as a mulatto who was lucky enough to be one of the lighter descendants of the often depraved sexual union between white men and black women. The prevalence of miscegenation and its evidence is in the largely light-skinned characters of the film. In this sense then, Paul *can* claim an affinity with the history of Ti Misery/Saint Sebastien as all of the island's inhabitants can. He embodies both sides of the figurehead's origins.

The Ambiguous Beaumont

Gyllian Phillips has argued that Legendre is "that postcolonial horror, the home-grown mixed type feared by the American regime."[103] I would suggest that Beaumont is also racially ambiguous. If he is, as I suggest, a Haitian mulatto, then he would have inherited his plantation after Emperor Jean-Jacques Dessalines outlawed land ownership by whites[104] following the revolution. Under a plan by President Alexander Pétion, a mulatto from the southern part of Haiti, to distribute the land to Haitians, countless numbers of mulatto and black revolutionaries inherited land that they then turned into sugar and banana plantations.

If he is indeed, mulatto, then his desire for Madeline reflects an American white male taboo against miscegenation that was rampant under colonialism. But while white men had access to black and mulatto women's bodies, sex between white women and non-white men was strictly prohibited and punishable by death. When Madeline is removed from her mausoleum and Dr. Bruner suggests that she is not dead but made to look that way so that someone could take her body after she was buried, Neil exclaims in horror, "Surely you don't think she's alive and in the hands of natives? Oh no! Better dead than that!"[105] Phillips rightly reads his horror as a reflection of the fear of miscegenation that was common before the 1960s and an "ever-present cultural anxiety about racial purity and the security of a white supremacist power structure."[106] As the audience knows that Madeline is in the hands of Legendre and Beaumont, the implication is that they are the natives to whom Neil refers.

Throughout most of the film, in fact, Legendre and Beaumont are depicted relationally. For example, during Neil and Madeline's wedding, as

One. *White Zombie* and *I Walked with a Zombie*

Beaumont escorts the bride down the stairs he professes his love for her. When it is clear that he will not be able to woo her with conventional means he gives her a rose with the zombie powder that Legendre has made for him. Later, while Beaumont is inside wrestling with the decision he has just made to zombify Madeline, Beaumont is shown outside making a wax replica of Madeline. The dichotomy between inside and outside and light and dark is presented with Beaumont being on one side and Legendre on the other. However, since they are both invested in the zombification of Madeline, albeit for different reasons, they are two sides of the same coin and equally implicated in the forces of darkness. The difference is that, while Legendre's intentions are known and evident from the first moments of the film—again, he personifies Baron Samedi who relishes his power to zombify others—Beaumont is an ambiguous character. He is presented as such throughout the film, whereby the struggle between good and evil is waged through him. For example, when he realizes the mistake he has made in trying to subjugate Madeline, he vows to "take her back," meaning, restore her to her former self. The ambiguity is finally resolved when good wins out once Beaumont's physical body—representative of his carnal desire—is almost completely consumed. Once his physical body is subdued, corrupted as it has been by sexual desire through his association with the island, his higher spiritual being is allowed to prevail.

Finally, where Renda reads Legendre's comment to Beaumont, "I have taken a fancy to you" in the scene in which he zombifies the latter, as a "come-on line"[107] I would suggest, that, although for most of the film, Beaumont is depicted as apart from and above the disfranchised population whom Legendre has zombified, in that scene, Beaumont is outed as inextricable from the land. In other words, Beaumont's status as a mulatto landowner—a child of Haiti—allows Legendre, as Baron Samedi, to also claim and zombify him.

Contested Masculinities

During Madeline's funeral scene in *White Zombie*, Beaumont and Neil stand on the stairs while pallbearers put her coffin into a mausoleum. In another realization of white men's fear regarding black men, Rhodes comments that Beaumont possesses the signifiers of sexual prowess and physical power, not only in his attire, but also in the swords and weapons hanging on his wall and a length of chain in his hand in the opening scenes of the film.[108] Not only do these accoutrements establish Beaumont's prowess, but the filmmaker reinforces his dominance and masculinity in the funeral scene visually by having him and Neil stand side by side where it is clear that the former is significantly taller than the latter. Beaumont's masculine superiority is later enacted when he succeeds in taking Madeline's body while Neil is in a tavern futilely embracing shadows in a drunken stupor. As Neil stumbles around in the darkness in the cemetery drunk with grief and alcohol later, the racially ambiguous Beaumont and Legendre are again presented relationally, working together to remove Madeline from the mausoleum with the help of the zombies. Beaumont has won; he has taken Madeline from Neil, proving that he is more of a man than her groom; again, a major fear of the white man.

As the film draws to a climax, the struggle over masculine prowess shifts from Beaumont to Legendre. For example, when Neil enters the room where Beaumont and Legendre sit after Legendre has administered the poison to zombify Beaumont, he suddenly falls backwards collapsing on a settee at the top of the stairs. Legendre senses his presence and rushes to him while Beaumont sits helplessly by clutching his useless hand almost completely paralyzed (that is, impotent). Legendre smiles and then makes the now familiar movement with his hands to summon Madeline who rises lethargically from her bed. Wearing a white flowing gown, which recalls her wedding gown[109] she makes her way through the mansion, past Neil, and descends the stairs to join Legendre. Under Legendre's power, Madeline takes the dagger that he had been using to whittle the figure of Beaumont a few moments before and raises it to plunge it into Neil's neck. Neil is saved by Dr. Bruner who is also associated with the island, and thus, with the power to influence its supernatural elements.

Neil finally confronts Legendre and his zombies and, as he backs toward the cliff's edge, pulls a gun from his waist, shooting at the zombies who close in on him. When all hope seems lost Dr. Bruner again, appears and hits Legendre over the head allowing Neil to scurry between the zombies' legs as they continue walking over the edge of the cliff. Richardson remarks about this scene that it would have been more effective "if Halpern had followed Haitian belief and given the zombies salt and let them tear Legendre to pieces!"[110] However, as an example of white men's

One. *White Zombie* and *I Walked with a Zombie*

inability to admit that power in Haiti lay in the hands of blacks, even asserting that evil is a white preserve and reflecting a persistent American myth of the period that black people could only serve, even this recompense is denied them.[111] They, along with the potential to control their own destinies, vanish over the cliff.

Masculinity is equally contested throughout *I Walked with a Zombie* in the two brothers, Wesley and Paul, who both want to possess Jessica. Paul and Wesley's rivalry is brought into relief early in the film when, on her day off, Betsy has drinks with Wesley at an outdoor café and she hears the song that sheds light on the animosity that has seethed beneath the surface since Wesley was first introduced. The song is sung by a street musician named Sir Lancelot:

> There was a family that lived on the isle
> Of Saint Sebastian for long, long while
> The head of the family was a Holland man
> And the younger brother, his name was Rand

Wesley tries to keep Betsy's attention focused on him, but she is more interested in the song.

> A woe, a me, shame and sorrow for the family
> The Holland man he kept in a tower
> A wife as pretty as a big white flower
> She saw the brother and she stole his heart
> And that's how the badness and trouble start

Like Madeline who is compared to a flower in *White Zombie*, the zombified Jessica is compared to a "big white flower." In addition to equating white womanhood with innocence, fragility, and beauty the metaphor also suggests that the women's zombification symbolizes their loss of innocence (their deflowering) as a result of their contact with the Caribbean.

When Sir Lancelot realizes that Wesley and Betsy have heard the song, he apologizes, saying that he never would have sung the song if he had known he was with a lady. But, the issue is not whether the song is true. It is about who hears it; namely one who may be the object of the man's affection. Wesley does not deny the song's truth, but says that he thinks that Paul planned the whole debacle just to watch him suffer.

Several hours later, Wesley is seen passed out at the café table with Betsy unable to wake him. Meanwhile the rest of the song from earlier is heard as Sir Lancelot makes his way toward Betsy and Wesley:

> The wife and the brother they want to go
> But the Holland man he tell them no
> The wife fall down and the evil came
> And he burned her mind in the fever flame
> A woe, a me, shame and sorrow for the family
> Her eyes are empty and she cannot talk
> And a nurse has come to make her walk
> The brothers are lonely and the nurse is young
> Now you must see that my song is sung
> A woe, a me, shame and sorrow for the family
> A woe, a me, shame and sorrow for the family

Young discusses these scenes with Sir Lancelot extensively as comments on black-white relationships in the Caribbean that are depicted in the film. As anthropologist Harold Courlander has shown in *The Drum and the Hoe* (1966), songs and the oral tradition often were used to, not only preserve history and cultural beliefs among the colonized, but also to serve as weapons of social criticism.[112] Sir Lancelot's song exposes the corruption of the masters who have historically portrayed blacks as behaving immorally. The emphasis on the love triangle essentially reverses the colonial discourse of the "oversexed native who has no respect for Western practices of monogamy."[113] Again, like Madeline, Jessica is compared to a flower. However, the song also points to the danger Jessica poses as a "New Woman" and her punishment for asserting her desire to be with Wesley: zombification.

Wesley's diminished position in the family in relation to Paul comes through when Mrs. Rand arrives at the café and directs the waiter, Ti Joseph, to get Wesley's horse and head him toward the plantation. She then introduces herself to Betsy solely as Wesley's mother. Her doing so establishes Wesley as a child still in need of mothering, unlike Paul who has established himself as "master." The two leave the café together, with Mrs. Rand commenting that, "Wesley is a very nice boy," again reinforcing his childlike status in the family. At the same time, her prevailing on Betsy to ask Paul to remove the whiskey decanter from the table also establishes the latter as an authority figure.

Wesley's childlike status in Paul's eyes reaches a climax when he tries to explain to Paul that the voodoo practitioners who are calling Jessica to them with their drums really do have power. Not only is his authority undermined by Paul who tells him that they believed such things when they were boys, but he is revealed to believe in voodoo and its power, signifying his possession by the island. The depiction of his possession is complete when later, after the *houngan* whispers something to his helper, Wesley rises mechanically from the table where he has been drinking, opens the gate for Jessica so that she can follow the sounds of the drum to the *houmfort*, and then removes the arrow from St. Sebastien before also leaving the fort. Both he and Jessica die in the end, inextricably connected to the Caribbean visually by the filmmaker having Carrefour follow them toward the ocean where Wesley drowns and implying that they will both be buried on the island in having their bodies brought back to Fort Holland as the film ends.

Island Possession Reversed

Fay remarks that, during the Occupation, "the marines who served in Haiti were viewed as beholden to a phantasmatic economy of their own"[114]; one that revolved around the specter of themselves being drawn into the belief systems that gave rise to such creatures as zombies. This fear is evidenced in Craige's *Cannibal Cousins* in which he writes about the toll that Haiti took on the Marines "in zombie-like terms" with "the degenerating magic of the tropical sun" affecting "the troops stationed too long in Haiti: 'Flesh melts from the bones, [the face] becomes the face of a corpse, with deep set eyes, like pools of smoldering fire.' Under this condition, Marines go mad like rabid dogs, become violent toward the natives, then turn suicidal. In general he finds that 'white men think queer thoughts and sometimes do queer things in the tropics.' The only cure is 'a swift return to the land of birth.'"[115]

This danger of the Marines succumbing to the tropics that Craige describes is realized in both films in which whites are presented as corrupted or rather, "possessed" by the island. For example, when the audience meets Dr. Bruner of *White Zombie*, a white missionary and doctor, it is in the context of Neil telling him about their coach driver's reaction to seeing men in the road digging a grave and declaring that they are zombies. When Neil asks if he does not believe it, Dr. Bruner hesitates: "Haiti is full of nonsense and superstition. They're always mixed up with a lot of mysteries that will turn your hair gray. I've been a missionary here for thirty years and at times I don't know what to think." His statement hints at the corrupting nature of life in the tropics, sinking those who come into contact with it into sin and superstition. Although Dr. Bruner has come to Haiti to save souls he has also grown to take on the black inhabitants' beliefs. He elaborates on his assimilation of black superstition and the inhabitants' appropriation of him in a later scene. In fact, almost all of Dr. Bruner's responses essentially reflect St. John's rhetorical question and answer about the corruptive nature of the Caribbean and more specifically, Haitian voodoo: "Who is tainted by Vaudoux-worship?' I fear the answer must be, 'Who is not?'"[116]

Although he is "kindly and good" Dr. Bruner's ambiguity, if not total corruption, is also implied visually. The lighting of the match for his pipe at various key moments in the film symbolizes his role as a representative of Christianity that "lights the dark." However, as Rhodes rightly remarks, it is problematic that "Bruner is not actually the giver of light; he relies on the matches from those who have traveled to Haiti."[117] Even more importantly, newly arrived to Haiti, Neil and Madeline represent the purity that they bring with them from the United States. It is clear by the end of the film that the couple will leave the site of their trauma and potential corruption as soon as possible thus, taking their light with them and leaving Dr. Bruner to seek his light from other "innocents." In this sense, Dr. Bruner is portrayed as a kind of cannibal, himself, feeding off the innocence of hosts as the Vampyre fed off of the innocence of his victims.[118]

Tony Williams notes about Dr. Bruner, that "As the white colonial figure and alter ego to Legendre, Bruner remains to restore normality and repression" (2005). As the missionary, he offers hope for a Haiti that will come into the light, a crusade that was administered by the Catholic Church beginning in 1896 and continuing intermittently until 1941 in the anti-superstition campaigns.[119] However, again, his goodness is not assured as the film insinuates that his corruption by Haiti may be too far along to be remedied and the light that he gives must come from the "civilized" outside.

Dr. Bruner also displays a deep knowledge of Haitian history and its culture. In addition, he speaks of a kind of adoption by Haitians who accept his power from within their worldview. I would suggest that, while this may be interpreted as Dr. Bruner's conscious appropriation of Haitian culture, his knowledge, incorporation into the culture, and ability to access

One. *White Zombie* and *I Walked with a Zombie*

information that would be off-limits to outsiders actually signifies the island's possession of him. He is the voice of authority, explaining to Neil, "The natives brought their superstitions from Africa. Some of them can be traced as far back as ancient Egypt. And beyond that yet in the countries that were old when Egypt was young." In addition, drawing directly on a scene from Seabrook's text, he pulls a book from his bookshelf and begins reading from it. Invoking the law (mistakenly identified as Article 249 of the Haitian Penal Code) that was used in posters to draw audiences to the film, the doctor says, "The law of Haiti acknowledges the possibility of being buried alive."[120] After explaining that "the natives think that [he's] a magician" because he is a preacher and that he can get information that no gendarme would be privy to, the doctor vows to get to the bottom of Madeline's disappearance. In addition, as Williams argues, he is linked to Legendre, not only visually in his clothing, but in the way that he uses voodoo or benefits from his association with it. Although he scientifically rationalizes Madeline's zombified condition, he resorts to voodoo to save her, signifying his belief in its power.

Like Dr. Bruner, Mrs. Rand is also possessed by the island. Although Dr. Bruner is a Christian missionary, he exhibits scientific rationalism that is associated with the West. Mrs. Rand, the wife of a missionary, is also depicted as scientifically rational in her running a medical dispensary although there is no indication that she has any medical training. Like Dr. Bruner, she also has a deep knowledge of voodoo and is accepted by its practitioners, even rising to a position of leadership.

Unlike with Dr. Bruner, the audience is not immediately exposed to the depth of Mrs. Rand's corruption. For example, when Betsy visits her in the dispensary that she "runs," Mrs. Rand seems to admonish a little boy with an amulet around his neck, asking, "How do you ever expect to get into Heaven with one foot in the voodoo *houmfort* and the other in the church?" After the little boy leaves, she turns her attention to Betsy, calling the wearing of amulets "native nonsense" and declares, "The *houngan* has his prescription and the doctor and I have ours." Instead of responding to Betsy's query about whether she believes in voodoo, Mrs. Rand answers with a question, "A missionary's widow? Not very likely, is it?" Turning the onus on Betsy to remain rational when Betsy asks if she thought voodoo could cure a sick person, Mrs. Rand echoes Paul when she turns and says, "Frankly, my dear, I didn't expect such a thing from a level-headed girl like you." Finally, displaying a hint of belief in the power of voodoo, when Betsy suggests that she will take Jessica to the *houmfort*, Mrs. Rand indicates that such a thing might be dangerous for both her and Jessica. Then, in a line that has been repeated innumerable times about Africans and people of African descent and was given as a justification for the American invasion in 1915, Mrs. Rand adds, "These people are primitive. Things that are natural to them might shock and horrify you."

Later, Mrs. Rand's entrenchment in voodoo is made clear when Betsy takes Jessica to a voodoo ceremony to ask Damballah, the *loa* of life, for their hearts' desires. When Betsy steps forward to ask for what she wants, it is Mrs. Rand who reaches out and pulls her into the *houmfort*. Dressed in her tailored suit and with her hands in her pocket, Mrs. Rand is the picture of authority. Her assistant, a man who has lit a lantern for her, stands silently by, looking down, his hands crossed in front of him in a sign of supplication. When Betsy expresses her surprise at finding her there, Mrs. Rand divulges her ambiguity in regard to science and spiritual belief. She explains that she took on the personage of Damballah as a way of gaining control over her servants after her husband died. She discovered the secret to control while trying to help a mother who would not listen to her advice to boil her baby's drinking water. She portrays "the natives" in childlike terms in need of protection from themselves when she concludes, "It seemed so much simpler to let the gods speak through me. I should've known there's no easy way to do good, Betsy." At Mrs. Rand's urging, Betsy returns to Fort Holland with Jessica and, as an example of her power, Mrs. Rand's assistant's directive to the *serviteurs* to "let them go" allows them to depart unmolested.

The depth of Mrs. Rand's corruption by voodoo and by extension, the island, is revealed at the end of the film when she confesses that Jessica's zombification is a result of her actions. Not only does she "talk more than a little voodoo to get medicine down a patient's throats" as Dr. Maxwell does, but she "entered into their ceremonies and pretended to be possessed by their gods." It would seem however, that the *loas* had the last word when one night she went to the *houmfort* and was possessed. She says, "The drums, the chanting, the lights. I heard a voice speaking in the sudden silence; my voice. I was speaking to the *houngan*. I was possessed. I told him that the woman at Fort Holland was evil and asked him to make her a zombie." Although Dr. Maxwell tries to discount Mrs. Rand's belief that she is responsible for Jessica's zombification, and instead, offers a medical explanation, Mrs. Rand is convinced of her guilt, thus signifying her full turning away from Western science and the completion of her mental, physical, and spiritual possession by the Caribbean.

Although Young reads the film's ending ambiguously, I read it as evidence of Mrs. Rand's full corruption by the Caribbean. Rather than civilizing and Christianizing the natives as she and her husband set out to do, her husband has died and she has been co-opted by their "superstitious" beliefs. The implication is that she has "gone native" without even realizing it; lured as she was by the drums and the lascivious dancing that had corrupted so many before her like Dr. Bruner.

Again, Dr. Bruner and Mrs. Rand have been drawn to the "dark side" because of their intimate association with the island and its people. They are contaminated like the doctor and Johnson of *The Love Wanga* whom I discuss in the following chapter, have been contaminated. And even though the white protagonists—Madeline and Neil in *White Zombie* and Betsy in *I Walked with a Zombie*—will be able to escape the corruption, perhaps because they have not been exposed to it long enough, Dr. Bruner, Mrs. Rand, the doctor and Johnson will spend the rest of their lives there. They are unable to return to a state of "innocence" that again, is associated with the Global North (the U.S. and Canada).

Women and the Nation

In her article, "The Cinema of Difference: Jacques Tourneur, Race and 'I Walked with a Zombie' (1943)," Gwenda Young, like most authors who have written about *I Walked with a Zombie*, focuses on Tourneur's recognition and celebration of racial difference. Relatedly, there is the issue of the representation of the liberated white woman let loose in the Caribbean.

As Ann Kordas remarks, the stereotypical "New Woman" who emerged in the late nineteenth and early twentieth century meant different things to different people. While some Americans welcomed their appearance, others found them to be dangerous, uncontrolled elements in American society. Still others feared that they were exposing themselves to harm.[121]

These fears about women combined with white male fears about uncontrollable and uncontainable black men gave rise to films in the 1930s and 1940s that associated the zombie with moral transgression, especially sexual transgression.[122]

Renda notes in her discussion of other cultural productions about Haiti from the same era—most notably, Eugene O'Neill's *The Emperor Jones*—that, "Haiti functioned as a proving ground for men, a site for struggles over racialized versions of masculinity."[123] As such, "cultural texts taking off from Haitian themes addressed themselves to women's proper place."[124] While Renda explores the disrupted role of women using a novel titled *The Goat Without Horns* (1925) and *White Zombie*, her observation is relevant to *I Walked with a Zombie* as well. In both of the films, the filmmakers attempt to put the white woman who has been let loose in the Caribbean back in her "proper place" by depicting her, on one hand, as a source of corruption to white men and on the other, corrupted by her contact with the Caribbean in general and Haiti, in particular.

According to Renda, Robert Beale Davis, author of *The Goat Without Horns*, believed that "romance, marriage and family relations constituted the foundation of all that was right with Euro-American society. What threatened well-ordered sexuality therefore threatened the West. Davis took aim at feminists who he associated with that grave danger: a liberated sexuality. For him, failing to mind their place in the world, modern women played with fire."[125] A similar warning is issued in *I Walked with a Zombie*, which places the "beautiful Jessica" at the center of a love triangle involving half brothers and Betsy, the girl-next-door, as an extension of the triangle through her love for Paul.

The very real danger of the Caribbean and the black man in particular is driven home when Carrefour enters into the intimate space of Jessica's bedroom where she and Betsy sleep. As a white woman, Jessica represents an entryway of contamination by outsiders; elements of corruption that Carrefour represents. The fact that Carrefour is allowed to roam about the room without detection signifies the insidious way that the purity of the white race vis-à-vis the white woman is potentially contaminated by the primitiveness of the black body and deficient intellect (as in the mindless zombie). Jessica has already been contaminated as a result of her lustfulness and Betsy is in danger of being contaminated. The scene is reminiscent of one of the early scenes when the shadow of a servant passed

One. *White Zombie* and *I Walked with a Zombie*

over Betsy's body while she was in her bedroom. This shadow contact by Carrefour signifies the impending danger to her, as yet, at least on the surface, maintained innocence. Whereas the threat from the earlier scene was neutralized in the shadow being revealed as that of a servant, in this later scene, the danger is allowed to linger, actually growing in intensity in the mindless form of the giant black male body, which Lizabeth Paravisini-Gebert observes is phallic.[126]

Such films seem to undermine their goal. As Dendle argues, films such as *White Zombie* and *I Walked with a Zombie* deny the possibility of complete containment by men of women. The repressed anima of the zombie woman surpasses its prescribed boundaries, just as women in society were surpassing traditional gender roles as a result of the depression shortly before *White Zombie* was released and World War II when *I Walked with a Zombie* was released. The films express white male anxiety over losing control over "their women" as, during both of these eras, women became more independent when they were forced to find work outside the home in order to support their families.

Like Jessica and Betsy, Madeline is also associated with the nation as synecdoche: at once a feminized Haiti as well as the U.S. in peril. About the scene in *White Zombie* in which Madeline is shown readying herself for her wedding, Williams observes that, dressed in underwear with a map of Haiti embossed on it, she is linked to a feminized Haiti to be taken and possessed by the U.S. as it is represented by Neil and Beaumont.[127] Fay also remarks that the film strives "to remind us of Madeline's affinity with Haiti and black culture, and it intimates that the plight of women may not be disconnected from the plight of the occupied."[128] In fact, as Williams notes, Madeline is the center of the conflict in the film as Haiti was at the center of the conflict between the U.S. and Germany as well as other nations at the time.[129] Furthermore, as Rhodes notes, "she does little to impact the film's narrative, but rather is acted upon."[130] She is presented as the archetypal white female, innocent, victimized, and vulnerable. She also represents the potential for corruption by sin and lethargy that the Caribbean poses. As Sheller notes, this potential is figured through feminine corruption,[131] a theme that also permeates *I Walked with a Zombie* and later, *The Love Wanga*.

While indeed, this struggle between two world powers over control of the little island of Hispaniola was very much foremost in the white

American male's mind at the time, I would also posit that the fight is between Haiti as an independent nation and the U.S.'s desire to return it to a colonial state through annexation, which was also proposed prior to the invasion. Subduing Haiti would not only allow the U.S. to restore the natural colonial order, but it would allow it entry into the ranks of, not just world powers, but colonial powers, although belatedly. Thus, Madeline represents the feminized nation of Haiti, not in relation to male prowess represented by Germany, France, and Great Britain, but that Haiti represented in taking its independence. As such, feminizing it by placing it on the body of a white woman was an attempt to present it as weak to the penetrating and colonizing advances of the U.S.

Redemptive Endings?

Madeline stands out from the zombified natives, not only because she is white, but because she is a woman. While "the natives," all male, are not able to rouse themselves from their zombified state even going so far as to fall to their deaths for lack of any agency, Madeline is never fully conquered by Beaumont or Legendre. Her restlessness when she senses that Neil is near, her suddenly becoming conscious as she is being commanded to murder her husband, and her moments of lucidity on the terrace as the war between Neil and Legendre wages, are evidence of the strong will that was attributed to the empowered woman of that era. At the same time, of course, cautionary tales are embedded within these depictions of empowered women as Renda argues about the novel, *The Goat Without Horns* and the film, *I Walked with a Zombie* where white women are portrayed as corrupted and corrupting influences on white men. But, unlike Jessica, Madeline escapes the warning partially by virtue of her allegiance to her man. The war for control for imperialist control is fought over the body of the woman and the U.S. emerges the victor.

With *I Walked with a Zombie*, the audience can assume that Paul and Betsy will go North, away from the corrosive and corruptive environment of the Global South where "everything good dies." Like Dr. Bruner from *White Zombie*, Mrs. Rand is too much a part of the environment to leave the island. So, although in some ways, she is still able to offer the light of Christianity and medicine to the "primitive natives," she, like Dr. Bruner, is irredeemable as a consequence of her prolonged contact with them. Again, Jessica, completely irredeemable, is condemned to social and physical death. Unlike Madeline of *White Zombie* who still has the hope of being a mother and wife to the innocent and pure Neil, Jessica, as a woman who pitted one brother against another out of lust is damned. Like the biblical Adam who ate the apple at Eve's behest, Wesley too is condemned. Although Paul is also corrupted by his history, Betsy, who has reclaimed her innocence, will be able to fix him once she has removed him from the corrosive environment that makes both white women *and* men lose their souls.

CHAPTER TWO

The Love Wanga
The American Occupation and Miscegenation

Debates about the racial identity of *White Zombie*'s Murder Legendre reflect the different sociopolitical and ideological conditions that he represents. For Jennifer Fay, he is "white and European"[1] and "his racial categorization represents larger concerns about labor and capital in depression-era America."[2] Conversely, Kyle Bishop contends that he is black, asserting that Madeline's zombification represents the "greatest fear of the colonizers—that the native will rise up and become the dominating force."[3] Gyllian Phillips presents yet a third option, arguing that Legendre is "that postcolonial horror, the home-grown mixed type feared by the American regime."[4] Cleeli Gordon, the villain of George Terwilliger's *The Love Wanga: A Story of Voodoo Filmed in Its Entirety in the West Indies* (1935), puts such discussions to rest as she is clearly a mulatto woman. Her mixed-race heritage is, in fact, central to the plot as it relates to her relentless pursuit of a relationship with a phenotypically white plantation owner named Adam Maynard.[5]

Phillips' reading of Legendre gets to the heart of the message of *The Love Wanga*. As she says, Legendre presents a

> primal source of horror related to miscegenation: when Madeleine, and later Beaumont, ingests the secret zombie powder, they are in a sense infected, or at least contaminated. The boundaries of their bodies are violated and invaded, leaving them without essential agency. Whereas miscegenation is a threat to the social order, through the production of mixed race citizens, the zombie metaphor shows the boundaries of identity associated with the skin as permeable and unfixed. The film poses an almost philosophical problem about the nature of bodily autonomy and racial social structures in American culture. Postcolonial culture produces the creole whose very identity undermines the black-white binary necessary to white supremacist power structures.[6]

Indeed, Cleeli challenges the black-white binary on which white supremacist ideology rested. I would propose that, in fact, miscegenation, the order of the day under the colonial system with a legacy that extended well into the twentieth century, complicates the directive to stick to one's own kind, as Cleeli is told to do repeatedly in the film. As such, I suggest that, while Cleeli is obviously mixed-race, Adam, her love interest, is, like Legendre, also possibly mulatto. The feasibility of my proposition highlights the problem with creole populations: one can never be sure who is who. This inability to distinguish with any certainty who is harboring black blood fundamentally undermines the black-white binary on which white hegemony hinges. If Adam is indeed, "black" as I suggest, then Cleeli, in choosing him, *is* sticking to her own kind. However, since he is portrayed in the film as white—perhaps passing—then both he and Cleeli offer insight into the historical underpinnings of the societies they represent: the U.S. and Haiti respectively.

The Negro Problem

The mixed-race person took root under the colonial system and may very well be ground zero for Cleeli as well as Adam's bloodlines. It was out of miscegenation that the Haitian *affranchi* class, which undermined the white colonial power structure, emerged. Prior to the Haitian Revolution the *affranchis* challenged the white colonialists for control of the island and posed a real threat to white hegemony. "Men of color" such as Vincent Ogé and Jean-Baptiste Chavannes are well-known martyrs for racial equality from Saint-Domingue history. In the end, the *affranchis'* joining with the black enslaved population ensured the success of the revolution.[7]

It was also out of miscegenation that African Americans who could pass for white in Jim Crow America emerged. In a racially schizophrenic country where the one-drop rule was law, but someone could be considered white on one side of a state line and black on another, white male America suffered anxiety around maintaining the purity of the race. Light-skinned black men being able to pass and have sexual access to their women with the evidence of their union being mulatto children was, like a black nation following the Haitian Revolution, the stuff of white nightmares. Black women who could pass for white were also problematic as the birth of a mulatto child to two "white parents" called the whole system of racial difference, and with it, inequality, into question.[8]

When the Marines, originating from an America that was preoccupied with their "Negro problem," landed in Haiti in 1915 they found a class of people, the mulatto elite, who were descended from the *affranchis* and who refused to fit themselves into the black-white binary on which white American racism depended. As such they were labeled uncontainable and uncontrollable monstrosities as part and parcel of the island nation. Cleeli represents that uncontainable, uncontrollable monster who threatens the natural order: the separation of blacks and whites. Her corruption is so complete, in fact, that she, like Jessica of *I Walked with a Zombie*, has to suffer a violent death in the end.

The Film

The Love Wanga centers on Cleeli who pursues her neighbor, Adam, after the two had a two-year romantic relationship when he lived alone on his father's plantation on "Paradise Island," an analogue for Haiti. However, rather than continue with the relationship, Adam decides to marry a white New York socialite named Eve Langley. Cleeli, refusing to be cast aside, sends a charm to Eve in an effort to kill her. After her plans are thwarted Cleeli raises two zombies from the dead to kidnap Eve with the hope of sacrificing her to Damballah, the voodoo snake god. When Le Strange, Adam's mulatto overseer who is in love with Cleeli, tries to rescue Eve, Cleeli shoots him and then continues with the ritual that will end in Eve's sacrifice. However, as she raises her arm to cut off Eve's head, Le Strange burns Cleeli's protective *wanga* (charm), which he had grabbed from around her neck as they struggled over Eve. Distraught, Cleeli heads into the woods with Le Strange in pursuit. Before he dies from his gunshot wound he strangles Cleeli, killing her.

A Bit of Background

The Love Wanga was an independent production made for Paramount Picture's English distribution arm. After it was completed, however, Paramount refused to release the film in the U.S. Cheryl Black, who explores the star of *The Love Wanga*, Fredi Washington's career, speculates that investors found the finished film too controversial. Washington, however,

Two. *The Love Wanga*

stated unequivocally that the film was banned precisely because of its depiction of interracial sexuality by an interracial cast.[9] Whatever the reason, the film's release in America was delayed until early 1942 when it was distributed briefly under the title *The Love Wanga* and *Drums of the Jungle*.[10]

If the audience notices that some of the characters' accents seem a bit "off" it is because Terwilliger was forced to film the majority of *The Love Wanga* in Jamaica, rather than Haiti, following some transgressive behavior by the filmmaker. According to Bryan Senn,[11] although Terwilliger initially won the confidence of the locals, he quickly raised the ire of their religious leaders when he asked to film their actual ceremonies. After several warnings (including a *wanga*[12] in the front seat of his car), Terwilliger was forced to move production to the neighboring island of Jamaica. However, even after they left Haiti the crew was plagued by problems including deaths, which one of the actors, Sheldon Leonard, intimates, may have been related to something that happened while they were still in Haiti. According to Leonard, the film's prop person tried to obtain certain objects such as stuffed snakeskins, goatskin drums, skulls and other exotica, but he could not buy them because they were sacred objects. Nor could he borrow them. Unwilling to take "no" for an answer, he stole what he wanted. Although they switched islands to finish the movie, it would seem that Haiti was not finished with them. The filming that was supposed to take six weeks turned into eleven weeks, plagued by attacks by hornets, one person's impalement on barbed cactus quills and two deaths; one by barracuda, one by yellow fever.[13]

The Love Wanga's claim to fame is that it is the second movie (after *White Zombie*) to feature zombies. It also clearly works through the fears and taboos that white Westerners harbored at the time. The VHS cover for *The Love Wanga* conveys the film's preoccupations, proclaiming, "Meet Clelie … naïve, young and beautiful … lithe, yielding and primitive.… Love hungry child of the tropics!" Also, as Mark H. Harris on his blog states, "It … deals with interracial relationships, the notion of 'passing,' and the supposedly inherent fiery lustfulness of black native women."[14] But again, as I suggest, this notion of passing is not limited to Cleeli, but can also be extended to Adam.

As a mulatto woman, not only does Cleeli represent a disruption of the black-white binary on which the white power structure is based, but as a wealthy female plantation owner, she also threatens the patriarchal structure. Finally, she epitomizes the "New Woman" who is sexually transgressive in having been, the audience can assume, sexually active outside the sanctity of marriage. This chapter explores Cleeli's racial and sexual transgressiveness as representative of, not only the fear, but the desire that white men harbored about such women as a driving force behind Terwilliger's treatment of the character. I read his Othering of her as integral to the Haiti that Terwilliger represents as uncontained and uncontrollable. Through his use of Othering, the filmmaker contributed to calming white fears of contamination by Cleeli as a mixed-race woman and, by extension, the impermeable black collective that inhabited the island and against which white American authors had been writing for a number of years before the Marine invasion. Finally, I consider how, as a production of a white American male, the film reflects and comments on the white American dilemma around what to do with the African American male.

Changing Womanhood

The Love Wanga marks an important digression in the treatment of female characters in the zombie films that both preceded and followed it. As Chris Vials remarks, after Seabrook's book in which he described the use of women in voodoo ceremonies as a disempowering process, an important shift with respect to femininity occurred in American film and radio in which, "The loss of either womanhood or female innocence was visited upon white women instead of Haitian women."[15] In effect, the physical and spiritual suffering of Haitian women was displaced onto white, female bodies.[16] While this loss of innocence was usually signified by zombification as in the case of *White Zombie* and later, *I Walked with a Zombie,* Vials also cites the radio programs, "The Zombie" and "Isle of the Living Dead" which presented white female corruption through the guise of the villainous white female plantation owner. Cleeli, though mulatto, also embodies corruption as the villainous female plantation owner. Not only does she hold a position that is reserved for white men, but the fact that she rejects her blackness repeatedly, is determined to violate the holy union of Adam and Eve, and then dares to attempt to take her revenge on a white woman makes her irredeemably transgressive. She simply does not know her place.

Cleeli's history with and persistent lustful advances towards Adam are contrasted with and dependent upon Eve's purity and innocence. As such, Adam's behavior with his fiancée also remarks on his past relationship with Cleeli. As the first father, he will bed his future wife out of obligation to the race; not because he enjoys the act with her. The obligatory nature of Adam and Eve's coupling, evidenced by their lack of passion for each other, contrasted with Cleeli's displays of fiery passion, which include frequent outbursts, her ripping her dress open so that Le Strange can gaze on her whiteness, throwing herself at Adam's feet, and raising zombies from the dead to kidnap Eve, reinforce this contrast. The audience can deduce from these scenes that Adam was attracted to the corrupted and lustful Cleeli because, free to objectify her, he was able to indulge his most base sexual instincts. Conversely, his white wife was free to remain pure and, as such, worthy of propagating his family.

Although white women, like black and mulatto women, were also objectified, the consequences for them were different. White women were more often placed on a pedestal rather than degraded as black and mulatto women were; a fact that several scholars, including Norma Manatu, have taken up in their research on black women in a U.S context. In fact, as Joan Dayan argues regarding the distinction between love and lust as it pertained to white versus black and mulatto women under slavery, the sentiment of love, when attached with women other than white "became emblematic of lust and debauchery. Yet, the mixed-blood or mulatto woman somehow became the concrete signifier for lust that could be portrayed as 'love.'"[17] Reflecting common beliefs held by the colonizer, the lawyer, Moreau de Saint-Méry who documented Saint-Domingue culture and politics, wrote that "The entire being of a Mulâtresse is given up to pleasure, the fire of this Goddess that burns in her heart only to be extinguished with her life.... To charm all her senses, to surrender to the most delicious ecstasy, to be surprised by the most seductive ravishing, that is her unique study."[18] In other words, so driven is Cleeli by her lustful desires that the only way that she can cease in her pursuit of Adam is in death; she has not choice. Therefore, she has to die in the end.

"Tragic" Mulattoes

Fredi Washington, the lead character in *The Love Wanga*, is an interesting personage in her own right. A woman who identified strongly with her African American heritage, before playing Cleeli, Washington, starred earlier in the film *Imitation of Life* (1934) as a young black woman named Peola who passes for white in order to find opportunity in a racist society. Unlike the characters she plays in both films, Washington was very proud of her blackness and turned down several roles where she was asked to pass for white. In her comments on passing and her role in *Imitation of Life* she says, "I have never tried to pass for white and never had any desire, I am proud of my race. In *Imitation of Life* I was showing how a girl might feel under the circumstances, but I'm not showing how I felt."[19] Finally frustrated with Hollywood's racism, she left for New York and became a civil rights activist and theatre writer.

Of course, a variation on the theme of rejection of one's blackness resurfaces in *The Love Wanga* as Cleeli, who is as light-skinned as Eve, proclaims her whiteness repeatedly while also denouncing her black heritage. Why Washington decided to accept the role is unknown. However, given her sociopolitical views and the reason that she gives for taking on the character of Peola in *Imitation of Life*, the audience can deduce that she recognized in the character of Cleeli an opportunity to subvert the racist ideology that demonized people like her and what they represented: the triumph of blackness.

We can return to our discussion from the Introduction of the monstrous as a barometer of cultural anxiety as Kevin Alexander Boon suggests. Again, Boon argues that "That which is defined as monstrous ... was not supposed to happen; that is, it is unnatural and as such a malformation of some universal design." The "monstrous" threatens the purity of the human form as that form is intended by whomever is responsible for that universal design."[20] Again, the very nation of Haiti "was not supposed to happen" and is thus, monstrous. Cleeli, as a female mulatto child of the nation, is also monstrous. She, in fact, embodies several monstrous conditions. She is a liminal character, not black and not white, yet both and as such, unclassifiable and uncontainable. She is also a Jezebel figure, one who, as K. Sue Jewell asserts, is also a tragic mulatto with her "thin lips, long straight hair, slender nose, thin figure and fair complexion."[21] While in some respects, her phenotype renders her acceptable to white audiences, she is nonetheless still perceived as tainted by the black blood that runs through her veins.[22] As Kamala Kempadoo notes, throughout the Americas, women of mixed descent were, in general, perceived more favorably by the European elite than pure African women. Nonetheless, again, they still had their black side to contend with. For Kempadoo,

> If white womanhood represented the pinnacle of femininity, couched in assumptions of fairness, purity, frailty and domesticity, and black womanhood the total opposite because of its presumed closeness to nature, dark skin, masculine physique and unbridled sexuality, the combination of western Europe and Africa produced notions of the "light-skinned" woman who could almost pass for white yet retained a tinge of colour, as well as a hint of the wantonness and uninhibited sexuality of exotic cultures. The "coloured" woman was then often described as possessing "a great physical attraction for the European."[23]

But for whom amongst the European elite is the mulatto woman acceptable? About this, Kempadoo is not explicit. I propose that the mulatto woman is acceptable to the elite white man, not the elite white woman. Not only can he see himself in the mulatto woman (as his potential offspring), but she embodies the qualities that he desires in a wife while also harboring those forbidden characteristics that he desires carnally. Conversely, for the white woman, the mulatto woman is essentially, a reminder of the white man's transgression of forsaking her for a black woman. She is a reminder of a rivalry that extends back to the time of slavery when white masters had black concubines and mistresses for whom they would leave their marital bed and the children in whom the white mistress could recognize her husband's features. Thus, the mulatto woman was cut by a double-edged sword: prized for her beauty as the embodiment of sexual transgression, but also reviled because of it.

The mixed-race woman was also a liminal creature; a monstrosity because her membership in the category of "mixed race," mulatto, "mustee" or "colored" legally placed her outside of white society and ideologically, outside of black society. She represented

> European impurity and moral, racial and social degradation, constituting an "unnatural transgression of the rules of social propriety." The mulatto woman (*la mulata*) represented the erotic and sexually desirable, yet was outcast and pathologized and emerged during slavery as the symbol of the prostitute—the sexually available yet socially despised body—the exoticized other, the trope of the exotic.[24]

While she may, until recently, have been categorized legally as black, the mulatto woman was also ideologically excluded from black society because of her tainted status as "part-white." As such, within the black community she was seen as a potential traitor to the race. Because of her constant companion of "not belonging," there has arisen the trope of the "tragic mulatto" who is characterized as sad or even suicidal because of her outsider status. Cleeli, a tragic figure, fulfills her destiny by, on one hand, rejecting her black identity and on the other, claiming to be white, trespassing boundaries that "Adam and Eve," as a synecdoche for "pure" white Western culture and gatekeepers, guard jealously.

Adam's Ambiguity

As I mentioned at the beginning of this chapter, I want to suggest that Cleeli is not the only mulatto in the room. As the son of a banana plantation owner who inherits his father's business, Adam's racial identity is questionable. The question arises from Haiti's revolutionary history when the nation's first leader, Emperor Jean-Jacques Dessalines, decreed at the nation's founding that whites were prohibited from owning land in Haiti. Later, under President Alexander Pétion's land distribution plan, several men who had served in the revolutionary army were given large plots of land to cultivate as they chose. When Adam tells Eve as they sail to the island that his father gave him his plantation, it could be this ancient practice of land distribution to which he is referring. Additionally, his skin color hints at the practice amongst the American black elite to strive to whiten the race such that one's black roots are suppressed after several generations. It also references the practice of passing that some light-skinned African Americans engaged in both during slavery and the Jim Crow Era (such as Peola from *Imitation of Life* does) in order to gain social and economic mobility.[25]

Although she is not portrayed as American, this skin-lightening scheme also seems to be the framework under which Cleeli operates. Although she is still recognizably black, more because of her frizzy hair than anything else, her skin is indeed white. Her marrying Adam, more phenotypically white than she is, would secure her place in white society. Terwilliger's projection of this particularly American practice of skin-lightening from within the racist framework of the United States evidences what several scholars have commented about zombie films from that era: that they are more reflections and comments on white American preoccupations and anxieties than the country that was presumably their subject.

If Adam and Cleeli are both indeed black, then their accommodations on the ship and Adam's marriage to a white socialite seem to suggest, not only the truth of the Haitian adage, "The rich black man who can read and write is a mulatto; the poor mulatto who can't read or write is black,"[26] but also the possibility of it being extended to include whiteness. As such, "the rich mulatto who can read and write is white." In the context of Haiti in which the black-white binary does not have the same meaning as in a U.S. context, even if Adam is mulatto he would be considered a master because of his lighter skin in relation to Le Strange who is also mulatto, but of a slightly darker hue and with curlier hair. It should also be noted that the actor who played Le Strange, Sheldon Leonard, was Jewish, thus further blurring the racial binaries and boundaries on which the film rests.

An Island in Need of Saving

The theme of an island paradise that was corrupted by its black inhabitants was propagated in the American media several years before the U.S. Marines invaded Haiti. For example, in 1908, an article reprinted from an address to the National Geographic Society, "Haiti: A Degenerating Island: The Story of its Past Grandeur and Present Decay" by Rear Admiral Colby M. Chester, U.S. Navy, painted Haiti as an oasis that was being ruined by its black inhabitants. Calling it one of the "most favored nations" because of both its location and its natural resources, he lamented that the island's inhabitants were not of an order befitting the country's natural riches.[27] In his section entitled "Haiti Is Degenerating to a Condition of Barbarism" Chester pointed out that, of 21 rulers from Dessalines to "the one now holding power," only four had completed their terms in office. He followed that with a truth that read like an accusation: "Haiti is getting blacker and blacker."[28] His statement can be taken to refer to both the skin color of the nation's inhabitants and his perception that the country was sinking deeper and deeper into a barbaric state as, according to him this encroaching blackness was the result of the practical extermination or forcible removal of the white element from the island. For him, in 1908, not only were the ancestors of the contemporary inhabitants of Haiti responsible for the "fierce strife known as 'The Horrors of the Negro Insurrection in Santo Domingo,'"[29] but the inhabitants of the twentieth century continued their insubordination against the natural order of things. In his view, Haiti was "the one country in the world where white blood [was] at a discount."[30]

National Geographic Magazine in which the article was printed was an important tool for winning popular American support for the invasion of Haiti as the National Geographic Society, which publishes the magazine, had and continues to have a reputation for "safeguarding American values and traditions."[31] This includes "an informed or knowledgeable citizenry, particularly in an epoch, which may have been devoted to the idea of America's *global responsibilities*"[32] (emphasis added). The U.S. used the rhetoric of Christian duty and the need to save Haiti from itself as justification for its military mission. In addition, the idea that Haitians were children in need of fatherly guidance was promoted. As Mary Renda notes, "Paternalist discourse was one of the primary cultural mechanisms by which the occupation conscripted men into the project of carrying out U.S. rule."[33]

As part of the machine of imperialism, Chester's article damned the Haitian inhabitants and was presented as evidence of the need for radical intervention by Christian souls who had the benefit of "hundreds of years of enlightenment and study of political science and economy and republican principles."[34] As Chester wrote for a white American audience, the plight of the barbaric Haitians "who have no higher ambition than to possess sufficient means to supply the demands of their appetites,"[35] who engaged in "the most disgraceful orgies" and practiced "blood sacrifice" and "cannibalism"[36] as they remained in touch with the "call of the wild"[37] was linked to the preoccupations of his white American audience: the American Negro.

According to theorists of the Frankfurt School, *National Geographic* is located within "mass culture—materials created and disseminated by powerful interests for the consumption of the working classes."[38] For these theorists, mass culture is degenerate and manipulative, invested in duping and misleading people into developing a false sense of an understanding of their situation in a capitalist society.[39] We see this manipulation at work in Chester's indirect way of pointing to the danger of *not* invading Haiti. He advised his audience: "It is well for us to consider whether we too may not expect some such acts of savagery to break out in our country if our own colored people are not educated for better things."[40] As such, the desire to intervene on Haiti's downward moral, economic, political, and social spiral was depicted as being driven, not only by a sense of Christian duty, but also self-preservation. Chester finished his exposition with a directive: "Let us ... not make a similar mistake to the one here enacted, lest our own wards go through the horrors which have so darkened the history of the Black and Brown republics."[41] The wards to which Chester referred were black people in the United States, a good number of whom remembered the days of slavery from first-hand experience and with whom the U.S. was trying to figure out what to do. In other words, if white Americans planned to hold on to their way of life then it was in their best interest to support a move to quell the bad example to the South lest their "own wards" revert to their natural state of savagery which, until then, their contact with white people had abated.

With the Marine invasion came a slew of eyewitness and fictionalized accounts of the depravity of Haitian culture, focusing on Vodou, and propaganda to justify the human rights abuses that were perpetrated against the Haitian population. A 1916 article in *The National Geographic Magazine* entitled "Wards of the United States: Notes on What Our Country Is Doing for Santo Domingo, Nicaragua, and Haiti" picked up where Chester's article left off. The author depicted the three Black and Brown neighbors of Chester's article as sorely in need of salvation that can only come from the United States, even at high financial and (white) human cost:

> It has not been without effort or without expense, nor yet without the actual sacrifice of blood and life that our country has stepped in to play the role of Good Samaritan to the peoples of Santo Domingo, Haiti and Nicaragua, who had lost the blessings of peace and were unable to gain them. In Haiti alone we lost one officer and six marines and had a number wounded.[42] How much money it has cost has not been ascertained officially, but the usual estimate is that it costs $1,000 a year to support an American soldier in the tropics, and thousands of them have been sent down there.[43]

Continuing with his claims of the U.S.'s purely altruistic intentions, the author asserted, "Wherever America has gone, whether to Cuba, whether to Panama, whether to Santo Domingo, Port Rico (sic), Nicaragua, the Philippines, or Haiti, the welfare of the people has been her first concern...."[44]

Gary D. Rhodes and Kyle Bishop agree that the Marines' overt goal was to modernize the island—build roads, hospitals, and schools—and to establish a stable democratic government.[45] However, as the above discussion of writings prior to the invasion indicate, and the means by which the work was carried out (through forced labor),[46] the Marines' mission was not only structural; it was also ideological. As such, along with modernizing the country and improving government systems presumably came the imperative to take over Haiti's banking system, fly the American flag on the national palace grounds for the duration of the occupation, and make the country safe and stable for the introduction of American tourists, businessmen, and immigrants (expatriates). Such developments would kill two birds with one stone: Haiti could be reclaimed for white Western imperialist aspirations and saved from its descent into unmitigated "blackness."

The Love Wanga takes Chester and those of his ilk's assessments and gives them dramatic form. In the film, the irrationality, barbarity, and superstition of Haiti's inhabitants is contrasted with the civilized, rational, and scientifically superior West before the film even begins with an upward scrolling introduction that polarizes the two:

> ... with the coming of science supernatural phenomena were explained and supposedly banished, yet in many out of the way corners of the earth there may still be found remnants of races that believe implicitly in the religious formulas that have come down to them from the dim and distant past. Of all these strange beliefs perhaps the most inexplicable and disturbing is that of the Haitians, known to whitemen as "VOODOO." Many weird tales of the mysterious deeds of "BOCOURS" or Witch Doctors, of strange epileptic seizures, or "LOAS," during which Haitians believe Gods or Demons take possession of human bodies, of "ZOMBIES," lifeless bodies of murdered negroes reanimated by Bocours for evil purposes, and of the potency of WANGAS or charms...[47]

The people who are the subjects of the film are immediately Othered. Despite the fact that Haiti is a mere 838 miles from the coast of Florida, it is described as an "out of the way corner of the earth." The inhabitants are described as having "strange beliefs" that are "inexplicable" and "disturbing" to the Western mind that is guided by science and reason. Their practices, also "weird," "strange" and depraved, allow for the murder and subsequent reanimation of corpses. This description of Haiti and its inhabitants would not have been new to the audience, instrumental as it was in the continued demonization of the island of "spiteful children" whom the U.S. Marines had just recently left in the hands of the puppet government of Philippe Sudré Dartiguenave.

The white and male eyewitness element is then introduced to the audience in the mention of people who have sat and "listened to the ominous rumble of the drums tell many stories of strange and frightening things they have seen." Such a statement carries with it the insinuation of anthropological research (the domain of white men at the time) and concomitant authority over the subject matter. As such, there is the intimation that the filmmaker has fearlessly delved into the dark underground world of *bocours* [sic], demons, and *wangas*, and come out on the other side unscathed because of his recourse to scientific logic. He, as the ultimate authority, is bringing that "weird"[48] world to the audience so that they do not have to subject themselves to the horrors he has faced. As such, the audience is free to be armchair travelers, voyeurs into this uncivilized and dangerous world that the U.S. Marines were charged with making civilized and safe for American domination and consumption.

Also, in much the same way that Chester's writings about the Haitian were based on his audience's preoccupation with the American Negro, Terwilliger was working with a number of tropes born of the peculiarly American sociopolitical condition in his film. First, for white Americans, a land ruled by its black inhabitants was considered not only monstrous, but unthinkable.[49] Secondly, in a patriarchal misogynist society, women were corrupted and corrupting by virtue of their gender. Finally, in a deeply racist society, mulatto women were more culpable than white women for their depravity because of the black blood running through their veins.

"Ain't no black magic gonna get the best of this charcoal blonde!"

Terwilliger's preoccupation with what he imagined was black American culture comes through in his inclusion of the characters Susie and Jackson, a maid and manservant from Harlem, New York. Jackson is obsessed with shooting dice while Susie is obsessed with Jackson. Both of them speak broken English, argue incessantly, and are superstitious. They are deathly afraid of going to Haiti which Susie calls "devil country" and of voodoo which they denounce. Jackson protects himself against voodoo using his own superstitions: throwing salt over his left shoulder, carrying a rabbit's foot, and reciting rhymes to ward off evil. Despite their propensity for backwardness, they are a testament to the effectiveness of white's civilizing influence. Loyal to whites, they save Susie's employer, Eve, from being sacrificed by the voodoo priest who takes over for Cleeli.

Ann Kordas explains the significance of the inclusion of such characters in these early zombie films averring that, following the abolition of U.S. slavery, "Fear of physical harm at the hands of African Americans and fear of economic hardship as the result of the inability to command African American laborers led many white southerners ... to yearn for a black labor force of contented, willing, docile workers."[50] In order to ease their fears, they invented a whole industry around "the image of the gentle, willing, white-loving laborer"[51]: Hollywood.

Susie and Johnson's role as informants who foil what might be likened to a slave uprising from the past (after all, Cleeli is about to upset the power structure) also implicates them in the continuation of their subjugation. They are the stereotypical "happy negroes" of slaveholders' propaganda pamphlets who betrayed plots of rebellion by others "of their kind" and were loyal to the master to the end. However, no matter how loyal, the film suggests that, ultimately, all blacks are driven by their carnal desires. As soon as her "mistress," Eve, is out of danger, Susie and Jackson head to a local party where, as everyone dances suggestively, Susie uses the love potion that Cleeli has given her on Jackson who proceeds to pick her up and carry her away. The audience can deduce that they are off to dance "privately."

Plantation Dreams

As I have suggested, the U.S. military occupation made the introduction of American business possible. The two were, in fact, inextricable. A man who exemplified the American desire to return Haiti to a nation of plantation labor was James P. MacDonald who, as Laurent Dubois writes, was a U.S. investor who secured a monopoly on all banana exports from the country at the same time that there was a boom in banana consumption in the U.S. MacDonald's plan to turn Haiti into a land of banana plantations was predicated on "the removal of the rural residents who had built their lives on growing high-quality coffee, cultivating livestock, and harvesting acajou and other woods for sale."[52] Dubois notes that MacDonald's project, and I would add, the myriad number of others like it,

> aimed to replace the local way of life with a new version of an old but still vividly remembered system: monoculture plantation production for export. There would be bananas

rather than sugar, and wage workers instead of slaves, but the overall effect remained the same: if the plan succeeded, many Haitians would be transferred from independent farmers into field laborers toiling for a foreign master.[53]

It is this new form of slavery with their plantations and masters to which the film refers, exemplified in, not only Cleeli, but Adam.

This idea of a new form of slavery comes through in the film's setting that gives the viewer the sense that the film takes place in colonial Saint-Domingue, signified by the expansive corn fields, gingerbread houses, overseers, and no sign of black life until night falls when ceremonies in which blacks dance with abandon or dumbly (as if zombified) abound.[54] The film exemplifies whites' longing for a return to a "before" time when everyone knew his or her place, sexual relations between white men and black women could take place with impunity and the kind of backlash that businessmen like MacDonald faced when he attempted to take people's land for profit was not an issue. For as Dubois relates, although the authorities successfully displaced many farmers without compensating them and burned or razed their houses, many fought back, attacking U.S. company buildings, "destroying sawmills and lumberyards, smashing tools, and trying to intimidate workers into abandoning construction sites."[55]

Though there is no indication of resistance on the part of the local residents in the film, *The Love Wanga*, nonetheless, deals with the very real threat of the destruction of the U.S. business project by transferring it to the supernatural realm vis-à-vis the *wanga*. In other words, where the destruction of equipment and intimidation of workers threatened the success of the plantation system as it was being conceived during the occupation in the physical world, the *wanga* and the dangerous practices that it represented for whites threatened the ability of the white man and woman to stay and make their home in Haiti. After all, it is doubtful that after being almost beheaded Eve will want to stay in Haiti and Adam, as her divinely ordained husband, will surely follow her back to New York. Moreover, since by the end, Cleeli and Adam's trusted overseer, Le Strange, are dead, the plantation will then presumably be abandoned. Therefore, in addition to "stick to your own kind," another lesson of the film is that if Haitians will not take development as it is being handed to them by Western businessmen, then they are doomed to remain primitive, ignorant and bereft of economic growth that imperialists propose comes with the imposition of their policies and systems. It would seem that this theme has not completely died as contemporarily, the nation is occupied by a multinational military force and large foreign-owned factories in need of exploited laborers are again being sought by the Haitian government in collaboration with the country's international paternalistic figures, most prominently, the U.S.[56]

The Myth of the Black Matriarch and Her Emasculated Men

Like the close relationship between the U.S.'s military intervention and the introduction of American business, the corrupted land of Haiti is linked inextricably to its inhabitants, and more specifically mulatto women. In the first few seconds of the film, following the written introduction, the narrator sets the stage, contrasting the breathtaking beauty of "Paradise Island" and the innocuous and simple occupations of its inhabitants during the day with the sinister activities that transpire once the sun goes down. As the scene switches from a black male zombie figure emerging slowly out of the shadows, his arms outstretched toward the camera to another black male zombie surrounded by darkness pounding mechanically on a drum, the narrator intones, "Mysterious figures slip silently from shadow to shadow, nature becomes ghostly and unearthly, alive with evil movement and shuddering incantations and gruesome rites. And seemingly from everywhere comes the pulsing, throbbing beat of the voodoo drums, drums, drums." The combination of the black male figures, their eyes blank and shrouded in shadow, and the incessant pounding of the drum framed by the narrator's ominous voice were meant to invoke terror in the film's audience. Many of those audience members had very little contact with black Americans, let alone Caribbean blacks, except as their maids and chauffeurs. The narrator's insinuation of the unknown and implied unknowable dark underworld of the blacks performed the general task of Othering the Caribbean, and Haiti, specifically while reinforcing the audience's terror. At the same time, the white fear of the black male is quelled as, the two zombies, empty shells of human beings, are rendered impotent. They do not act by their own volition, but are merely pawns for the real threat to white Western civilization: the corrupted mulatto woman, Cleeli.

The zombies thus, represent the emasculated black man in relation to

Cleeli, the "black matriarch," a stereotypical figure that sociologist E. Franklin Frazier introduced in the 1930s and American politician and sociologist Daniel Patrick Moynihan popularized in a report on the black family in the U.S. in 1965.[57] According to Moynihan, black men are emasculated by black women who assume control of the family and the finances, are often more educated, and have better jobs than their male counterparts. He notes that the dysfunction of the black family has its roots in slavery when, since they did not own themselves or their labor, black enslaved people were not allowed to exert any control over the make-up or conditions of their families. In other words, black men did not have the power to play the role of head-of-household and exert the kind of power associated with it in a patriarchal society. Many black women had to raise their children on their own and be prepared for the seemingly inevitable eventual disappearance of their men. These black female-headed households continued after slavery with the U.S. government's implementation of forced labor that affected mostly black men and then Jim Crow laws that made it difficult for black men to display their manhood in a traditional patriarchal way as breadwinner, disciplinarian, support system. Conceived as the film is through a racist American lens, Cleeli assumes the role of black matriarch at various points throughout the film, dominating Le Strange and bullying the voodoo priest into digging up the men that she zombifies.

Cleeli's power at the expense of black men, even in the supernatural world, is reinforced by the scene that immediately follows the introduction of the black male zombie when she is seen at the center of a voodoo ceremony receiving her protective *wanga* from the aging voodoo priest. The priest's handing his power over to Cleeli, a young woman, displaces him and posits her as the next generation who will continue the tradition of maleficence, driven by the whims of her heart, as we see in her determination to kill Eve so that she can have Adam.

"Voodoo" and Misreadings of the *Loa* Damballah

The unacceptability of voodoo being used against white women that was first proposed in *White Zombie*'s advertising[58] is raised here again in *The Love Wanga* with Cleeli trying to use her superstitious charms to kill her adversary, the proverbial first mother, Eve. As the introduction states,

"One case so reported is of the LOVE WANGA, or charm invoked by a native priestess against a white rival, as visualized in this picture." As such, Cleeli is posited as a threat to the pure white mother, and by extension, the white race. In this sense, Cleeli's association with the filmmaker's misreading of Damballah, the Vodou *loa*, aligns her with the snake from the Garden of Eden that corrupted Eve and caused her as well as Adam, to be exiled from Paradise.

In Haitian Vodou, Damballah is a benevolent *loa* who, amongst *serviteurs*, is thought of as an aged noble father who helped God (*Bondye*) when he created the universe. As such, he is believed to have preceded the world and is venerated.[59] His praise songs exult him as the great serpent and refer to his affinity with water because he is believed to come out of the underworld to drink after a rain.[60] When he arrives at ceremonies he comes as a snake, plunging first into the basin of water that is prepared for him and then writhing upon the ground or mounting a tree, a primordial source of all wisdom.[61]

The filmmaker's misreading of Damballah as the serpent from the Garden of Eden opens up two avenues through which to consider Eve's fate. In one reading, if both Adam and Eve are to be considered pure in their origins as "the ur-parents of all humankind,"[62] then if Cleeli had succeeded in killing Eve, Adam, the first father, might have been driven back to Cleeli's arms and subsequently produced yet another impure offspring, sullying his bloodline. The second suggestion is that Eve's being saved may actually be the problem in a way that is comparable to Madeline being saved in *White Zombie*. Already corrupted by her contact with the island and more specifically, the serpent with which Cleeli is associated, Eve is bound to the corrupted place ironically called "Paradise Island." Thus, Neil's proclamation that Madeline would be better off dead than in the hands of the natives rings true here as well. As such, Eve cannot return to the United States, contaminated as she is by her contact with Haiti, symbolized by the corrupting serpent.

Contested Womanhoods

Cleeli and Eve's fates are, in fact, linked. Again, the rivalry between the two women extends back to the colonial era when masters would leave

Two. *The Love Wanga*

their marriage beds for the slave cabins. The exploitation of black and mulatto women's bodies by white masters and racist white men under Jim Crow for their most base sexual desires in turn spared white women from what were considered degrading acts. Furthermore, as Vials suggests, during slavery the Caribbean plantation was a space that broke up white marriage bonds.[63] Even if married whites stayed together in name, the sanctity of the monogamous union was violated by the perceived inescapable lustfulness of black women on the plantation who lured white men away from the marriage bed. The audience gets a hint of this dynamic when it is revealed in the film that, for the two years that Adam lived in Haiti prior to his marriage to Eve, he had an affair with Cleeli. As such, the film draws parallels between black women who were sexually victimized under slavery while being accused of being lustful and luring the white man from his marriage bed and Cleeli, a mulatto woman who hopes to do the same. Although Adam used her for companionship while he was alone in the Caribbean and then tosses her aside once his white fiancée arrives, Cleeli is depicted as the lustful aggressor who will not take "no" for an answer. Interestingly, however, the film inverts the rivalry between the black woman and the white woman. Whereas during slavery, Eve would have been jealous of Cleeli because of the threat that she posed to their marriage, in this postcolonial Haiti, Cleeli is at war with a woman who is not even aware that there is a battle, so secure is Eve in her position as Adam's future wife.

Cleeli and Eve's rivalry comes to a head late in the film when Cleeli confronts the catatonic woman whom the zombies have delivered to her. After comparing their skin color, Cleeli grabs Eve's face and asks, "A passive white blooded thing like you make Adam happy? Adam needs a woman of fire, of passion, like me.... I could have won him if he'd stayed down here. He was so lonely. But you took him away from me. Well, you won't have him. Do you hear? You won't have him." The scene is both verbally and visually pivotal. Eve is still pure, trying to resist her possession, but quickly succumbing to it, repeating "drums, drums" as Cleeli manhandles her. The scene also contrasts her physically and morally with Cleeli. As the stereotypical upper class white woman, she is refined, ineffectual, and delicate and with a weak mind that is easily manipulated (seen also in *White Zombie* and *I Walked with a Zombie*). Conversely, Cleeli, though thin, is very strong physically, mentally, and spiritually. This contrast is reinforced visually in the scene in Cleeli's speech about her passion and determination to get Adam back. However, for all of her strength, the scene ultimately speaks to the inability of black women to compete with white women for white men's affections. The filmmaker seems to want to redeem white relationships here, implying that while they are in the Caribbean alone white men rely on black women to comfort them, but their hearts will always belong to their female counterparts. As such, the sanctity of the white family remains in tact. Of course, if Adam is black, then the suggestion is that black women cannot compete with white women for *any* man's affections. As a white socialite, Eve represents the ability for Adam to truly and completely leave his black side behind; a feat that Cleeli is trying to accomplish.

Parallels can also be drawn between Cleeli and Susie. While on one hand, Cleeli, as an upperclass Haitian voodoo priestess is contrasted with Susie, a black working class maid who is afraid of voodoo, on the other they are presented as two sides of the same coin. Reminiscent of Cleeli's behavior with Adam, the scene in which Susie throws herself at Jackson links the two. As such, the high classed mulatto is equated with the black maid, thus implying that no matter their skin color or class, blacks are doomed to certain (unsavory) behaviors. This linkage is maintained throughout the film as Susie pursues Jackson, enlisting the help of Cleeli to make him love her in exchange for the former's help with getting rid of Eve. By the end of the film Susie is able to successfully use one of Cleeli's powders to attract Jackson. However, it would seem that Cleeli's charms and potions are only meant for other superstitious blacks and her trying to use them against whites is her undoing.

"I'll Be Your Slave" or Possessions of the Body

The issue of possession surfaces repeatedly in the film with Cleeli claiming Adam for herself, first telling him, "You belong to me, Adam, and no one else but me" and later declaring to Le Strange, "If I can't have him no one else will." Le Strange, however, claims Cleeli, not only for himself, but for the black race. As he tells her, "You're black … you belong to us, to me" and finally "no one else is going to have you, is that clear? I'll kill you first." The desire to possess is also found in Susie trying to make

Two. *The Love Wanga*

Jackson love her through her use of magic. In addition, Cleeli offers to enslave herself twice in the film: once to Adam and once to Le Strange. The first time she offers herself to Adam is during their initial conversation when Adam rejects her. She tells him, "I ask for so little, only to be with you. I'll be your slave, anything." The second time is as a last resort, when Le Strange is about to kill her. As he closes in on her, she tells him, "I'll be your Cleeli, I'll love you." This willingness to offer herself, first to a plantation owner who is presumably white and then a mulatto overseer, has implications both in the realm of gender and race. A mulatto woman offering to willingly enslave herself to a white man invokes the white imperialist fantasy of returning blacks to a state of enslavement. It also speaks to white men's wish to return women to the state of servitude that existed prior to World War I that Renda discusses in *Taking Haiti* (2001). At the same time, both offers, if taken up, would link her intimately with the power structure, distancing her from her black side. This distancing would be insured by her connection—even as a servant—to Adam, and less so in her connection to Le Strange. Though the more desirable arrangement would be with Adam, she pledges herself to Le Strange so as not to be killed.

The island, governed as it is by voodoo, also possesses the white inhabitants. Not only does Eve fall prey to Cleeli's *wanga* twice even though she has no idea what it is, but Johnson, Adam's butler is not only knowledgeable about, but also thoroughly believes in voodoo's power. When Eve finds a death *wanga* in her purse, Johnson explains what it is, warns her not to touch it, and then instructs her to throw it away. When Adam witnesses Eve's rapid physical demise and recovery after he interrupts the death spell that he catches Cleeli weaving, he also becomes a believer, asking Susie if any of Eve's dresses were missing. Implicit in his question is the thought that it may be being used for nefarious purposes, as Johnson explained was possible.

Once she recovers from her physical illness, Eve is possessed in still other ways; first by the voodoo drums whose rhythm threatens to overtake her and then the black male zombies who kidnap her, physically picking her up and carrying her away from the sanctity of her white environment signified by her socialite aunt. Even the doctor who tends to Eve during her illness admits that he has failed to find scientific explanation for many of the phenomena that he has observed on the island over the years. As with *White Zombie* and *I Walked with a Zombie* and the characters of Dr. Bruner and Mrs. Rand, the suggestion here is that whites who come in contact with the island are corrupted by it. Moreover, if they stay long enough, they are unfit to return to white American society.

Finally, there is the spirit possession seen, first, at the beginning of the film during the ceremony in which Cleeli receives her *wanga* and then, late in the film when Cleeli is preparing to sacrifice Eve. In the initial ceremony, Cleeli is seen swaying back and forth and the name of Damballah, the voodoo serpent is chanted. In the later scene Cleeli wears a headdress with a serpent on it and on her dress, an appliqued snake. Again, this invocation of Damballah, a *loa* who is considered benevolent and "the great father of whom one asks nothing save his blessing,"[64] reflects a misreading of the god by the filmmaker who imposes a Christian reading on the serpent. This misreading makes possible the interpretation of Adam and Eve as representative of the first mother and father who are exiled from Heaven. Of course, the question that begs asking here then, is "whose Heaven is being invoked?" Is it the Heaven of Paradise Island where white men have free access to black women's bodies and where black men are zombified or is it the United States where white men also rule and the illusion of the pure white race can be maintained, although with anxiety around who is really white?

Stick with Your Own Kind

Not only does *The Love Wanga*'s major narrative tension center around racialized womanhood, but equally, the admonition that Cleeli hears repeatedly to "stick with [her] own kind," denoting the taboo against miscegenation, in American law, even if not in practice. The first time she is told to "stick with [her] own kind" is when she confronts Adam on the boat on the way to Paradise Island from New York after she is shown lurking in the shadows eavesdropping on Adam and Eve's conversation. The scene establishes Cleeli as sneaky and conniving; a woman who will stop at nothing to get what she desires. Even though Adam repeatedly advises Cleeli that they cannot be together, assuring her that she is desirable and deserves happiness, and even asking her if his being married makes a difference in her desire for him, she refuses to be deterred. Considered in

Two. *The Love Wanga*

relation to the scene that immediately precedes it in which Eve is heard enthusing about getting married on the island rather than amongst her socialite friends in New York and about how romantic the Caribbean is, the scene in which Cleeli tries to thrust herself on Adam despite his protestations establishes her as the kind of woman that he would not marry.

Despite being dressed in furs, occupying a first class cabin and putting on high class airs, she nonetheless engages in voodoo magic on the ship, tucking her *wanga* into her evening gown before she confronts Adam and hypnotizing Susie. Upon her return to Paradise Island she goes almost immediately to consult with the voodoo priest to tell him that she has failed in her mission to "get rid of the white girl." Moreover, throughout the film, her speeches about her whiteness are almost immediately preceded or followed by references to voodoo, the evil practices of the blacks. For example, in her first conversation with Le Strange upon her return to the island, she repeatedly declares her whiteness and thus, her worthiness to be with Adam. She asks rhetorically, "Black am I? Is this black?" (She touches her face.) "Or these?" (She holds out her hands.) "Or this?" (She tears open her dress to expose her chest). But for all of her declarations of whiteness and her love for Adam, in an example of the inevitable triumph of her blackness, she succumbs to her lust for Le Strange and kisses him passionately. In fact, only voodoo drums wake her from her lust-induced stupor, reminding her of her goal; that is to claim Adam for herself, and by extension, for the island.

Later, when Eve falls ill and Adam goes to see Cleeli, he finds her making a *wanga* to kill his fiancée. Again, though she affirms her whiteness initially, asking him if she is not as beautiful and as white as Eve, she has just been shown indulging in the "black arts." It is only when she realizes that there is no possessing Adam that she claims her blackness. Despite her getting down on her knees before Adam and begging him not to throw her away as if she were a "black wench from [his] fields," he abandons her, returning to Eve. Later, when Le Strange tries to comfort her, she remembers that Adam threw her away "like black trash." She then asks, "Black am I? Alright, I'm black. I'll show him what a black girl can do." Not only does Cleeli's inner dialogue reflect her understanding of the difference between white standards and black standards of behavior, but also the theme that has run through the film: that her black blood, her femaleness, and her inherent association with the Caribbean make her a corrupted and corruptive monstrosity.

Even though Cleeli has betrayed her white side in her use of the supernatural elements to try to kill Eve, her claiming of blackness in this last moment marks another level of her depravity. She is now free to unleash all of the evil that comes with her black side, exemplified by her raising the dead and attempting to cut off Eve's head. In other words, the film seems to say, she cannot escape the barbarity within her. Even though she looks white on the outside, inside her tainted blood drives her to commit evil acts. Again, a voodoo practicing mulatto woman who will stop at nothing to spread her evil—in short, a monstrosity—must die at the same time and at the hands of her male mulatto counterpart.

The Uncertain Fate of the Ur-Couple

The film ends with alternating scenes of Susie and Jackson at a party and Le Strange murdering Cleeli. Curiously, Adam and Eve are not featured in the final scene of the film. Their absence can be read as the film not being about them directly, but about the fate of Haiti if left to its own devices. Again, *The Love Wanga* and films like it were part of the propaganda machine that justified American military intervention as well as the encroachment of American businesses in Haiti. Devoid of any scenes of modernization, the film seems to seek to remind the white American viewer that, despite the sacrifices that the military and business owners were making in occupying the island to the Global South, the alternative would be a continuation of the superstition and primitivism that they found amongst these people whom they considered their wards when they first arrived. In that sense, the film is very much about Adam and Eve who represent the primordial couple who sacrifice themselves to develop and civilize "the natives," even if only by distant (and safe) association. For a mulatto Adam, this ending is quite optimistic, as it means that he has successfully passed into white society. For whites, Adam's passing is the ultimate fear as it signifies the monster's breaching of their own citadel,[65] the white woman.

CHAPTER THREE

Heading South[1] and Zombification or "Haiti is open for business"

By the time the American rock band, Steely Dan, recorded their song "Haitian Divorce"[2] in 1976, Haiti had long been a fascination in the American imagination, most notably as a favorite subject of novelists and filmmakers with an eye for horror. But it was also a site of profound sexual exploitation; from the time that Christopher Columbus "discovered" the island that he named Hispaniola the colonial invaders had sexual relations with members of the native populations based on unequal power dynamics.

"Haitian Divorce" tells the story of a young woman named Dobs who gets married very quickly and gets divorced equally quickly in Jean-Claude "Baby Doc" Duvalier's Haiti. The song speaks to the otherworldliness of Haiti; the exotic paradise where the foreign woman can drink "zombies from cocoa shells" and then smile at a "Charlie" for an otherwise nameless fuck for the night. It is only after her ego is subsumed under the haze of the very strong alcoholic drink that she allows the encounter that results in the "semi-mojo," a mulatto child, as evidence to everyone "back home" in the U.S. of her transgression. The song invokes the cinematic gaze which, after the foreign woman smiles, backs away and fades to black, leaving the audience to imagine what transpires between the white Northern female tourist and the repulsive (greasy chair, kinky hair), yet enticing symbol of base masculinity: the exotic Caribbean man. In 1970s Haiti, the fear that white American males had taken pains to suppress—the black man's seemingly unquenchable thirst for the white woman—was not only coming into the light, it was bearing "strange fruit."[3]

The Haiti of 1976 was one where anything went as long as one had the cash; something that the vast majority of Haitian people lacked. Enter the white North American woman who has made at least two regrettable decisions in her life. The first was mistaking lust for love and marrying another Northerner, Clean Willie. The second mistake was giving in to her carnal urges a second time and being left with the evidence of it for the rest of her life in the form of a mulatto child. Following the logic of the song and the films that I have discussed thus far, the white woman of the 1930s and 1940s is still corrupted and corruptive decades later. Clean Willie, Dobs' short-term husband, and the Haitian Charlie are both portrayed as silent objects caught up in her lustful web. The danger inherent in the single white woman in the Caribbean finds its full expression, not only in Steely Dan's song, but also in film, with French director Laurent Cantet's *Heading South* (2005), based on several stories from the collection, *Vers le Sud* (2006),[4] by Haitian-Canadian writer, Dany Laferrière.

This chapter draws on Christopher Moreman and Cory James Rushton's introduction to their edited volume, *Race, Oppression and the Zombie* (2011) in which they aver, "Despite the proliferation of potential meanings, the zombie is associated with capitalism above all else"[5] to propose that *Heading South* depicts female sex tourism as a contemporary consumptive practice. As Jen Webb and Sam Byrnand write, "Capitalism … works as an analogue of zombiedom because it … is predicated on insatiable appetite, and the drive to consume."[6] They continue with an interpretation of capitalism and its appetite for consumption that gets to the heart of my discussion of female sex tourism and its relationship to zombification: "Capitalism has [a] heartless all consuming character … that doesn't care, and doesn't weigh human costs. It is simply zombie—hungry, and hence, focused on feeding and expanding regardless of the consequences."[7] While Webb and Byrnand posit that capitalism is the zombi, I would suggest that it also works *through* its zombis, who in turn, consume others who are also zombified. My close reading of the film suggests that the U.S.'s "taking of Haiti"[8] in the early twentieth century and carried out primarily by Marines and American businessmen, was followed by a different but equally sinister invasion in the 1970s. This new invasion, carried out by white North American female tourists who flocked to the Caribbean, targeted the sexual labor of young men commonly labeled "beach boys."[9]

Though in the latter half of the twentieth century, cash replaced guns, the consequences were the same. Both invaders exploited Haitian bodies and denied Haitian subjectivity. I posit that while Cantet explores the exploitative relationship between the "native" and the tourist on one level, he also pushes his project further to complicate the dialectical relationship between "us" and "the other," "here" and "there," "inside" and "outside" and in the process, subverts the relations of power that are embedded in these distinctions.

The Film

Heading South focuses on three vacationing white women: Ellen, a professor of French literature at Wellesley College in Boston, Massachusetts, Brenda, a divorcée from Savannah, Georgia, and Sue, a factory manager from Quebec, Canada. Legba, a "beach boy" named for the Vodou *loa* of the crossroads, is the object of Ellen and Brenda's affection. Albert, the maître d' of the resort where the three women stay, acts as another crossroads figure, mediating between the reality of life in Haiti and the fantasy created for tourists. The film features monologues by Brenda, Ellen, Sue, and Albert, which give the audience insight into their histories and their thoughts. Interestingly, Legba, who is ostensibly the main protagonist, does not have a monologue. By the end of the film he and an unnamed Haitian woman whom he loves are dead and Ellen and Brenda leave the island. Ellen returns to Massachusetts, disillusioned, while Brenda heads off to other islands in search of more Caribbean men. The film brings together the liberated and transgressive white woman and the zombified black man in a late twentieth century setting with sex at its center.

Unlike Laferrière's collection in which Legba is featured as just another character in several discrete stories, Cantet centers him. Although Legba does not have a monologue, one way that Cantet sets him apart is by showing the audience his life outside the resort; something that is not done with the other characters. It is worth noting that, even though the film is set in the 1970s, it debuted in 2005, one year after MINUSTAH began its occupation of the country.

1970s Haiti and Before

The United Nations began promoting international tourism in the 1960s as a strategy to help Caribbean nations participate in the global economy. As part of the strategy, Caribbean governments were encouraged to diversify their economies as a way of overcoming "economic crises that threatened to cripple the small nation-states" through the acquisition of foreign currency.[10] Baby Doc (1971–1986), François "Papa Doc" Duvalier's son and heir to the presidency-for-life, recognized opportunity in the recommendation and opened Haiti to foreign tourism. While the U.S. military invasion lasted 19 years, this second invasion lasted for about 20 years. As Dr. Paul Farmer writes, by 1992, the year that Haiti became associated in the American press with AIDS, Port-au-Prince counted tourism as one of its chief industries.[11]

Tourism in Haiti truly began in 1949 when Port-au-Prince celebrated the two hundredth year of its founding with the inauguration of the *Cité de l'Exposition*. During that year at least 20,000 tourists visited the country with slightly fewer in 1950 and 1951. During the next several years, approximately 250,000 tourists would spend an average of three days and $105 in Haiti, bringing in approximately 25 percent of Haiti's foreign currency.[12] An increase in political instability in 1957 caused the tourist industry to decline. However, in 1970, Papa Doc, hoping to again court American dollars, welcomed U.S. Vice President Nelson Rockefeller to Haiti and promoted the country as an ideal site for, not only U.S. assembly plants, but also the American middle class, to vacation. It was close, beautiful, and again politically stable as a result of Duvalier's terror tactics carried out by the Tonton Macoutes, the Duvaliers' paramilitary army.[13] By 1970 the annual number of visitors was about 100,000. By the end of the decade, excluding brief layovers and "afternoon dockings," the average annual number of tourists reached over 143,500.[14]

During that time Haiti was but one of several locations that were marketed as an island paradise where tourists could "'find new experiences' in 'unspoilt' new destinations."[15] As with most of the other "island paradises," while tourists from abroad made their way to the island to escape their everyday lives back home, the majority of the people in Haiti were abysmally poor with no hope of escaping their daily realities. The combination of the two—abject poverty and the injection of foreign dollars through tourism—gave rise to what Farmer calls "institutionalized prostitution"[16] which, according to Stephen Clift and Simon Carter (2000), spawned a "sex industry infrastructure."[17] Speaking specifically about Haiti, Farmer continues: "As Haiti became poorer, both men's and women's bodies became cheaper. Although there have been no quantitative studies of Haitian urban prostitution, it is clear that a substantial sector of the trade catered to tourists, and especially North Americans."[18] Outside of Port-au-Prince where resorts like *Club Mediterranée* opened in the 1980s, there flourished not only female prostitution but also the phenomenon of the "beach boy."

Beach Boys

Beach boys are usually young and physically fit young men who range in age from 17 to 25. The more successful have the ability to learn other languages easily and can carry out a rudimentary conversation in four or five different languages.[19] In "In Search of the Big Bamboo: How Caribbean Beach Boys Sell Fun in the Sun" (2000) Klaus de Albuquerque paints a picture of a typical beach boy in the largely Anglophone Caribbean. He says, they "cruise the sands in search of unattached tourist women" and are easily recognizable because of their distinctive wardrobe of "T-shirts, baggy swimming trunks, Teva sandals, gold bracelets, and brand-name sunglasses, preferably Oakley or Ray-ban. They are without exception physically fit."[20] After listing some of the menial jobs that a "beach boy" might do, Albuquerque concludes that their "relatively low wages" are "insufficient to maintain the enviable beach boy lifestyle" as they "require the latest clothes and shoes, immodest jewelry, meals and drinks at pricey tourist restaurants and nightclubs."[21] He adds sarcastically, "female tourists earn them *these necessities*"[22] (emphasis added). Albuquerque writes the entire article from the perspective of a Northern white male, never once venturing to ask what could drive these young men to sell their bodies, who, as Jacqueline Sánchez Taylor contends, do not enter into sexual exchanges "through personal desire but in order implicitly or explicitly to obtain money or goods."[23]

Drawing on the trope of the voracious black male, Albuquerque works under the assumption that these young men are drawn to these mostly white female tourists out of sexual desire and financial greed rather than need. The underlying question in his description of the beach boy's attire and lifestyle is "why can't they be happy with what crumbs we throw at them?" By "crumbs" I mean the "relatively low wages" on which no one could possibly live and which beach boys must share with family members and friends who are also forced to make do with menial jobs for which they may earn about $2.00 a day, if they are lucky.[24] About the tourist industry in particular, Kamala Kempadoo (2013) points out that Caribbean men and women employed in jobs such as barman, waitress, cook, cleaner, maid, gardener and entertainer, work for meager wages:

> Male and female labour and energies constitute a part of the package that is paid for and consumed by the tourist during the period in which she or he seeks to relax and enjoy—in the leisure time the tourist has set aside to recuperate and restore the mind and body in order to maintain a healthy and productive working life on return home. Caribbean sexuality also constitutes a critical resource within this panorama, and it is in arrangements and representations of this aspect of the tourism industry that new articulations of exoticism are evident.[25]

It would seem that Albuquerque's underlying assumption is that only foreigners should have access to the trappings of capitalism. Missing the link that Farmer, Kempadoo, and Sánchez Taylor point out in their own research, Albuquerque assumes that "beach boys" cater to women tourists because it is easy and pleasurable money that supports their implied extravagant lifestyle. *Heading South* redresses many of the issues that Albuquerque's essay raises through its deployment of the trope of zombification as a rendering of the victim into a laboring shell of a being who is alienated from his or her labor. It also explores how the master is equally zombified in his or her enslavement of another. The film's portrayal of the female sex tourist in this respect, invokes the famous abolitionist orator Frederick Douglass who remarked in his 1845 autobiography, that slavery not only degrades the enslaved, but also the master.[26]

Life Is Cheap Here

In both Papa Doc and Baby Doc's Haiti, the life of the average Haitian was cheap. Illustrative of Farmer's words about the cheapness of both male and female bodies that is enmeshed with the violence that permeated Haitian society at the time, the film opens at the point of entry for the

Three. *Heading South* and Zombification

new master: the airport named for Papa Doc. There, Albert is seen writing Brenda's name on a chalkboard in preparation for her plane's arrival from the U.S. A well-dressed, handsome middle-aged Haitian woman approaches him and explains that her husband was arrested at his job as a sanitary inspector at the Public Health Department and never heard from again. The practice about which she speaks was common in Haiti under the Duvaliers.[27] The mother and her 15-year-old daughter are now very poor and she cannot pay her rent or her daughter's school fees. The woman offers her daughter as a gift to Albert, hoping that he will take care of her.

As a condition for being allowed to exist in the misty zone between aliveness and death under the Duvalier regime, Haitian people had to behave as if they did not see and did not hear. Thus, the blank look that Albert gives the woman betrays no sign of recognition or emotion about what he has just heard and he continues with his task. As an employee in the tourist industry he is charged with shielding the foreign tourist from the reality of life for the poor majority. Responding to the Haitian mother and her plight would be forbidden in that context as it would detract from his labor of welcoming, protecting, and attending to the tourist's every need. It would also expose him to the wrath of Baby Doc who would read his response as political consciousness or an awakened state; forbidden territory.[28]

Albert lives in a country where the job of the Tonton Macoutes was to silence voices of dissension with the ultimate goal of numbing the masses to their oppressed state; effectively zombifying them so that they could be used by The State. As such, they swept through the country like locusts murdering and disappearing people, raping and taking whomever they wanted to be their concubines; murdering the parents if they refused. The audience witnesses this reality later in the film in a scene between Legba and his ex-girlfriend when she explains that a colonel in the army saw her at a funeral wake and before she knew what was happening he had taken her as his concubine. In anticipation of Legba challenging the colonel for her, she warns him that he would be killed. It is also to this constant danger that the mother alludes when she says about her daughter, "Unfortunately being beautiful and poor in this country, she doesn't stand a chance. I always take her with me so I can watch over her, but they won't think twice about killing me to grab her." The threat that the Tonton Macoutes pose is made visible when Albert looks in the direction of the

Haitian woman's daughter and spots behind her, several men dressed in the signature clothing of the Macoutes—blue shirt and pants with blue hats flipped up on one side—chatting with army officers.

Shortly after the mother leaves, Brenda arrives flanked by a baggage carrier dressed in a uniform of a red shirt and cap. Several such service workers are visible in the background. The airport is orderly as many white tourists mill around also in the background gathering their luggage. Brenda passes soldiers and looks back slightly to make sure that the baggage carrier is following. In these first few moments, the events that unfold in the rest of this tragedy are set into motion. All the elements—political, sexual, physical, and economic violence—are bundled together. The remainder of the film unfurls and brings into sharp relief each element until the end when a disillusioned Ellen arrives at the airport on her way back to Massachusetts, presumably never to return to Haiti and Brenda sails away from Haiti on her way to conquer other islands of black male bodies.

The Island Paradise Setting

The St. Lucian poet, Derek Walcott, has referred to beach resorts as "beautiful little groins of land."[29] Walcott's likening the beach resort to a groin is most appropriate as it reminds the listener that the groin is a concentrated site of pleasure on the human body when one is engaged in sexual intercourse. It also reminds the listener that these small bits of heaven, "little groins," are dependent upon ignoring the rest of the body and their less than sexy functions: urinating, releasing gas, defecating, spitting, shedding. All of these other functions, however, are necessary to the existence of that small site of pleasure. Similarly, the tranquility and security of beach resorts is dependent upon keeping the less savory aspects of life in the Caribbean at bay and out of sight of the tourist. Although resorts are central to socioeconomic networks, their paradisiacal illusion is assured by limiting the encroachment of what lies beyond. As Gavan Titley comments "the Caribbean would not be the Caribbean without the beach" and "Caribbean beaches are not only usually represented as spaces of freedom and indulgence, but as spaces of exclusivity."[30] They are liminal spaces, "safely beyond the everyday and apparently insulated from the increasing irruption of the everyday upheaval into the tourist haven."[31] The "everyday upheaval" of Haiti from which the tourist of the 1970s was protected included people living on below-poverty wages, being terrorized by Duvalier and his henchmen, and the banality of violence under such conditions. Although Albert and the other wait staff, as well as Legba and the other tourists' lovers in the film may live in the city, their experience of poverty and the political repression they endure are never meant to touch the fairytale in which the women reside. The beach resort is a liminal space between the reality of life in Haiti and their "real" lives back home.

Exchanging Plantations for Beaches

Following a drive through the city, Albert and Brenda arrive at *Hôtel Petit Anse*, a beach resort that is surrounded by palm trees. Away from the cacophony of Port-au-Prince there is only the sound of the ocean waves, the leaves blowing in the breeze and the occasional bark of a dog. Recalling the scene at the airport, Brenda leaves Albert to get her bags and tumbles headlong toward the entrance hoping to resume a sexual relationship that she had begun three years prior with the-then 15-year-old Legba. Her stepping through the canopy that announces her destination signifies her entrance into another world where she, as a white woman tourist, is free to let herself go. As Sue remarks later in the film, "There's nothing to worry about. Here, everything is different." With this line, Sue voices the marketing of tourist settings as both romantic and culturally different and "where different social norms apply." This Othering of the Caribbean facilitates "a sense of freedom from constraints for the traveler that is reinforced by a reduction in normal inhibitions...."[32] Albert follows silently and just as she did in the airport with the baggage carrier, Brenda looks back only briefly to make sure he is there. As they know well their roles as servant and mistress, she needs only make this small gesture. Nonetheless, it is a necessary one that early on, establishes a hierarchy of power in their brief relationship.

The Exoticized Caribbean

Kempadoo argues for a tracing of the history of prostitution through the discourse of exoticism as a way of examining the ways in which colonial and global relations of power and ruling have contributed to the masculine control of female sexuality. I would extend her theorization to ponder how exoticizing "the Other" has feminized the Caribbean man and masculinized the Western female sex tourist to such an extent that they deserve separate consideration in thinking about processes of global relations of power. Kempadoo focuses primarily on the sexual uses of slave women by white men and to a lesser extent, white women during the colonial era. However, in order to fully understand exoticism's role in maintaining colonial relations of power, it is important to apprehend the intersectionality of racialized, sexualized, and gendered processes at work at the time. Though it is identified as a white masculine discourse, exoticism was also mediated through the white imperial feminine imagination.[33] In fact, while extensive work has been done on white colonialist men's sexual relations with black and mulatto women, less attention has been paid to white colonialist women's relations with black men, mostly because such relations were hidden as a way of upholding the system. Nonetheless, white women did engage in sexual relations with black men with black men often paying for the transgression by being castrated, dismembered, or executed.[34]

These relations of power that were established under slavery continue in the contemporary Caribbean tourist industry. In *Paradise and Plantation* (2002) Ian Gregory Strachan writes about the portrayal of the Caribbean as a paradise in the tourist industry contemporarily as a continuation of the Caribbean as a plantation during the colonial era. Furthermore, Frank Fonda Taylor argues that, "Caribbean tourism is "intrinsically" a "neoplantation" enterprise.[35] If the plantation allowed Europe to enjoy an economic paradise in the Caribbean, the tourism industry has learned this lesson and puts it into practice with equal aplomb.[36] Thus, while today, the Caribbean is no longer the cornerstone of what Karl Marx called Europe's "primitive accumulation" of wealth, it finds itself again "coveted for its natural resources—this time, not for gold, silver, pearls, tobacco, cotton or sugar, but for sun, sand ... sea"[37] and I would add, sex.

Referring to the wholesale vending of Caribbean land and its people to the American tourist, Walcott in his speech for the 1992 Nobel Prize in Literature, commented, "In our tourist brochure the Caribbean is a blue pool into which the [American] republic dangles the extended foot of

Florida as inflated rubber islands bob and drinks with umbrellas float towards her on a raft. This is how the islands from the shame of necessity sell themselves...."[38] Indeed, where in the colonial past, the Caribbean islands were stolen and their enslaved inhabitants forced into roles of servitude, today Caribbean people are portrayed as offering themselves up willingly to be consumed by the European imperialist. This is the world for sale into which Brenda enters as she steps through the canopy—an alternate reality where all of her dreams are to be fulfilled in the tradition of the popular TV series, *Fantasy Island*, which, I think, not coincidentally, premiered in 1977.

Reading Legba

The reader will recall my discussion of Legba in relation to *I Walked with a Zombie* and Carrefour in Chapter One. Again, Legba is considered Master of the Crossroads, guarding the realm between seen and unseen worlds, life and death, and with origins amongst the Fon and Yorùbá people of West Africa. Amongst the Fon, Legba is associated with fecundity and procreative prowess. As the procreative and primal energy of all things, his chief domain is in the realm of sex. His fecund energy is enacted through his supplicants during ritual dances where "the performers hold a carved phallus between their legs and perform copulating movements."[39] The virile energy of the Fon Legba seems to have diminished with his crossing of the Atlantic Ocean during the transatlantic slave trade. Where the Fon say that Legba "everywhere dances in the manner of a man copulating,"[40] and his carved phallus is a sign of virility, in Haiti he is seen as old and in need of a cane to support himself. Unlike Legba of Dahomey (now Benin Republic), Papa Legba or Legba of the Old Bones, as he is commonly addressed in Haiti, is very old, and is depicted as an aged limping *loa*.[41] Although Legba is aged and in need of a cane to keep himself upright, he nonetheless, maintains his power as Guardian of the Crossroads.

Where the Legba of Africa is full of life, the Legba of the diaspora who shuffles down the road, is impotent, with "sores on his body," and maggots gnawing at his flesh,[42] would seem to describe the condition of a zombi, not a god. I propose that the Legba of Cantet's *Heading South* conflates the virile Legba of the Fon and what seems to be a misreading of the Legba of the diaspora who, on the surface, resembles a zombified being. Although Legba of Cantet's film is physically virile for foreign female sex tourists who are consumed by the world of carnal desire, the filmmaker seems to posit him as spiritually impotent, unable to offer hope to the next generation of Haitians, represented by Eddy, his young protégé.[43] However, I would propose that Legba displays a different kind of spiritual strength in ultimately choosing his girlfriend over his continued exploitation (zombification) by the tourists. In the remainder of this chapter I explore Legba as well of the other Haitian characters' zombification before suggesting that they are not the only ones who suffer. Rather, I posit that the female tourists are also zombified. And while one of them receives the grain of salt that reawakens her humanity, another relishes her condition of liminality, mistaking the condition for being alive, and continuing willingly along her path of mindless consumption of others under the aegis of capitalism.

The Inert and Feminized Caribbean

In his discussion of a postcard from the Bahamas featuring a young, beautiful black woman sleeping on a deserted beach wrapped only in the island flag, Strachan suggests that the young woman is being offered up to be consumed by the male tourist. Conflated with the nation, the woman as well as the land is feminized, waiting to be penetrated by the Northern west that the white male represents. The young woman may be visually consumed, but it is not enough to devour her visually. She must be physically consumed as well. Because she seems to be asleep, it is the male tourist's job to awaken her "just as the land must be stirred from its inertia...."[44] Such discussions of the feminization of the Caribbean and its need of the European male to awaken it from inertia recall discourse that was widely circulated during the colonial period when colonialists conquered the indigenous populations and the lands they inhabited. For the colonialists, the indigenous populations were squandering their natural resources by not exploiting them fully. As such, not only were the people mired in a state of inertia, but they spread their inertia to the land as well. It was therefore, the colonialists' job to save the indigenous populations and the land from their lethargy, even if it meant killing them both in the process, which is what they did.

Feminist analysts have discussed scenes such as that in the postcard from within a broader critique of the gendered international tourism industry, citing travel as a historically masculine domain.[45] But while Cynthia Enloe argues that sex tourism is "one strand of the gendered tourism industry"[46] and focuses on the exploitation of women within the system, *Heading South* offers another side of sex tourism; that which feminizes the male body to be consumed by the Northern female. By extension (as per Strachan's discussion), the island on which his available body lays is also feminized. Also, as in Strachan's formulation, the feminized man, like the land, must be awakened from inertia. Where again, during colonialism and the American Occupation, the awakening was achieved with guns and forced sexual relations,[47] contemporarily, it is done through international tourism and "consensual" sexual relations.[48]

The postcard woman's awakening would be signaled by her eager responsiveness to the prospective tourist's advances, necessary to fulfill his or her fantasies of desirability. But while these conditions and outcomes must be met in order for tourism to work, the "native's" ability to awaken is circumscribed. In the language of the zombi, the master actually desires the native's inertia that makes him or her easier to consume. In other words, while the awakened body is desired, an awakened consciousness is not. As Legba remarks in a conversation with his friends, the female sex tourist does not want a beach boy who thinks and expresses himself. She wants a mindless body that will fulfill her fantasies.

If not asleep, the woman in the postcard is, at the very least, not returning the tourist gaze, which allows the tourist to consume her visually with impunity. Though in *Heading South*, the consumed native is male, he, Legba is feminized, connected as he is with the unspoiled white sand of the beach resort; the only place the female tourists are meant to see him.[49] The feminization and projected inertia of the land and those associated with it come together in the privilege of the gaze as a function of power. The audience is clued into this power as soon as Brenda emerges on the beach shortly after having shed the constraints of her life at home in the United States. Her hair, which was tightly wound up and clipped when she arrived, hangs free. She no longer wears a jacket, trousers, and pumps with a purse on her shoulder. Instead, she now dons only a one-piece bathing suit, a beach bag, sandals and a sheer cover-up. When she finds Legba, he appears to be asleep, his back to her, thus relaying his vulnerability. Like the woman from the postcard, he is virtually naked, wearing only a gold chain and Speedos. Brenda is able to approach him without being detected. As such, she is able to drink in his lithe, muscular form, devour him with her eyes without having her gaze challenged. The scene establishes her as a master who has come to raise the zombi from his inertia/grave to begin working. Indeed, as if by magic, Legba opens his eyes when she softly calls his name. When she asks if he remembers her, Legba, fulfilling his role as an extension of the will of his prospective master,[50] smiles broadly, sits up, and responds, "Sure" and then asks her if she has been at the resort a while. The fact that the audience is never told if Legba actually does remember Brenda also speaks to the question of the zombi's memory, a question which has been debated by scholars.[51]

Silenced "Zombis"

Legba's long-term "master," Ellen, interrupts his time with Brenda to ask him if he is hungry. She then acts as an intermediary ordering sandwiches and drinks for him even though the waitress stands before them, able to see and hear him herself. Since Legba is outside the world of the resort, those who work inside cannot acknowledge him. He is thus rendered invisible even as the establishment depends on his sexual labor. Just as the zombi master depends on the zombi's labor, Legba must not speak even while he is critical to the resort's success.

When the audience is first introduced to Ellen she is with two other women and their beach boyfriends. One named Jessica reads while her boyfriend, Chico, sits silently at the foot of her chair. The other woman has her boyfriend, Charlie, put sunscreen on her back. All of the women are, by the looks of them, well over 40 years old and their lovers look either to be teenagers or in their early twenties. The two sides of the zombi are illustrated when, as the women talk and joke in English, Chico looks on, obviously with no idea of what is being said, but Charlie laughs. While Chico is silent, a much-cited mark of the zombi, Charlie mirrors his master's actions. Ellen switches to French to tell Chico that he "should take care of her," referring to Sue who has set up her beach chair nearby. Displaying the charm that Albuquerque speaks about, when Ellen asks Legba if Sue is fat he sagely replies, "Fat or skinny, I love beautiful women." Ellen remarks, "As usual he takes no risks." Actually, in this instance, Legba the man is manifesting the *loa* Legba who lets humans choose their own fate; not making a decision for them. What is seen as not taking a risk is an aspect of the *loa* Legba's habit of presenting options. When Legba asks Ellen if she wants to know what he really thinks she declines, saying, "Leave me to my illusions." The illusions on which her summers in paradise rest are in her physical desirability. On one hand Legba will indeed wear the mask that will support her illusion/delusion. On the other, like Charlie, he fulfills his master's desires.

During Ellen's ensuing tirade against fat women she mentions a Dutch painter who painted fat women. Demonstrating the ignorance that Albuquerque attributes to "beach boys" who are uneducated and unworldly, at the mention of Rubens, Charlie, exclaims, "A what?!."[52] Ellen explains patiently and then continues with her denigration of fat women. After listening to a bit more of her tirade Charlie and his "girlfriend" who looks like she is well into her 50s or 60s walk off hand-in-hand toward the ocean. Perhaps here Cantet is making a comparative statement about the age of the women who come to the Caribbean as sex tourists and Ellen's distaste for fat women. While Ellen cannot imagine a fat woman in bed with a man, equally possible is that others cannot imagine women her age in bed with younger men. While she rages against one form of "handicap" in this sense, she is blinded to her own "handicap." Although the age and status of the female tourist may be irrelevant to the beach boy, as Polly Pattullo suggests, their relationships are often a source of shame to members of their community.[53] Indeed, although there may be a certain amount of irrelevancy regarding the tourists' age, there is still, as Albuquerque remarks, a hierarchy of preferred sex tourists with wealthy, attractive French Canadians in their 30s topping the list. Thus, the older the sex tourist is, "the less discriminating she can afford to be."[54]

Although Ellen is clearly attractive she is fifty-five years old compared to Brenda who is in her forties and therefore, poses a threat to the former's position as Legba's master.[55] In fact, a struggle for dominance over Legba, and by extension, the island ensues between the two almost immediately. When Ellen introduces everyone to Brenda, the filmmaker's decision to have the camera rest on Brenda staring longingly at Legba to the exclusion of the latter comments on Brenda's position of power in relation to him. The audience has no idea if he returns the gaze. It also becomes clear why Brenda is visiting Haiti when Ellen asks her if she came alone and Brenda responds affirmatively. Ellen's reply, "Well, welcome to Paradise. You're going to have a ball," and repeated by Sue several times throughout the film, refers to the "bacchic release" promised in brochures about tourism in the paradisiacal Caribbean: "happiness, eternal youth, sexual adventure, nonstop sunshine and partying."[56]

Brenda's revealing that "she knows the place" because she was there three years ago extends the struggle over possession from Legba to the island. Ellen, believing that she knows all of the tourists, is at first disturbed that she does not recognize Brenda, but is reassured when she learns that Brenda had visited at a time when she does not normally vacation there. Her acceptance of Brenda's explanation seems to suggest that while she, as Legba, and by extension, the island's master is away, the two are free to be used by others. As Ellen lays back, smug in her regained power over her knowledge of who goes and comes to "her island paradise" and invoking the proprietary relationship that marked the language around the Caribbean in earlier films, Brenda looks again at Legba. This time the camera *does* turn to Legba who returns the look but then turns away quickly, taking a bite from his sandwich. The gaze is again, at issue as, while Brenda is free to look at Legba all she wants, he either refuses or is unable to return the gaze. His inability to hold her gaze links him to the zombi and its unseeing stare. Also, again, silencing here is an issue as the two women who can both speak French speak in English even as three people sit close by who the audience assumes do not speak their language. Their exclusionary use of the language, even though it does not seem to be deliberate, disempowers the three others who have no access to the conversation. As such, they are silenced like the zombi is silenced, not even speaking amongst themselves. This is especially prescient for Legba as he is the object of both women's desires. He is objectified, silenced in a battle that has just been subtly declared over his body.

Not only can Legba not return the gaze, but he seems, at least on the surface, to not be able to speak. While all three of the white women are later given the time and space of monologues to recount their histories, their feelings about their lives "back home," and their impressions of the island, Legba, although one of the lead characters in the film, is not given such a forum. Instead, Cantet develops Legba's character through the exposition of his labor, either with the women or for short periods while he is in the Haiti that exists beyond the resort walls. While on one hand, we may read Legba's voicelessness as a silencing by the filmmaker that reinforces the image of him as zombified, in the moments when the audience does hear his voice, it becomes clear that he is actually more self-aware than the women. Nonetheless, the reality of life under the Duvaliers forces him to assume the façade of zombification so that he can stay alive. That said, his inability to express himself both inside and outside the resort speaks to the reality of his zombification. Though not dead, he is also not truly alive, but instead resides in a liminal state where glimpses of his personality emerge for brief moments. It is only at the end of the film when he truly "tastes salt," choosing the woman that he loves over the façade of living, that he awakens. Murdered because of his choice, he and his girlfriend are finally released from their torturous state by physical death.

Zombified Men

The exoticization and exploitation of the black male body in relation to the land come into focus when Brenda, Ellen, and Sue have dinner and discuss the differences between men "back home" and those in the Caribbean. The scene shifts from the three women giggling conspiratorially to Albert behind the bar as three unattractive white men sit at the bar and drink the local beer, *Prestige*, and then back again to focus in on the women's conversation. The filmmaker sets up a triad with the three white women, the three white men, and the older black man as the anchor or point of reference. On the island the whites' relationships with each other are mediated by Albert, an older version of Legba, as guardian of the gates. However, unlike in Vodou where the gates divide the visible and invisible realms, the gates that Albert guards divide the foreign-owned establishment from the world outside. As I discuss later, his role denotes a betrayal of his revolutionary political and spiritual heritage.

When Sue tries to convince Ellen that there are several men (meaning white men since the "beach boys" are not allowed to eat in the restaurant) in the room who are attracted to her, she retorts that they are "not in the least bit horny." This is the most important, if not the only quality, she is looking for in a partner. Feeding fuel to the illusion to which Ellen referred earlier in the film, Brenda chimes in, "I think you're very beautiful." Ellen thanks her just before Sue says, "But at the same time, let's be honest. Here I don't even notice whites. They are nothing beside the blacks." While Ellen offers that there are many black men for Sue to choose from in Montreal, Sue rejects her suggestion, adding that the men on the island are "very different." Brenda's agreement and suggestion that men on the island are "closer to nature" recalls racialist discourses that again, date back to the colonial period when native populations and African people were linked inextricably with nature and the environment. As such, just as nature made itself available to be consumed by the colonizer, so too were the people who were associated with the land supposed to offer themselves up like ripe fruit to be picked. Furthermore, as many scholars of "primitivism" have noted, "whether white assessments of African or African American/Caribbean arts and cultures are positive or negative, they are always based in the racist assumption that anyone of African descent is necessarily closer to some past, originary state of mankind."[57]

Brenda's comment also speaks to the naturalization of the Caribbean that was cultivated by Europeans for centuries. She voices Deborah Root's assertion that the Caribbean was historically presented as a kind of Ur-tropics where "the inhabitants are identified with the natural world of luxuriant growth and fecundity and the adventure of entering the tropics (for the white tourist) becomes a sexual adventure with dark others."[58] This objectification of naturalized black bodies was useful during slavery when blacks were portrayed as being able to work the land and sustain hard labor better than native peoples or Europeans and then again during the American Occupation when Haitians were conscripted into the *corvée* system.[59] The connection was more explicitly linked with sexual interest with the spread of sex tourism, according to Sheller.[60] These naturalized black bodies at "a dime-a-dozen"; embodied commodities available at a low price, are a key component in sex tourism.[61] Ellen brings these linkages into relief when, in her retort to Brenda, she says "The big difference, sweetheart, is that here you see them stripped to the waist." Brenda's ignorance of her own racism is also communicated when Ellen responds to Brenda's protestations with "I know you don't know it, but I'm sure of it and I'm also sure that that's precisely why you've come back here.... So stop pretending. You didn't come here just to get a nice tan." Also, commenting on the cheapness of black life, she adds, "I mean, think of all those cute guys. They're a dime a dozen. Take your pick.... If you're too shy to pay them just give them gifts." Her comments articulate in the 1970s what the Irish writer, Patrick Leigh Fermor, wrote about his own encounters with black male bodies in the late 1940s, when sex tourism was taking off: "The young men were nearly all beautifully built, and looked their best when they were working without their shirts, and displaying magnificent shoulders and torsos that taper down to flat stomachs and phenomenally narrow waists."[62] Brenda also echoes Fermor's words in her description of Legba's body as long, lithe, and muscular during her monologue later in the film. It becomes clear in Fermor's account and Ellen's remarks that these lithe bodies (including those of children) are available for sexual hire, a message that Brenda gets loud and clear and acts upon.[63]

How to Objectify a God Without Getting Tired[64]

Legba's objectification is depicted several times in the film. For example, in one scene, following their lovemaking, Ellen decides to take his picture as he reclines naked. She does not ask his permission; just tells him to lay still so that she can snap his photo. Undoubtedly she will return to Massachusetts with the photo so that she can look at it whenever she wishes. She actions reify him in the way that the "taken" photo freezes him in a moment of her liking. Legba's response to her directive to lay still with "Whatever you want" reinforces their unequal relationship. Although he is the man and is thus perceived as being more powerful in relation to his female client, he has no power to decide whether his photo will be taken or not, nor for what purposes.

His objectification is also found in Brenda's monologue in which she recounts how her "relationship" with him started when she was visiting Haiti three years before with her husband, Mark. In his First World beneficence, Mark took pity on the young boy and invited him to eat with him and his wife. Brenda remarks that Albert was not happy about it (this issue of Albert and Legba's contentious relationship arises again in a later scene when Albert refuses to serve Legba in the restaurant). Brenda, blissfully ignorant of the complicated nature of class, color, and race on the island misreads his actions and accuses him of racism. She is also ignorant to the ramifications of her actions for the hotel and the workers; namely, of the very real possibility that Alfred could be fired for serving the known sex worker.

Brenda claims that she and her husband "kind of adopted Legba." The audience has no idea what Legba's situation was when Brenda and her husband met him as they have only Brenda's narrative to educate them. Her narrative is, however, unreliable because of her ignorance about the reality of Haiti. She did not come to Haiti to learn about its politics, culture, economic realities; she came there for a good time. The resort setting makes sure that she remains ignorant of the harsh reality of life outside of it. Although she says he was, it is doubtful that Legba was in school. She remarks that he had not eaten for two days when she met him and if she came to Haiti in September he would have been in school rather than spending time with Brenda and her husband.

As she begins to tell the story of her first sexual encounter with Legba she seems uncomfortable recounting it to the nameless, voiceless face behind the camera, but also aroused by the memory. While she tells her story her breath quickens:

> His body fascinated me; long, lithe, muscular, his skin glistened. I couldn't take my eyes off him. And the later it got the more I was losing my mind. He was lying there beside me. His eyes were shut. I remember every move I made as if it were yesterday. I edged my hand over and placed it on his chest. Legba opened his eyes and immediately closed them again. That encouraged me. I moved my hand down his body. Such soft young skin. He was motionless. Then I slid two fingers into his bathing suit and touched his cock. Almost immediately it started getting hard in the palm of my hand until it just popped out. His hands were beside his body and he breathed faintly but very regularly. I looked around to see that no one was coming and I threw myself on him. I literally threw myself on him. It was so violent I couldn't help but scream. I think I never stopped screaming. It was my first orgasm and I was forty-five. He opened his eyes and he was exhausted too, shy and frightened. I kissed him all over. I was crying.

The visual cues in the scene are just as important as the monologue as the audience witnesses a full range of emotion while Brenda tells her story and the extent that she exercises power over Legba finds full expression. She begins nonchalantly telling just another tale of meeting a young boy and being kind to him. She even chuckles at the memory of how much he ate. However, as the story progresses and her involvement with Legba unfolds, her amusement gives way to other, more complex emotions. In the beginning of the narrative she looks directly at the camera for the most part. However, as she starts to remember and recount her sexual encounter she looks away, into the distance, down at the floor and then back again at the camera. At some moments she tells the story almost trance-like, as if she is transported to the past. She breaks down in the end when she admits that until then she had never had an orgasm. Like Sandra, the female character of the Barbadian novelist, Kwadwo Agymah Kamau's *Flickering Shadows* (1996) who spends "most of the novel with a sexually inadequate white husband, and finds deliverance in a virile black man who leaves her spent, weak-kneed and satisfied," Brenda, a wife from Savannah, Georgia, also finally finds satisfaction with a black man—or rather—a boy with "The Big Bamboo."[65] Legba was only fifteen years old at the time.

This sexual exploitation of children that Brenda describes is not unusual. As Sheller argues, the sexualized black Caribbean body also encompasses children who are part and parcel of the allure of travel, often expressed through the sexualized images of children in advertising.[66] Seemingly innocent images of children used in tourist propaganda can be read alongside accounts of child prostitution to present a picture of their uses in promoting tourist destinations.[67] Eddy, a younger version of Legba who was preyed upon by an older woman (Brenda) when he was about Eddy's age, represents the possibility of his usage by tourists as well.

Brenda does not seem to be able to make a distinction between the fully grown man of her fantasy and the child whose innocence she has stolen, blinded as she is by her own desire. And because she is in a country where boundaries between what is acceptable and what is not are almost non-existent, she does not have to think twice about her actions. Even though Legba was just a child when he had sex with Brenda he served to sustain her romantic fantasy of the primitive within the primitive paradise as country and body; the perfect embodiment of the possibility, to paraphrase bell hooks (1992). As Sue says to Brenda while passing her on her way toward the ocean in a later scene, "Here everything is different." Furthermore, as Julia O'Connell Davidson argues, questions about child sex tourism are very much questions about power. The sex tourists who exploit both adult and child prostitutes are not only empowered to do so by economic, social, and political inequalities (between rich and poor nations, between men and women, between adults and children, between non-prostitutes and prostitutes, between white and black, and ethnic majority and minority). They are also motivated by ideologies which reflect and reproduce those same inequalities of power.[68]

Finally, Brenda's description of the sex act with Legba connotes zombification. The entire time she takes and devours his body, he shows no emotion. His arms remain by his side, he keeps his eyes closed and thus, does not confront her ravenous gaze. He is a passive body; a recipient of her aggression. Her screaming can thus, be contrasted with his silence throughout. While she is able to fully express herself in the most primal of ways, he remains silent and impassive. His silence allows him to be interpolated by Brenda, his master, both during and years after the act.

Impotent Revolutions

Although Albert has a monologue, it is not delivered directly to the camera as it is with the women. Moreover, where the women's monologues are delivered from the privacy of their rooms divulging their secrets, Albert's monologue takes place in the only other place the audience has seen him (besides the airport), the restaurant. As he prepares food for Legba, Brenda, and Sue, his voiceover tells his story by way of his lineage. He explains that he was born in Cap-Haitian in Northern Haiti to a family of patriots. The confluence of the setting of Albert's monologue, the personal history that he divulges in relation to the country's Haiti, and the indirect way that it is delivered brings Haiti's distant history of the first American invasion and subsequent occupation and its direct relationship to the foreign invasion in the 1970s into relief. As Albert says,

> My whole family fought the Americans during the 1915 Occupation. I think my father never shook a white man's hand. He saw them as lower than monkeys. He used to say: "I always look behind a white man to see if he has a tail." My grandfather didn't bother with that. To him, a white man was an animal, period. When he talked about "the white man" he really meant the Americans. The invaders, the occupiers, people who dared tread on Haitian soil. If he knew I was a waiter to Americans he'd die of shame. This time the invaders aren't armed. But they have more damaging weapons than cannons: the dollar! So everything they touch turns to garbage. The whole country is rotten.

The monologue summons several images: one, is how proud Haitians are of their revolutionary history; both the war of independence and their resistance during the American Occupation. In fact, one would be hard-pressed to find a Haitian person who cannot tell him or her the story of

Bois Caïman and the revolutionary fathers. The name of Charlemagne Péralte, leader of the *Caco* Rebellion during the Marine Occupation is also readily accessible. When Albert talks about how the Americans have not returned with guns, but with money, he recalls the words of the Haitian artist and *houngan*, André Pierre, who presents a few gourdes to the camera in the film, *A Pig's Tale* (1998)[69] and says, "You want to see Lucifer? Here is Lucifer." In the literature and films about sex tourism we also see how young men and women sell their bodies for money, the real "devil."[70] While Albert does not sell his body for sex, he *does* sell his labor in an establishment that caters to white foreigners. This is not only an affront to his heritage, but it also places him in the realm of the zombi. Although he is not completely silenced, the fact that he does not deliver his monologue directly circumscribes his voice. In addition, as the audience witnesses, he is impotent in the face of the demands of the tourists whom he is paid to serve.

Zombified Women

Ellen's monologue recalls earlier military and journalist writings as well as zombie films such as *White Zombie* in which white characters claimed Haiti as their own to define as they saw fit. Her speech conveys a sense that she "knows" Haiti. Calling the country a "dung heap" she explains that she had been drawn to the Global South, but considered Port-au-Prince "an animal park." For the past six years she has spent her summers at *Hôtel Petit Anse*, remarking that it is "clean and calm and the ocean is beautiful." It is there that she feels "finally at home." Later she remarks that she had once ventured outside the resort, but wishes that she had not. The implication is that she is privy to the world both inside and outside the resort and can speak authoritatively about both.

Ellen's monologue also exemplifies what the Caribbean represents to the white tourist, which according to Titley, "is an index of images and associations suffused with escapism and the extraordinary license of leisure, sustainable only through insulation and limitation."[71] The resort is an escape from her life in Massachusetts where the only guys she interests are "natural born losers or husbands whose wives are cheating on them." Sue speculates during her monologue that Ellen also feels out of place because of her British accent in an American environment. Thus, Ellen has made a conscious decision to be comfortable with the "insulation and limitation" that is necessary for her to maintain the illusion of "being at home."

Where it would seem that as a liberated woman Ellen has no use for the dramatics of "the emotional" girls at her university that she criticizes in her monologue, I would argue that she is jaded by her history as a professor of girls whom she perceives as being more interested in catching husbands than learning and the married men she meets back home who "are not the least bit horny." She has been deadened by her experience in the U.S. and is looking for the metaphorical salt that will awaken her in the Caribbean. However, what she ends up doing is zombifying someone else. Her realization of her complicity in the Other's zombification through violence that is predicated on the illusion that is created by the resort prompts her to leave and probably never return. By the end, she is guiltily aware of not only the pleasure that she has derived from her exploitative relationship with Legba, but also the social cost of her consumerism.[72] The emotional pain that she experiences when Legba is killed is her awakening.

Conversely, Brenda seems to relish her zombified state. During her monologue it becomes clear that her life with her husband is unfulfilling. She does not mention having a job, so she may be a housewife. The fact that she had not experienced an orgasm until she had sex with Legba speaks to her own deadness in the company of her husband who does not care about her needs and perhaps treats her in their bedroom the way that she treats Legba; as a body to ride until he is satiated. As such, she transfers her own zombification to the disfranchised boy. Despite several opportunities for her to do so, she never awakens from her deluded conviction that Legba cares for her.

After Legba dies, rather than return to her master in the U.S. (her husband), she chooses to assume the role of master over others: black men on other Caribbean islands. Her actions, however, are also evidence of her continued deadened state, which makes her predatory in the tradition of George Romero's zombies. As Bishop asserts about *Dawn of the Dead*, "Romero consciously draws the audience's attention toward the relationship between zombies and consumerism. The insatiable need to purchase, own, and consume has become so deeply ingrained in twentieth century Americans that their reanimated corpses are relentlessly driven by the same instincts and needs."[73] Several critics concur with this analysis. For example, Steven Briodowski comments that Romero's film takes "obvious satirical jabs at modern consumer society, as epitomized by the indoor shopping mall where a small band of human survivors take shelter from the zombie plague sweeping the country."[74] Most of the people who read the film this way take a decidedly Marxist position that capitalist production breeds a form of commodity fetishism that has an exploitative and depoliticizing effect on consumers.[75] Perhaps then it is no accident that Cantet chose to portray women as the cannibals (man-eaters as it were), as they are most commonly associated with consumerism.

Consumerism from a radical Marxist viewpoint may indeed be a Eurocentric luxury, and patronizingly aloof from the concerns of women shoppers in particular, as Meaghan Morris argues.[76] However, such detractors may also want to consider the effects of Northern consumer mentality on not just themselves, but on the rest of the world with whom they come in contact beyond the shopping mall and who they may treat as just another commodity. As Stephen Harper comments about *Dawn of the Dead*, Romero is not only interested in decrying commodity fetishism as spiritually deadening or politically inert, but also exploitative.[77] These are themes that run like a thread throughout Cantet's film as well, with deadly consequences.

Perhaps reflective of her low self-esteem, attributable to her weight and undesirability to white men back home, unlike the other two women who begin their monologues with their own stories, Sue begins by wondering what Ellen's life is like in Boston. She muses that when Ellen is in Haiti she is "like a sun, a fixture of the landscape." She then echoes Ellen when she confesses that she finally feels at home in Haiti, because when she is there she is the center of attention, a magnet. She feels beautiful and desirable in a way that she never could in the North at the bars that she used to frequent. Her sense of herself in this setting reflects a feeling that has been discussed in the literature about female sex tourism; that the female sex tourist gets to feel beautiful and sexually desirable and uses sex tourism to reconstruct her identity. Thus, as Sánchez Taylor says, "The 'Others' become a mirror which reflects back the female tourist's chosen sense of femininity"[78] or put more simply by Sue, "whatever her mood, life revolves around her."

It would seem that for Sue, Haiti provides the salt that she needs to awaken to her degraded state in Canada. Unlike Ellen and Brenda, she is a most obvious "cog in the wheel"[79] as a working class female; a manager of a warehouse that makes spare parts for kitchen appliances. She relates that she works with many men and slept with one of them one night. The next day the man acted as if he did not know her. She surmises that perhaps he was afraid that she wanted to marry him before switching to discussing her experience in Haiti, which is diametrically opposed to her life in Canada. She says, "It doesn't show, but here I feel like a butterfly. Free, alive, unattached. And then there's Neptune (her boyfriend). With him things are simple. I think I love him. Yes, I truly love him. Elsewhere it would be laughable, but not here. It isn't here because we all become different. So much the better." Her monologue and comments up to that point reflect Sánchez Taylor's comments cited above regarding female sex tourism, sexual desirability, and reconstructed identity. They also speak to bell hooks' reading of consumer cannibalism:

> To make oneself vulnerable to the seduction of difference, to seek an encounter with the Other, does not require that one relinquish forever one's mainstream positionality. When race and ethnicity become commodified as resources for pleasure, the culture of specific groups, as well as the bodies of individuals, can be seen as constituting an alternative playground where members of dominating races, genders and sexual practices affirm their power-over in intimate relations with the Other.[80]

As such, Sue's awakening is predicated on her deadening of another. Haiti is Sue's alternative playground where she, as a member of the dominant race, affirms her power that is disavowed in her native Canada. Not only is her job unfulfilling, but her personal life as well. Thus, she seeks freedom and aliveness in the Caribbean through her consumption of the Other who she has convinced herself she loves.

Tasting Salt

There are a couple of times in the film when the audience witnesses the consequences of Legba "tasting salt." The first time is when he sits with the women sipping his drink while they mull over the possibility of going into town. When Sue mentions that two of the other tourists had been to a lavish party at the president's palace the night before and then

Three. *Heading South* and Zombification

turning to Legba who has been studying his drink as if it were a scientific experiment, not once looking up to interject, asks, "Legba, do people know this squandering goes on?" Legba responds disinterested, "I don't know. Probably." Ellen persists: "How do people stand for that?" In a rare moment when Legba is not simply a mirror of the women's desires, he suddenly looks up and asks sharply, "Who says that we do?" Shortly thereafter he finishes his drink and rises to leave. To Ellen's suggestion that he take Brenda with him, he responds, "Some other time." The women are oblivious to the fact that, as an obscene example of corruption, Jean-Claude Duvalier's regime was kept in place by the brutality of the Tonton Macoutes. That is what Legba refers to when he questions the people's complacency with regards to the corruption of the palace. Again, what lies outside the resort—the violence that makes their pleasant stay possible—is not their concern. Nor do they have any notion of what Legba and the other beach boys endure beyond the walls of the resort. It is outside of their purview for however many weeks they are in paradise. As such, embedded in Legba's question is also a rebuke; an accusation of the women's collusion with the corruption and violence that they criticize out of ignorance.

The second time that the audience witnesses Legba's tasting of salt is when he decides to relinquish his liminal state of being to be with the woman he loves. His decision proves to be fatal because the woman is the concubine of a colonel in Duvalier's army. As she seduces Legba while the two ride in a government-issued car, the audience sees the chauffeur looking through his rearview mirror at them. Before she lets Legba out downtown in front of the ministry buildings, she makes him promise to meet her again. Although Legba does not say anything he kisses her on the cheek before he gets out of the car and the camera follows him as he walks away. The scene marks a pivotal moment in the film as it signals Legba's decision to "taste salt" by standing up to the political system that deprives the vast majority of Haitians of a life where they do not have to sell their labor and their bodies cheaply, but rather, are free to love whoever they want—a revolutionary idea.

Knowing that he will die for his decision, he visits his mother who lives in a hovel in Port-au-Prince and gives her all of the money that he has earned as a beach boy. Read through the symbolism of the zombi, although he has been a zombi for the past three years, from the time that Brenda raped him, Legba remembers his life before and returns to say goodbye to it before seeking out his grave, as the zombi is wont to do.

Death's Sweet Release

The symbolic capital of the fantasy Caribbean is shattered at the discovery of Legba and the Haitian woman's murdered bodies at the resort. For the tourists, the violence of the outside world has been allowed in. As the vacationers look on at the bodies being loaded into an ambulance, Brenda and Sue arrive. Although Albert tries to stop her, Brenda pushes past him and opens the ambulance, pulling back the sheet covering Legba and kissing him on the lips. She then steps down and walks away supported by Sue. Meanwhile, Ellen, still in the clothes from the night before, stands in the restaurant, philosophizing about Haiti. For her, Brenda's romantic notions about Haiti are responsible for Legba's death. Again, summoning her knowledge about Haiti's political reality that seems to escape Brenda, Ellen asks rhetorically, "Don't you realize no one's ever allowed to grow too tall in this country?"

But for all of her knowledge of Haiti, Ellen's ignorance of Legba's reality is evident in her assumption that she could have prevented his murder. "If I'd kept quiet he'd still be alive," she surmises. As an example of another consequence of the resort experience whereby the tourist is made to feel as if that world exists only for their pleasure, it is as if Legba existed only for her. Because Ellen is unaware of Legba's reality, she is able to rationalize that if he had spent the night with Brenda he would still be alive. She is however, self-aware enough to, at least suspect that he loved the young woman with whom his body is found. It seems that at that moment she decides to return home, preferring the known of Massachusetts to the unknown and unknowable of Haiti. Legba's death has turned her world upside down. Where she had always been able to count on the island paradise that had been constructed for her in the resort and Legba's attentions, both of which position her as master, this is no longer so. The real world has irrupted into her insulated haven where she was the center of attention, "finally at home."

Three. *Heading South* and Zombification

"No refuge from reality"

According to Gary Younge, people who come to the Caribbean are afraid that "global inequalities will interrupt their rest and relaxation."[81] Although the resort is supposed to be "safely beyond the everyday and apparently insulated from the increasing irruption of the everyday upheaval into the tourist haven" the violence of life in Haiti manages to invade the tranquility of paradise.[82] If anything, the women's experience proves that walls built around resorts will not save them from the reality of the people whose labor and bodies they exploit.

The image of the Caribbean that is portrayed in tourist brochures is also crucial in framing it as an investment opportunity. In the way that Haiti was open to being "taken" by the U.S Marines in 1915 and Papa Doc Duvalier declared that Haiti "could be a great land of relaxation for the American middle class" in 1970, contemporarily, former President Michel Martelly repeatedly declared that "Haiti is open for business."[83] As part of Martelly's plan to "'rebrand' Haiti from a development basket-case to a Caribbean success story"[84] he proposed establishing "urban and rural development zones and industrial manufacturing parks to create 1.5 million jobs in five years."[85] Summoning the words of Legendre about his zombies, these parks would consist of exploited laborers who earn about $7.00 for an eight-hour day, the relatively low wages of Albuquerque's imagination under inhuman conditions such as those that are exposed in anthropologist Mark Schuller and Renée Bergan's's film, *Poto Mitan* (2009). At the same time, in the inaugural meeting of the Community of Latin American and Caribbean States in 2011 Martelly announced in English that, "Tourism is a sector that can bring a lot of money, and we have lots of things to show the world.... We have a very rich and diversified culture, we have beautiful sights, a historical past. We have the most beautiful coast."[86] These industrial parks that are also displacing current residents from the sites where they are being built will likely reduce a notable sector of the young male and female population to "beach boys" and "beach girls" in a Haiti that also hopes to revive its tourist industry. They will be another product to whom consumers will have access as part of the Haitian "package deal" if the country is to succeed. At the same time, as people from the North who are driven to consume in their native lands and beyond flock to the opened market, the cycle of exploitation will continue.

Reading Meaning

As I have argued in this chapter, the disavowal and subsequent consumption of the Caribbean Other that is responsible for the success of the zombie figure in the American imagination has found another home in the tourist industry. The only way the exploitative relationship between the North and the Global South is going to change is if, as Sheller argues in *Consuming the Caribbean,* the North works to build "a more ethical relationship based on acknowledging complicity in relations of domination and with that an intimate responsibility to others."[87] The first step in building an ethical and equitable relationship is for members of the Northern population to acknowledge Caribbean people's humanity; a feat that has not been attempted from the days of slavery when the enslaved were dehumanized in order to justify colonialists' ruthless consumption of the original inhabitants before continuing with the African population. A close reading of films about the Caribbean in relation to the North as I have done with *Heading South* reveals the complexity of the unequal and unethical relationships that persist and the detrimental effects of those relationships on an individual and collective level. The themes that such films explore are tied inextricably to the existing socioeconomic and political conditions and reveal our collective responsibility to rethink our relationships both locally and globally.

Chapter Four

The Serpent and the Rainbow and the 1986 Revolution

Wes Craven's 1988 thriller, *The Serpent and the Rainbow*, picks up where films from the early twentieth century left off in proposing that one of the worst fates for a white person would be to succumb to the corrupt lure of the "island natives." However, rather than the vulnerable white women of *White Zombie*, *I Walked with a Zombie*, and *The Love Wanga*, *The Serpent and the Rainbow* portrays a white male scientist as in danger of being consumed and relatedly, subsumed by the Other: the primitive and superstitious Haitian. The film's catchline, "Don't let them bury me.... I'm not dead" accompanied by a picture of the ghostly protagonist, Dennis Alan, being entombed in a coffin served to draw audiences in to the tune of almost $19,600,000.

Although the film, as part of the horror genre, was consumed by the general American population for entertainment purposes, I would suggest that, like William Seabrook's *The Magic Island*, which anthropologist Franck Degoul characterizes as quasi-anthropological,[1] *The Serpent and the Rainbow* performs work beyond that of entertaining. Rather, the film, in positing Dennis as representative of white Western male scientific authority, also portrays Haiti as a land of feminized, primitive, and superstitious natives whose cruelty is endemic to their race. The film's intentionality is made clear on the DVD's back cover, which reads

> Wes Craven ... directs this terrifying story of one man's nightmarish journey into the eerie and deadly world of voodoo.
> A Harvard anthropologist ... is sent to Haiti to retrieve a strange powder that is said to have the power to bring human beings back from the dead. In his quest to find the miracle drug, the cynical scientist enters the rarely seen netherworld of walking zombies, blood rites and ancient curses.
> Based on the true life experiences of Wade Davis and filmed on location in Haiti, it's a frightening excursion into black magic and the supernatural.

There are several tropes invoked in this product description: that of the solitary adventurer (à la Indiana Jones) risking his life to secure knowledge from Othered primitive cultures for the benefit of mankind. His intellectual superiority is denoted by the reference to his affiliation with an Ivy League institution, his cynicism, and his grounding in the world of the tangible. For him, "seeing *and* experiencing is believing." All of the protagonist's positive attributes are contrasted with the nightmarishness of the journey into the eerie and deadly domain of voodoo, with which his audience is well aware because of voodoo's entrenchment in the American popular imagination dating from the time of the first American Occupation. Finally, in stating that the film is based on the "true life experiences" of Wade Davis and filmed on location in Haiti, the filmmaker invokes the documentary genre, thus leading the audience to believe that what they are witnessing on screen is essentially, a reenacted reality. For those who went to see the film—many of whom had probably never been to Haiti—*The Serpent and the Rainbow* offered them the ability to witness the corrupt and macabre world of blacks from a safe distance.

Anna Fahraeus has argued that, rather than stable, racial stereotypes about blacks are "historically contingent and are revamped or morphed into new variants depending on their political and social contextualization."[2] My exploration of *The Serpent and the Rainbow* at this juncture highlights the plurality, adaptability, and differentiated nature as well as the function of filmic images, which facilitate black stereotype(s), as Fahraeus suggests looking at stereotypes from different eras does.[3] Related to the perpetuation of black stereotypes in general, the film also reinvigorates notions of superstition as endemic to the nation of Haiti. As such, it misappropriates several of the Haitian *loas*, Baron Samedi and the Ghedes, and vilifies them as conditions for the triumph of the white male scientist who is guided by reason. Finally, the film conjoins the Haitian secret of zombification and the native woman as symbolic of the nation that must be protected against foreign invaders who want to possess her.

The Film

The Serpent and the Rainbow, based on the book by ethnobotanist Wade Davis by the same name, is about an anthropologist named Dennis

Four. *The Serpent and the Rainbow* and the 1986 Revolution

Alan who is commissioned by a medical company, *Biocorp*, to travel to Haiti to find out how zombies are made. When he first arrives in Haiti he meets with his contact, a medical doctor named Marielle Duchamps, and the two embark on an action-packed quest to discover the secret to zombification. Along the way, they become romantically involved. Ultimately, Dennis is successful in bringing the zombie powder to the U.S. where it will be potentially used to "save lives," as the CEO of *Biocorp* tells him is why he wants it.

Bryan Senn has praised the film, noting that Davis acted as Craven's guide and technical advisor and Craven and his producer "attended real voodoo ceremonies"[4] in an effort to treat the subject fairly. I however, read both the film and its inspiration a bit more critically. For me, the book and the film are inextricably connected, deliberately joined as they are in the public's mind. Not only is Davis implicated in the finished product based on his direct involvement in the process, but Craven's invocation of Davis's work as his inspiration in the film's publicity also implicates the author in the film's conceptualization, setting, and plot. Craven reinforces the connection in opening the film with the epigraph: "The following story is inspired by a true story." All of these elements: the DVD cover, Davis's involvement in the making of the film, and the film's epigraph, make a direct link in the audience's mind between the book and the film.

Several scholars have offered criticisms of Davis's work, drawing attention to the sensationalism of his narrative that made it ripe for its adaptation to film. Both Robert Lawless and J. Michael Dash criticize Davis's book with Lawless remarking that it reads like the first draft of a Hollywood movie, with Davis himself as an Indiana Jones–type hero."[5] As Dash comments, in Davis's book, Haiti once more, "found itself intensely associated with the stigma of bodily malfunction."[6] Furthermore, as Dash argues, "Haiti is not a real country for Davis. As an apologist for Duvalierism, he prefers to see Haiti as a zone of salutary dislocation, the supreme fulfillment of a young North American's *nostalgie de la boue*."[7] Dash also remarks that Davis's text harkens back to the earlier travel-writing era out of which the zombie emerged in its remaining "true to the spirit of the travel books of the thirties in its infatuation with primitivism and its disdain for modern, industrial society."[8] I agree with these critics that Davis's text was ripe for adaptation to the screen and even though he did indeed later condemn the film, calling it one of the "worst Hollywood films in history"⁹ and fled to Borneo to escape the hysteria and media after it was released, his work has had far-reaching consequences, helping to keep Haiti locked in the cage of primitivism and demonization that the international community has put it in since the revolution.

Davis was right to be horrified by the way that Haitian culture was misrepresented in the film and which also undermined the work that he was ostensibly trying to do with the book.¹⁰ As David Inglis concludes in his excellent evaluation of both *The Serpent and the Rainbow* and Davis's more scholarly work, *Passage of Darkness*, "the general tenor of scholarly criticism was that *Passage* as much as *Serpent* involved an untenable situation where 'fact nestles alongside fiction and warranted generalizations accompany unwarranted generalizations in a spectacular, though often ungainly dance.'"¹¹ He concludes that the amount of notoriety that Davis enjoyed was out of proportion to the contribution that his study made to the advancement of scientific knowledge. Moreover, with regard to Davis's attempt to distance himself from the film, Inglis avers,

> Davis had no right to complain about what the film-makers had done to the book, because his text already owed more to Hollywood than to serious scholarship in the first place. Having the temerity to present himself as "a dashing man of action as well as intellect," and to cast himself in the then very current garb of Indiana Jones, combining the role of "average academic turned wily world traveller," Davis had unintentionally cast "an almost comic slant to the 'double persona' problem of anthropologists."¹²

Despite his disavowal of Craven's work, in recent years, Davis has again been complicit in the Othering of Haiti that made the comment by televangelist Pat Robertson following the earthquake that struck Haiti in 2010 possible.¹³ In stating that enslaved workers of Saint-Domingue made a pact with the devil in order to secure their freedom from the French, Robertson reinvigorated long-held beliefs that Vodou is satanic and responsible for the political and ecological crises that have plagued the nation since its inception. As Davis rightly suggests

> So Pat Robertson is saying by that comment that voodoo itself is the devil. Voodoo is not a black magic cult, nor does it have anything to do with a Christian notion of the devil.
> All he's saying by that comment is that all African religion is devil worship, and he's revealing not only his ignorance about what voodoo really is, but also his bias that any religion not his own is devil worship.¹⁴

Indeed, Davis did attempt to expose the racist beliefs behind such a claim. Nonetheless, as Chris Vials argues, though Davis refutes Robertson's claims in *National Geographic*, "In many ways emblematic of the mainstream coverage of the disaster, Davis ... continues the politics of disavowal, albeit with a multicultural inflection, that fails to truly recognize the continuities of the past into the present era and is thus complicit in the logics of empire."[15] Such a position allows for the continued Othering, ingestion and spitting back out of the imagined culture that has been produced for the consumer's own purposes—in Pat Robertson's case, a brand of Christianity that demonizes anyone who does not subscribe to its doctrine.

"We are the mirror of your fears" I: Guarding Haiti's Secrets

Again, while *White Zombie* and *I Walked with a Zombie* were about the struggle to control the white woman let loose in the Caribbean, *The Serpent and the Rainbow* is preoccupied with what happens when white men are let loose. Concomitantly, it is interested in neutralizing the threat to white masculinity that the black man, embodied in the film's antagonist Dargent Peytraud,[16] chief of the Duvaliers' Tonton Macoutes, represents. As a continuation of the imperialist desire to possess the nation with which women were conflated in early zombie films, Craven presents the twentieth century white male imperialist desire to penetrate and consume one of Haiti's most guarded secrets, according to Degoul: the process of zombification. In my reading of the film, this "secret" is conjoined with the Haitian woman who is also associated with the nation.

As one of Haiti's most sought after secrets that has also been used to define the nation in many ways, zombies and zombification represent its deep recesses; the guarded secret garden which women's bodies have traditionally been viewed as. The amount of literature that has been written about zombies and zombification provides a clear indication of the power that it holds in the American imagination. As Dennis remarks in his voiceover when he deplanes upon his return to Haiti after smuggling the formula for zombification out of the country, "He's [Peytraud] gonna get to me wherever I am. I know that now. I've stolen his darkest and most powerful secret."

In "'We are the mirror of your fears': Haitian Identity and Zombification" (2011) Degoul argues for a rethinking of zombification. He discusses how the process, exogenous to Haiti in foreign understanding of it originating in the U.S., has been used against the Haitian people. However, he argues that zombification has been re-appropriated by the Haitian population as a collective identity and deployed against foreign invaders. Moreover, the secret of zombification is jealously guarded against its consumption by *blancs* (outsiders or foreigners).[17]

According to Degoul, zombification, which stands, in the American imagination, "as an emblem of Negro Haitian savagery,"[18] is

> equally associated in Haiti by drawing the same connection, but in a way that, in fact, reverses the terms of discourse. Positively appropriated, this allocation of practices conditions an affirmation of Haitian power that, simultaneously, protects Haiti from the iniquity of all involuntary occupation of its soil and imposes respect for sovereignty outside its natural borders—all by means of the fear that zombification instills.[19]

Zombification is thus, a secret, uniquely Haitian knowledge that can be used to chase away invaders. Not only is it a source of pride because of its uniqueness, but its knowledge is jealously guarded against "researchers of the world who try to penetrate its secret."[20] To illustrate this point, Degoul relates a story about a young student/seeker who, in search of the secret of zombification, is killed by a *bokor* through the use of a powder and brought back to life, but never learns how the zombie is made. For Degoul, the story provides a lesson. By demonstrating the effectiveness of the practice to the researcher—essentially, a demonstration of an otherworldly force that is posited as inaccessible to him or her as a foreigner—the *bokor* "affirms Haitian supremacy from its possible annihilation by the 'Other,' non–Haitian, with whom, by means of intervention, Haiti experiences constant conflict and tension."[21] The possibility of Haiti guarding any of its resources from American consumption is unimaginable to the imperialist mind. As such, its riches must be acquired at all cost, even one's own life. Relatedly, the idea of Haitian supremacy over anything, let alone Western science, is also unthinkable to the imperialist mind. As such, as Davis proved, not once, but twice with his publications, he would do whatever was necessary to penetrate the wall that Haitian *bokors* had put up around the practice of zombification.

However, despite their best efforts, ultimately the process of zombification continues to elude researchers. The impression of several *houngans* who Degoul interviews is that "the Other, the foreigner, enters into the domain of Haitian magical knowledge and witchcraft, which he wants to experience and benefit from."[22] Sure of themselves, they are able to obtain "the factual reality of the questioned operations," but they are excluded from "the arcane mystery"[23] of how zombification is accomplished. The implication is that no matter how many trips into the "netherworld" people like Davis and his filmic counterpart, Dennis, make, nor how much money they pay for the knowledge, they will never gain access to its true depths. Degoul surmises that Haitian people's

> collective conception relative to the Other, this definition of a particular form of alterity, explains that the anthropological research completed on zombification and Vaudou, as well as the desire demonstrated by certain "blancs" to be initiated into its rites, takes on the quality of suspicious intrusions into the very core of their Haitianness. What have they come to learn? What exactly are they searching for, these foreigners with their tape recorders, notebooks, unceasing questions, sometimes even trying to become an oungan or mambo by lending themselves to the secret rites of passage? Their interference remains suspect in the eyes of collective public opinion.[24]

Degoul's assessment regarding the hubris with which outsiders like Davis (i.e., an ability to intrude onto the very core of Haitianness) approached the subject of zombification, reflects the feminization of the nation in the mind of the researcher. At the same time, it suggests a revolutionary reading of the zombie. The foreign anthropologist enters Haiti confident that he will be admitted into its deepest recesses. However, what he finds is not the willing objects of his queries, but so-called "subalterns" who exercise their alterity in, not only, not acquiescing to his demands, but actively blocking his access to that which they hold dear: a collective identity. A zombi/zombie, alienated from himself, would have no notion of an individual identity, let alone a collective one. This would seem to suggest an interiorized awakened consciousness that has yet to be recognized by outsiders who continue to try to zombify the subaltern subject.

Situating Haiti

Craven conflates the presidencies of François "Papa Doc" Duvalier and Jean-Claude "Baby Doc" Duvalier which together, lasted from 1957 to 1986. Papa Doc, as he was affectionately called from his days as a country doctor who treated tropical diseases like yaws, typhus, and malaria, rose to power in 1957. Following an attempted coup d'état in 1958, Papa Doc's persona shifted from that of the kindly doctor to master of the macabre in associating himself with the Vodou *loa* of the cemetery, Baron Samedi. In addition, he created his own volunteer paramilitary group, the National Security Volunteer Militia, popularly known as the Tonton Macoutes, based on a Haitian bogeyman who is believed to kidnap naughty children at night and take them away in his sack called a *macoute*. His assuming the persona of Baron Samedi, donning a black suit and hat and speaking in a nasal voice in imitation of the *loa* when he possesses a supplicant, was an effective strategy for consolidating power. As president of a country where, at the time, it was common to hear that "Haiti is 85% Catholic and 110% voodoo," as Marielle voices in the film, such a strategy was highly effective.

Papa Doc's spiritual tactics worked in tandem with his worldly tactics to ensure his attainment and maintenance of power. As his association with Baron worked on the spiritual level, in the physical realm, he used murder, disappearance, and exile to keep the population in check. In fact, during his presidency, Papa Doc is believed to have ordered between 30,000 and 60,000 murders and countless other exiles. The macabre practices that he deployed against those whom he saw as political detractors have also been a source of his fame. Not only is he rumored to have had peepholes carved into the walls of the interrogation chambers at the infamous Fort Dimanche[25] so that he could watch detainees being tortured and submerged in baths of sulfuric acid, but he is also believed to have sat in on the tortures of detainees.

Before Papa Doc died in 1971, he named his son, Baby Doc, as his successor. The son continued many of the policies instituted by his father. That changed when Jimmy Carter was elected president of the United States in 1976 and took an approach to foreign policy in Latin America that emphasized a commitment to human rights. Desirous of American aid, Baby Doc eased his repressive policies. However, with the election of Ronald Reagan in 1980, Baby Doc understood that foreign policy was about to change and carried out a sudden wave of arrests and attacks on those who had spoken out against his regime in the previous years. He ransacked and shut down opposition radio stations as well as imprisoned and tortured journalists.[26] The tension that had been building in the country came to head when, in November 1985, during a student demonstration, several students were killed. Their murders lit the spark that awakened thousands of Haitian poor from their *seemingly* zombified state.

Four. *The Serpent and the Rainbow* and the 1986 Revolution

Thousands of students poured into the streets in the revolutionary city of Gonaïves and other towns, proclaiming that a new revolution was imminent and that Duvalier must go. As evidence of their awakened state, according to Martin-Luc Bannardot and Gilles Danroe, the student demonstrators shouted "Long live life! Down with death!"[27]

By February 1986 Baby Doc was compelled to invite the leading Vodou *houngans* to the National Palace to meet with him and his wife Michèle to get advice on how he should respond to the continuing political unrest. According to Laurent Dubois, he got an earful, with the leader of the delegation, the supreme priest of Vodou in Haiti, Max Beauvoir, laying out the grievances of the impoverished majority against the regime. A few days later, according to Dubois "Beauvoir delivered the verdict: 'The spirits are annoyed and angry.'"[28] In fact, "Since March 1985 the spirits have wanted you to leave.'"[29] After the U.S. embassy gave Duvalier a similar message, he agreed to be flown out of the country on a U.S. military plane and relocated to the French Riviera with millions of dollars from the Haitian treasury in tow.

Baron Samedi and the Ghedes

As I explained in Chapter One, Baron Samedi is a principle *loa* in Haitian Vodou as the guardian over the realm of death and rebirth. His uniform of choice is a frock coat and striped trousers, formal apparel once worn by government officials at funerals. Sometimes he wears smoked glasses to protect his eyes from the tropical sunlight because he spends so much time in darkness. As guardian of the realm that separates life and death, Baron is head of the pantheon of spirits called the Ghedes who cover their faces with thick coats of white powder, stuff their noses and ears with cotton plugs to simulate the dead, and also wear the color black.

In order to instill fear in Haitian citizens Duvalier claimed to not only be a *houngan*, denoting his power over the supernatural realm, but he also regularly appeared in public wearing a black suit and tie with a white shirt and talked with the strong nasal tone associated with Baron. The Tonton Macoutes can be read as his Ghedes who swept through the country killing and disappearing people with impunity.

Misappropriations

Linkages between Haiti's political and spiritual dysfunction in the filmmaker's imagination are drawn immediately in the opening scene, which depicts Haiti in 1978 where coffin makers are shown polishing their wares in an outdoor marketplace. A thug exhibiting only partial signs of the Ghede (his arms being painted white) comes through with his henchmen and, at gunpoint, takes one of the coffins that has been painted red, another color associated with Baron. Not only is the zombification of the masses indicated when the man who was shown polishing the coffin simply watches as they leave, but Craven makes sure to give the audience a glimpse of Haiti's degraded state, panning the camera around to reveal shacks and mounds of trash along the river. The scene is followed by one in which the same thug, dressed in full Ghede regalia, makes his way through a crowd, gun in hand, shooting it periodically as he shouts "Macabre!" His helpers come behind him carrying the coffin that they stole earlier as the crowd stands around looking; again, an indication of the zombification that has been induced by the terror tactics of François and Jean-Claude Duvalier whose faces are shown on a billboard side by side hovering over the shacks below. The billboard establishes the parameters for the filmmaker's conceptualization of the film, which, again, conflates the presidencies of the father and the son. Thus, while it was Papa Doc who, in fact, associated himself with Baron Samedi and the Ghedes, in the film, Baby Doc is also associated with the *loas*. The billboard also alludes to the tactic of surveillance that both presidents used to maintain both mental and physical control over the population. In such an oppressed sociopolitical context, the method of zombification is not a magical powder, but rather processes that harken back to the time of slavery and which the zombi/zombie is said to summon a memory of: terror and dehumanization that ultimately results in alienation of one from one's humanity.

Marielle Duchamps as Erzulie and the Nation

Yet another *loa* featured in the film is Erzulie, the *loa* of love, who I discussed in Chapter One in relation to *White Zombie* and *I Walked with a Zombie*. About Erzulie, Joan Dayan has proposed that, as a spirit that

Four. *The Serpent and the Rainbow* and the 1986 Revolution

originated in an experience of domination, she gives the history of slavery substance.[30] In *The Serpent and the Rainbow*, Dr. Marielle Duchamps, a mulatto woman and Dennis's guide and lover, is associated with her. Marielle's working under the auspices of love that Erzulie represents is established almost immediately in the film when the *loa* possesses her when she and Dennis visit the "nightclub" of a powerful *houngan* named Lucien Celine. She later explains that her father dedicated her to Erzulie when she was only four years old and the first time she was possessed she was only eight years old. She is a favored child of Erzulie and as Celine remarks, "To Marielle, possession is as natural as breathing." Such a close association with the *loa* establishes her as inextricable from the nation's sociopolitical and spiritual history and a worthy guide for Dennis.

This linkage between Marielle's personal history and the country's sociopolitical and spiritual history is reinforced later in the film when the couple make a Vodou pilgrimage to an area above King Henri Christophe's Sans Souci Palace in Milot in northern Haiti and then Sau d'Eau, Erzulie's sacred site. King Henri Christophe had Sans Souci built between 1810 and 1813 and the Citadelle Laferrière built between 1805 and 1820 as a fortress to guard against what he believed was the possibility of reinvasion by the colonizer. While he was right on one hand, he was incorrect on the other. Indeed, there was an imperial power that sought to retake Haiti; only it was not France, but rather the U.S., which it did during the early twentieth century in occupying the country for nineteen years. As I argue in Chapter Three, the U.S. did it again in the 1970s through the tourist industry. Here, I would argue that it was done yet again in the 1980s through researchers like Davis who sought to take her secret knowledge and that is depicted in the film. Today the U.S. is doing it in its leadership of the multinational military force that occupies the country while it determines the outcome of Haitian elections and opens the way for foreign-owned businesses to rule the economy. This reality is touched upon in the last film that I discuss in this study, *Zombi candidat*.[31]

In addition, since the audience now knows Marielle's spiritual history and has seen her possessed in an earlier scene in the film, when she and Dennis make love at Sau d'Eau it is unclear if it is Marielle or Erzulie whose face they see. Her connection to the *loa*, as well as the ease with which she moves amongst the peasants, her comfort in these sacred sites, and her letting Dennis in on cultural "secrets" again links her to the nation;

the good and rich part of the country. As Peytraud reminds Dennis, "She's home, she's Haitian."

Political and Spiritual Dysfunction and a Degraded Haiti

The political dimensions of Haiti's dysfunction, linked as it is to its spiritual dysfunction,[32] are illustrated when the Tonton Macoutes/Ghedes pass Peytraud after dropping the burning coffin that they stole earlier outside a hospital where a white doctor is pronouncing a man named Christophe Duran, a champion of the disfranchised poor, dead. Also in the room is Christophe's sister and a *mambo* dressed in red, again, invoking Baron. During the funeral, Peytraud, dressed in a black suit, tie, and white shirt, a scowl on his face, summons the image of a nefarious Baron Samedi. The same *mambo* from the hospital is also dressed in black. While the other Haitians that have appeared in the film until now have been metaphorically zombified as a result of Duvalier's terror tactics, Christophe has been literally zombified, buried alive and doomed to a state of liminality. This literal zombification is a consequence of his not succumbing to the Duvaliers' metaphorical zombification; in other words, keeping his mouth closed and turning a blind eye to the injustice that he witnessed.

The dichotomy between the Western scientific world and that of the primitive superstitious Other is made clear when the CEO of *Biocorp*, the company that commissions Dennis to travel to Haiti to secure the formula for zombification in order to "save lives," states unequivocally that "we … deal in science and medicine, not magic." The implication is that, where in the hands of the superstitious Haitians the knowledge of zombification is used to hurt each other, "a sign of the Negro atavism that pushed the Haitian to cruelty,"[33] in the hands of white Western male scientists, the knowledge that is wasted on Haitians would be put to good use.

Once he arrives in Haiti, Dennis's voiceover as he walks through the streets of Port-au-Prince contrasts the degraded state of the country with Marielle who he spots standing in front of her clinic for the insane. A kind of Pocahontas figure, she will help Dennis gain access to a side of Haiti that is normally inaccessible to *blancs*. In her association with the

Four. *The Serpent and the Rainbow* and the 1986 Revolution

nation that is on the verge of being penetrated by the white Western male explorer, her role as a guide conjoins her with the inner sanctum that he is after: the secret of zombification. A man would not be fit to guide him because he would be in competition for mastery over the island; such rivalry is absent from Dennis's relationship with Marielle. In fact, the two's later entering into a romantic relationship signifies his triumph, at least on one level. However, in the end, the representative of the true depths of Haitian culture, the secret of zombification, eludes him.

In this, Dennis's initial encounter with the island, the Otherness of Haiti is conveyed both aurally and visually. Stereotypical scenes of Haitian life: women holding live chickens, the ubiquitous baskets associated with Caribbean market scenes being carried on heads, heaps of rotting garbage blocking the streets, mark a visual display while Dennis's voiceover summarizes its history: "It's one of the poorest countries in the world, it's got revolution in the air, its got a ruthless dictator in the palace." Consequently, he expects the oppression that he senses. The sense of oppression that Dennis feels is reinforced visually by the sudden appearance of Tonton Macoutes in the distance and a poster of Baby Doc plastered on Marielle's clinic walls, seemingly keeping an eye on everything. This suspicion of surveillance is confirmed later when Peytraud confronts Dennis about his visit to the clinic.

In recent years, the same trope of profound Haitian degradation that Craven uses has resurfaced with Hamilton Morris remarking in his reinvigoration of the B-horror movie that inspires the title of his article as well as Davis's work in "I Walked with a Zombie: Travels Among the Undead" (2011):

> Even now, three months before the January 2010 earthquake that will destroy much of Port-au-Prince the chaos of waste in the streets seems without compare. The roads, alleys, and canals are littered with a skin of organic matter, peels, husks, and shells of every imaginable food. Banks of plastic miscellany line the sides of the roads waist-high with a coverage so complete it would seem the soda bottles must have crystallized in the atmosphere and fallen upon the earth like snowflakes.[34]

Morris's words can, in turn, be compared to those of journalist Amy Wilentz who in 2011 compared Haiti to a latrine in need of someone to clean it up.[35] In the film as well as in the two journalist narratives, Haiti is compared literally to a wasteland that has no hope if left to itself. It needs the intervention of *blancs*, outsiders, to clean it up physically, socially, politically, and spiritually.³⁶ In the film, as in Davis's book, that savior is, as it has always been, the white male who is portrayed as up to any challenge.

This message is reinforced when Dennis meets his first zombie, a woman named Marguerite who died fifteen years earlier and was recently found wandering around a popular market. Craven's depiction of Marguerite seems to have been culled from Seabrook's text where he tells the story of a young woman who had died years before and was found wandering around, naked and confused.³⁷ Where, prior to Dennis's arrival, Marguerite had been standing by a window in the clinic, motionless, and according to Marielle, devoid of memory, a few words of heavily American accented French from Dennis and she seems to come alive. While Dennis reads a warning in her eyes that follow him as he leaves, I would suggest that they are pleading for deliverance from the tortured state in which she, as representative of the disfranchised and terrified masses, is trapped. He, as a white man, represents salvation in the way that the American president, Jimmy Carter, represented a reprieve from the Duvaliers' reign of terror.

However, the desire for Haiti to remove itself from the shadow of the U.S. is depicted in the scene in which Dennis has been brought to Peytraud's office to be interrogated. Their exchange posits Peytraud as representative of the corrupt state apparatus, and Dennis, U.S. imperialist interests. As Peytraud informs Dennis, while rising from his chair behind his desk and coming around to face him, "This country lives on the edge, Dr. Alan. One weakness in the wrong place and over it goes right back into slavery again, just like with the French." Amid Dennis's weak protest, Peytraud steps close and menacingly continues, "The United States would like anarchy here, I'm sure. Well, this isn't Grenada, Dr. Alan." He deliberately draws out the last line: "I'm here now. There are people like me who make sure that doesn't happen." As he takes Dennis's passport from his own pocket he jerks his head to let him know that he is dismissed.

Not only does Peytraud's speech refer to Haiti's colonial past, but also the tense relationship between the U.S. and Haiti during both François and Jean-Claude's reign. While the U.S. held Haiti's purse strings it was demanding more of a role in Haiti's politics even though it was aware of the government's corruption and violent repression of the masses and intellectual class. But whereas the U.S. was able to enforce its rule by invad-

Four. *The Serpent and the Rainbow* and the 1986 Revolution

ing Grenada, Peytraud is warning that Haiti will not be as easily invaded and controlled. The zombi/zombie is a perfect metaphor for the U.S.'s desired invasion and control of the country. As Stephanie Boluk and Wylie Lenz argue in their introduction to *Generation Zombie* (2011), "despite attempts to claim ownership over the zombie, it has eluded containment ... it's very nature seems to have a built-in resistance to such efforts."[38] Similarly, Haiti has refused to be contained and controlled despite the international community, led by the U.S.'s repeated attempts to do so. While this resistance to co-optation can be read positively in the way that the country refuses to be contained, the corruption and violent repression that have kept those in power are not to be celebrated. In either scenario, it is of course, the masses who are disfranchised, zombified as it were.

Again, not very subtle in his message, Craven further connects Haitian politics and spirituality when, in Dennis's voiceover at Celine's nightclub, he explains that Celine is "powerful in both politics and voodoo." Celine is an allusion to the real-life Max Beauvoir, a biochemist and *houngan*, with whom Davis lived when he was doing his research. While the character in the film owns a nightclub, Beauvoir had a *peristyle* named Mariani, just outside of Port-au-Prince that, while he was alive, many foreigners frequented for Vodou/voodoo ceremonies. According to Morris, Beauvoir's *peristyle* was "once an attraction that would bring both UN workers and tourists from all around the world to watch nightly shows of dancing, hot-coal eating, and possession-induced dove decapitation (Bill Clinton in his autobiography, *My Life*, recounts a visit during which a possessed woman bit the head off of a chicken.)."[39] Not only did Davis stay at Beauvoir's home, but was introduced by him to the *bokor* who would make the zombie powder.[40]

Degoul's discussion of Haitians jealously guarding the secret of zombification surfaces when Dennis remarks about Celine that he "does a little bit of everything *except give out information*"[41] (emphasis added). To Marielle, Celine is simply being difficult, but as Celine tells Dennis regarding Peytraud, "Be careful my friend. In Haiti, there are secrets we keep even from ourselves." The scene signals that the struggle over the nation has begun when, Peytraud, having just arrived, introduces a drum rhythm that summons violent spirits. One of the men who is dancing tries to attack a possessed Marielle with a machete, but is saved, initially, not by the powerful Celine or even another dancer, but Dennis. It is only then that Celine intervenes and puts the would-be assassin down and then tends to Marielle. In other words, Celine can only finish the work that Dennis initiates. Furthermore, this displacement of power portrays Celine as ineffective, with the forces of evil destined to triumph without outsider intervention. The portrayal is reinforced at the end of the film when Celine is only able to provide limited protection to Dennis against Peytraud, is zombified himself, and then becomes an instrument of Peytraud who blames Dennis for the revolution that has begun. It is ultimately Dennis who destroys Peytraud who symbolizes the Duvalier regime on the physical level and evil forces in the spiritual realm.

A Zombie Who Remembers?

When Dennis and Marielle finally find Christophe, the man the audience has seen zombified in the beginning of the film, he is in a cemetery in his village because he is "obsessed with death," according to Marielle. Christophe is unique, not only because he can move on his own volition and speak, but more importantly, because he possesses memory. Again, the debate about whether a zombi/zombie can remember his or her life before zombification persists with most scholars concluding that they do not. However, Laënnec Hurbon posits that they do, based on his own experience with a relative of his who was zombified and returned to her home.[42] What Christophe remembers exactly is unclear as he talks only about being buried and then undergoing the zombification ritual, which includes being whipped. Although he refuses to leave the cemetery he is able to relate the "factual reality of the questioned operations"[43] of zombification to Dennis and Marielle and tells them that it is achieved by applying a poisoned powder to the skin. His adding that the powder seeps through the skin to the soul is "the arcane mystery" that will continue to elude Dennis, however.

Marielle's suggestion that Christophe is "obsessed with death" comments on the obsession that pervaded the entire society under the Duvaliers' rule when anyone could be killed for seemingly innocuous actions or remarks.[44] I would also posit that his saying over and over that he remembers refers, not to his physical zombification, but the terror of life that he suffered before he was zombified. That life along with the reasons

Four. *The Serpent and the Rainbow* and the 1986 Revolution

for his zombification become clear later in the film when Dennis asks Marielle if she knew Christophe before. She reveals that she knew *of* him because, although a poorly paid grade school teacher and not "important" he "wasn't afraid to speak out for the people, for freedom. He was very much admired." For Marielle, "That's why they made him what he is. Now, instead of inspiring courage he only inspires fear." This is the memory to which Christophe refers and is why he is obsessed with death. Rather then return to the "land of the living" that is governed by forces of death like the Duvaliers, Peytraud, and the Tonton Macoutes, he prefers the social alienation of the graveyard where he can be free from the terror that the regime engenders.

The spiritual side of his torture is also alluded to when Dennis asks rhetorically, "Why would they do such a thing to him? Why would they make anyone a zombie?" Implied in the unanswered question is Degoul's suggestion that, again, in the American mind, zombification is "an emblem of Negro Haitian savagery"[45] and a sign of the atavism that pushes the Haitian to cruelty.[46] As such, his questions leave the impression of the inescapability of the ruthlessness of blacks towards other blacks. Again, "natives" harm other "natives." As a white man asking these questions, the other side of the question is the implied response that, "We would never do that to each other." Under such circumstances, Neil's suggestion that Madeline would be better off dead than in the hands of the natives seems to apply here to Christophe. Better to be zombified and residing in a graveyard than "alive" and subjected to the Duvaliers' soul-killing cruelty.

Undermined Authority

Interestingly, although filmed in Haiti, none of the major actors in the film are Haitian. For example, Marielle Duchamp is played by Cathy Tyson, the daughter of a Trinidadian man and an English woman, Dargent Peytraud is played by South African actor, Zakes Mokae, Christophe Duran is played by American actor, Conrad Roberts, and Raul Winfield, also an American actor, plays Lucien Celine. Finally, Louis Mozart, the *bokor* that Celine sends Dennis and Marielle to for the potion, is played by Brent Jennings, yet another American actor. While the choice perhaps makes the film more accessible to American audiences, it undermines the authority that the film has tried so hard to establish with its description and epigraph. The actors' over-the-top accents give the film a farcical feel, which undermines the authority over the knowledge that they claim to possess as well as the validity of the ceremonies and rites that they perform.

Not only does Craven's choice of actors undermine the film's authority, but the filmmaker also chooses to undermine the authority of Mozart's power throughout most of the film. Not only is he revealed as a charlatan almost immediately, but he is later outwitted by the *blanc*, Dennis. Craven perhaps tries to redeem him towards the end by having him teach Dennis the real way to make the potion and then risk his life to give it to him with just the latter's wristwatch for payment. However, the idea of his dishonesty, a stereotype about the black man and capitalized on in Hollywood, is already firmly planted in the audience's mind.

The idea of the charlatan *bokor* has also been propagated from within the culture as a way of protecting the secret of zombification, according to Degoul. In the story of the young student/seeker in search of the secret of zombification from earlier, Degoul remarks that the "moral of the story is that a sly, crafty bôkô will always be a sly, crafty bôkô."[47] But while Degoul goes on to posit that the *bokor*'s powers were truly effective and he grew rich at the expense of the young guinea pig, Craven's version of such a *bokor* dismisses the possibility of Mozart getting rich from his knowledge. Rather, the film suggests that it will just be given away. As such, Haitians are denied the possibility of owning their knowledge and profiting from it themselves. Rather, in the tradition of the loyal black that we find in *The Love Wanga*, whites will inevitably find someone to relinquish Haiti's secrets to them for practically nothing (in this case, a watch). In so doing, he redeems himself in the eyes of white America who will recognize that he is not as crafty and dishonest as they thought (that is, until he has to prove himself again).

The Indiana Jones Complex and Dennis Possessed

Dennis reminds the audience of the filmic archeologist explorer Indiana Jones whose catchphrase, "It belongs in a museum," establishes him

Four. *The Serpent and the Rainbow* and the 1986 Revolution

as the keeper and preserver of endangered heritage about which ignorant "natives" know nothing or which they use to harm other "natives." Despite several warnings, Dennis refuses to "back off," as he tells Celine, from his quest to learn the secret of zombification and take it back to the U.S. where it will be put to good use. Not only is his hotel room broken into and voodoo symbols drawn on the wall with what looks like blood, but the very real threat of a henchmen just outside his room forces him to flee through the window. Even physically wounded later in the film he continues in pursuit of the formula, remarking flippantly to Marielle, "Hey, this recipe took a thousand years to get right, I want to learn it." Later when he is brought to the police headquarters and interrogated by Peytraud he tries to hide behind his American hubris. However, he is quickly subdued when the sounds of torture from another room break in on his attempt at a joke. Nonetheless, even then, he continues on his quest.

Related to Dennis's persistence as an Indiana Jones figure is, as a white person, running the risk of being seduced by the lure of the corrupt Caribbean. Like the whites of *White Zombie*, *I Walked with a Zombie*, and *The Love Wanga*, Dennis eventually succumbs to the lure and is possessed by the island several times: once, willingly, at Sau d'Eau when he and Marielle make love during the pilgrimage, and then unwillingly, when Peytraud kidnaps and tortures him. In the first instance, he and Marielle are at the pilgrimage for Erzulie and, following Marielle's washing his face with the waterfall's healing waters, the two make love in a nearby cave. The cave symbolizes the inner recesses of the island, where her secrets are hidden. During their lovemaking, Marielle takes on a look that the audience saw earlier when she was possessed by Erzulie. The implication is that her possession while making love with Dennis is passed on to him mimetically. As such, he is also possessed. His possession by the *loa* exposes him to the dark side of Haiti's spiritual tradition, zombification.

The second instance invokes the image from *The Love Wanga* when Eve is kidnapped by the zombies. But while she was restrained by the zombie's arms, Dennis is restrained by straps around his neck, his wrists, and ankles to a chair in Peytraud's lair. The final stage of his possession (the nail in the coffin, as it were) is when Peytraud's henchman straps Dennis's head to the chair, signaling total control over his being. In this scene for which the film is best known, the camera focuses in on Dennis's underwear bundled around his ankles with Peytraud wielding a mallet while the Macoute fetches a railroad spike for him. It is in this scene that the fight over masculinity and the nation is waged most vulgarly with Peytraud driving the spike through Dennis's scrotum, a fact that is not made clear until later in the film when Dennis states, "The wound Peytraud inflicted was struck for fear, not injury. I'm alive, intact." Until then, the audience is left to believe that Dennis's "manhood" is ruined and after witnessing the lovemaking scene between him and Marielle earlier, knows that this would prove disastrous for him with all of his adventures still to be had. Though the element of individual male virility is at stake, it is more so the imperialist nation's power over the feminized nation that is the real prize.

Dennis's possession is complete when he internalizes Haiti's belief system, signified by his dreaming that he is enclosed in a coffin with Peytraud throwing dirt onto him. His subsequent submersion in blood as he screams and ingests it, signifies his immersion, body, mind, and possibly soul in Haitian voodoo. As such, he has taken his final leap into his corruption and exposes himself fully to zombification, which, as a white Western man of science, until then, he would have been able to claim exemption from. Whereas he had arrived in Haiti believing that he would possess her, Haiti ends up possessing him. With his surrender to her charms as well as her darker side, he becomes privy to her secrets to an extent. For example, Marielle gives herself to him and Mozart can teach him how to make the powder. Nonetheless, his access is still circumscribed by his outsiderness and he never gains full access to the magic of the powder.

Because of his (limited) insider status, Dennis can return to the U.S. and speak authoritatively about the practice of zombification, which he does when he runs tests on the powder at *Biocorp*, providing the voiceover for the scene and then later at the CEO's home. But the other side of his insider status is that Peytraud now has access to him and cannot only enter his dreams when he is on the island, but also alter his reality and bring him back to the island when he chooses. Even though back in the U.S. with his friend advising him to stay away from Haiti for as long as he can, in Haiti, Peytraud successfully performs a ceremony that will force him to return so that he can punish him for stealing the zombie formula.

Four. *The Serpent and the Rainbow* and the 1986 Revolution

Revolution Interrupted

In the final moments of the film, Dennis's extrication from the grave where Peytraud has buried him after zombifying him is followed by scenes of revolution in the streets of presumably Port-au-Prince as the Duvaliers flee the country. These scenes of revolution provide the backdrop for the final showdown between Peytraud and Dennis, representative as they are of the struggle between good versus evil, over male virility, and for control over the nation symbolized by Marielle and Haiti's secret knowledge of zombification. Peytraud has the body of Celine say when he attacks Dennis, "It was your work that caused this." We can interpret the "this" as the revolution that is taking place outside and quickly making its way toward Peytraud's lair to destroy him. The implication is that Dennis's removing the formula from Haiti has released the zombified population from their stupor. This would in turn mean that the disfranchised masses are not the agents of their fate; it is rather Dennis who released them from their zombification. In a film that depicts a potentially revolutionary consciousness on the part of the disfranchised masses, such a suggestion disempowers the "revolutionaries." Moreover, relegating the Haitian population to the background while centering the "noble war" that is being waged by Haiti's masters, the old and the potentially new, with a mulatto woman at its center, re-zombifies them ideologically even as they are in the midst of potentially liberating themselves. As such, the revolution is a failure; a reality that was borne out over the ensuing years following the Duvaliers' exile. Labeled "Duvalierism after Duvalier" the years following the 1986 revolution were characterized by serial coups d'état and continued political repression. More recently, following the 2010 earthquake, the unthinkable happened when Baby Doc returned to the country and, not only evaded prosecution for his crimes, but lived lavishly in the hills above Port-au-Prince until he died of a heart attack in 2014. Haiti's government, at the time, neo-Duvalierists, in collaboration with the U.S., essentially turned back the clock on Haiti's revolutionary history.

Although it would seem that Dennis is successful in his quest to penetrate Haiti's secrets: he emerges from Peytraud's lair after defeating him, triumphant with Marielle by his side and has managed to smuggle the zombie powder out of the country to have it analyzed, Haiti, nonetheless, seems to have kept her secrets safe. Just before the credits role, the audience is informed that although "the zombie powder and its active ingredient tetrodotoxin is currently under intensive research" in both the U.S. and Europe, to date, "the process by which it works remains a mystery." Rather than any kind of potential revolutionary message on the part of Craven, this fact can be read as Haiti in her own interiorized awakened state, ultimately resisting her possession and consumption by outsiders.

CHAPTER FIVE

Zombi candidat à la présidence ... ou les amours d'un zombi and the Resurgence of *La politique de doublure*

Zombi candidat à la présidence ... ou les amours d'un zombi (2009)[1] directed by Haitian filmmaker Arnold Antonin and based on a screenplay by the prolific Haitian writer, Gary Victor, comments on the historical and sociopolitical quagmire in which Haiti is stuck. Unlike the other films in this study, *Zombi candidat* explores the figure of the zombi through satire. It also ends more optimistically than the others that are conceived of and directed through a foreign lens.

Drawing again on Franck Degoul's discussion of the zombi as a form of Haitian collective identity, I explore *Zombi candidat* as a film that empowers rather than disfranchises the zombi. I also suggest that the film offers commentary on Haiti's internal political system that is guided by *la politique de doublure*, as it has since the nineteenth century. Finally, I argue that, like the earlier films, *Zombi candidat* conflates women and the nation in an enduring symbolism that, disassociated from class-based struggles, offers contemporary audiences no solution to the crisis of zombification of the masses that the film portrays. As several scholars have argued, the trope of the zombi seems to be reinvigorated during periods of upheaval and crisis.[2] It, thus, stands to reason that in a country like Haiti that has endured a seemingly never-ending series of upheavals and crises since Columbus first landed on the island's shores, the zombi has also endured.

The Film

Zombi candidat is about a young taptap³ driver named Pierre Zéphirin who is killed and then turned into a zombi by Syrus, his lover, Swamen's, husband. However, it would seem that Zéphirin's zombification is never complete. Enlivened by his love for Swamen, Zéphirin escapes from his master, a *bokor* named Zèl Loray, and goes in search of her. Following his escape he meets a journalist named Nicole with whom he shares his story and who agrees to help him reunite with Swamen. Unfortunately for Zéphirin, Baron Samedi, *loa* of the cemeteries, has also fallen in love with Swamen and enters into competition with Zéphirin over her. Meanwhile, a group of politicians in need of a presidential candidate decide to make him their puppet. However, they soon learn that he is not as malleable as they had thought and have Swamen kidnapped.

"We are the mirror of your fears" II: Rethinking the Zombi

As I discussed in earlier chapters, in "'We are the mirror of your fears': Haitian Identity and Zombification" (2011) Franck Degoul argues for a rethinking of the zombi. Rather than seeing it as simply a reflection and commentary on the condition of enslavement as many scholars do, he considers, not only how the world perceives Haiti in light of its practice of zombification, but also how Haiti positions itself in relation to the exteriority of this perception by its use of the way the practice is imagined. His primary site of exteriority is the United States because of its sustained shaping of the way that Haiti is imagined politically, economically, and culturally. As such, he adopts the position that, in fact, the zombi and zombification are exogenous to Haiti because of the way that the figure has been imagined from outside a Haitian sociocultural context. Citing its introduction to the American public during the first American Occupation, Degoul proposes that although it comes "from outside its sociocultural space, this association of magical zombification with the Haitian being—which is most notably developed in film and literature made about Haiti—encases, in a remarkable manner, the phenomenon within the Haitian context."⁴

Five. *Zombi candidat à la présidence*

As a response to American-constructed misrepresentations of Haiti, with the spiritual belief system of Vodou at the forefront, ethnographer and medical doctor, Jean Price-Mars founded the Indigenous Movement in an attempt to re-appropriate and celebrate Haitian culture; its religion and folklore, specifically. Despite such efforts, as Emmanuel C. Paul has argued, prejudices are often interiorized by the implicated populations who have been submitted to the process of colonial acculturation.[5] As such, readings of the zombi, both from within and outside of Haiti, as an example of "the Negro atavism that pushed the Haitian to cruelty"[6] that originated during the Haitian Revolution and were revived during the American Occupation, endure. Nonetheless, while it may be true that Haitian people have internalized exogenous prejudices about themselves, it is also true that they have consistently found strength despite conditions that were meant to weaken them. The Haitian Revolution where enslaved people who were subjected to one of the cruelest slave systems in history took their freedom is a perfect example of this. Another example is the prolific and masterful quality of visual art that emerges from the masses (*pèp la*); many of whom live on less that $2.00 a day, contemporarily. Based on Degoul's findings, it would seem that zombification is another example of Haitian people's ability to interiorize a trope that was meant to disempower them and use it as a source of empowerment; in other words, to "flip the script." Put simply, Haitians have both internalized and interiorized or appropriated the zombi.

Through his interviews with and anecdotes by several *houngans*, Degoul deduces that, since the time of the Occupation, Haitian people have used zombification to defend themselves against outsiders. It was used against the Marines as soon as they set foot on Haitian soil in 1915, exemplified in the story that Degoul is told of the first army officer who walked on Haitian soil and is still working as a zombi in the sugar fields in Léogâne.[7] The story uses the zombi as a trope to comment on the unequal power relations that were inscribed at the time of the American Occupation. It suggests a kind of homegrown or underground resistance to the Marines, which, when joined with more overt means of resistance found in the *Cacos*, presented a formidable force against what they viewed as an invasion by outsiders. The specter of zombification is still used today in relation to the Dominican Republic, Haiti's next-door neighbor, which is also seen as an outside force. As one *houngan* tells Degoul, "Dominicans are afraid of us." Referring to a musical group's video, the *houngan* says, "…in the video we see a Dominican who … is armed, and then the Haitian holds in his hand (mimes a powder that he blows in this person's direction, who is clearly a soldier)."[8] When the Haitian blows the powder on the Dominican, the Dominican turns into a zombi. Of course, again, like the story that Degoul relates from the American Occupation, this tale comments on the uneven power relations that exist between Haiti and the Dominican Republic. This dyadic relationship has existed for decades, coming to a head in 1937 when Dominican soldiers massacred thousands of Haitians on the border between the two nations (The Parsley Massacre). It has again been brought into sharp relief in the past few years with the Dominican Republic stripping Haitians born in the D.R. of their citizenship and deporting them en masse. This official decree from the D.R.'s Supreme Court has been accompanied by increased violence against Haitians living and working in the country.

Whereas, according to the two afore-discussed stories, historically zombification has been used to repel or punish outside invaders, I would also posit that, as a form of collective identity, it is also a potential tool of the Haitian masses—the disfranchised—that can be deployed internally against the elite class who seek to exploit their labor; in other words, zombify them. I would also suggest that it is this dynamic that the audience witnesses in *Zombi candidat* in Zéphirin's denying his bodily labor to the Haitian politicians who try to turn him into a puppet president.[9]

Baron Samedi, the Ghedes and Life and Death in Haiti

While in previous chapters, I discussed the more macabre side of Baron Samedi and the Ghedes that is depicted in the films, in this chapter I elaborate on the playful side of the *loas* that is portrayed in *Zombi candidat* from a different sociopolitical and spiritual orientation. Again, in *Zombi candidat*, Baron Samedi, identified explicitly as a *loa*, rivals Zéphirin for Swamen's love. As such, he and his entourage, the Ghedes, are major characters in the film. As the guardian over the realm of death and rebirth, Baron's symbol, a black cross, sits "at the entrance of every Vodou burial ground" to remind visitors where they are. Maya Deren

Five. *Zombi candidat à la présidence*

explains that he governs the invisible forces of magicians and facilitates the raising of zombis from the grave.[10] As I have argued, it is this side of Baron as the zombi master, that early zombie films exploited. However, the other side of his role as facilitator of zombification is, as "Lord of Resurrection" whereby he can also heal if it is warranted. This is because, as Deren explains, the Ghedes, of which Baron is the head, are also just. Thus, if it is not time yet for a man to die, even if he has had a magical spell cast upon him, and if that man humbly asks him to intercede on his behalf, Ghede will refuse to "dig his grave no matter how much the magicians under Baron Samedi, may insist on it."[11] In fact, this absence of sanctioning by Baron Samedi may explain why he does not recognize Zéphirin as a zombi when they first meet. It may also explain why Zéphirin is never truly zombified.

The Ghedes are simultaneously the spirit of the dead, protectors of small children, guardians of human sexuality, and irrepressible social satirists. "They are licensed to beg, to steal, to tell dirty jokes, and to engage in various other forms of antisocial behavior."[12] Furthermore, the "Gede are *famni*, 'family,' par excellence. As spirits of death and sexuality, they connect Haitians to the macro-family extending backward through time to the ancestors and forward in time to descendants yet unborn."[13] They triumph over suffering through humor. "Thus a raucous Gede laugh can emerge from a devotee who only an instant before was possessed by a somber, awesome *lwa*."[14] While they are a constant reminder of death, the Ghedes are also masters of the human libido and lampoon sex. Their eccentric behavior turns death into satire. Because death is unavoidable, making fun of it helps mortal beings face it.

However, their open celebration of human sexuality affirms the continuity of life, even in the presence of death. As the masters of human sexuality, the Ghedes not only oversee death but also the source of life itself. Therefore, they represent the balance between life and death. Taking the Ghedes' characteristics into account, I base my discussion on the premise that their rule over the film is central to its conceptualization as a satire that also starkly portrays the poverty, corruption, and death that they lampoon.

Life and Death's Symbiosis

The symbiotic relationship between sex and death are running themes throughout *Zombi candidat* with Zéphirin and Swamen's passionate lovemaking causing the former's death, and then the two being brought together—one from beyond the grave—because of the passion they shared in life. As Zéphirin comments to Baron after Swamen announces on television that she has converted to Christianity and cannot see him, "Once she remembers our orgasms she will forget everything she said."

In real terms, the interconnectedness of life and death is illustrated in the fact that, following the 2010 earthquake in which over 200,000 people perished, there was reportedly a three-fold increase in births from four percent to twelve percent in the next year. While doctors and United Nation Population Fund officials were bemoaning the increase in births, pointing to the prescient concern about the lack of health facilities, the increase in violence against women and girls since the quake, and the potential spread of sexually transmitted disease, the other side of the coin is the realm over which the Ghedes reign. The comments by Gabriel Bedegian, Chief Technical Advisor on Population Development at the UNFPA brings this aspect of the increase in births to light when he counsels that, rather than assume that most or all of these pregnancies are the result of rape, consider the possibility that "the increase is best explained by people seeking to use sex for comfort after the catastrophe and ... promiscuity could also be a reason for the increase."[15] Bedegian's statement points to a very natural and understandable reaction to such a traumatic event where the loss of life was so immense. While his use of the term, "promiscuity" is an unfortunate choice because it connotes sexual looseness often associated with people of color, his point that people found comfort in the celebration of life through sex is an important aspect of the death/birth equation.[16] It is also completely within the realm of the Ghedes. As Patrick Bellegarde-Smith explains on NPR, the interconnectedness of death and sex is real. He relates conversations with friends of his who are nurses, doctors and even visitors to intensive care units where death is so close. After witnessing trauma and death they go home and do things that they "perhaps, should not do," meaning they let their inhibitions go and give free reign to their sexual desires.[17]

Ghede is, in fact, a phallic deity and Lord of Resurrection. Deren explains,

> Life for Ghede is not the exalted creation of primal ardor; it is a destiny—the inevitable and eternal erotic in men. He is lord of that eroticism which, being inevitable, is therefore, beyond good and evil and is beyond the elations and depressions of love. Of this,

he is neither proud nor ashamed; if anything he is amused by the eternal persistence of the erotic and by man's eternally persistent pretense that it is something else.[18]

It is this sexual/erotic aspect of the Ghedes that is just as much a part of death that is absent in the depiction of the *loas* from the American and European filmmakers that I have discussed thus far. In fact, the de-sexing of the white woman who is zombified under the auspices of the Ghedes in *White Zombie* appears to be deliberate, based as she is on the de-feminized girl of Seabrook's narrative. As Vials notes, Seabrook's narrative of de-feminization is transferred to white female bodies which are de-sexed through zombification ... the sexual excesses of the island are incompatible with [the white woman's] delicate frame...."[19] Essentially, Madeline's zombification in *White Zombie* actually disavows half of the Ghedes' power and thus, half of their domain. As such, we might consider that her being de-sexed and "rendered sterile"[20] makes sure that she does not procreate with the black male, an inevitability once she is corrupted by her contact with the oversexed Caribbean. The danger of Madeline's fertility is in her ability to taint the race by engaging in a sexual union with "the native" that produces mulattoes like the incorrigible Cleeli who will then try to claim whiteness. Similarly, it threatens the propagation of "white" as a racial category and with it, its privilege.

Reclaiming the Filmic Gaze

Zombi candidat is an example of a reclaiming of the filmic gaze that Fatimah Tobing Rony discusses in *The Third Eye: Race, Cinema, and Ethnographic Spectacle* (1996) and which she defines as evidence of "the third eye." She asserts that for a person of color growing up in the United States, the experience of viewing one's self as an object is profoundly formative. Recalling Paul's assertion regarding interiorized prejudices, she suggests that W.E.B. Dubois's description of double consciousness—that is, looking at one's self through the eyes of others—can be taken a step further: "The racially charged glance can also induce one to see the very process which creates the internal splitting" that takes place within the person of color's consciousness.[21] The veil through which one views one's self allows for "clarity of vision even as it marks the site of socially mediated self-alienation."[22] Rony proposes that "the third eye turns on recognition: the Other perceives the veil, the process of being visualized as an object, but returns the glance. The gesture of being frozen in a picturesque is deflected."[23] In other words, the way to overcome one's zombification is to become self-consciousness about the splitting or alienation from the self that characterizes the "zombi." It is that self-consciousness that distinguishes the zombi that is trapped in a haze and the one who has "tasted salt" and been awakened to his or her degradation. With that awakening he or she can perceive the veil and lift it in order to gaze back at the objectifying subject, join his or her split consciousness, and finally, enact revolution.

Though neither the writer, Victor, nor the filmmaker, Antonin, grew up in the United States, the U.S. has been an almost constant presence in Haiti since 1915 in official capacities as well as in the form of privately owned businesses, anthropologists, writers, military personnel, doctors, visual artists, tourists, journalists, etc. Haitians have been undoubtedly influenced by this constant foreign presence and are well aware of how foreigners have portrayed the country in the international arena. Drawing on the tradition of third cinema, Victor and Antonin not only return the gaze, but they also speak back to these foreign interlocutors through the zombi, a thingified person that the U.S. has appropriated and who is not supposed to be able to do either. Therefore, while earlier films silence and objectify the zombi and effectively write the black male subject out of the narrative, even when he is centered, or alternately vilify him, this film emerges from within the culture and centers the black male subject, giving him a voice.

Zombi candidat, Third Cinema and the Subaltern

In addition to the zombie film genre, Antonin's project can also be situated within the genre of Third Cinema as it is defined by Fernando Solanas and Octavio Getino. According to Solanas and Getino, Third Cinema "*recognises in that* [anti-imperialist] *struggle the most gigantic cultural, scientific and artistic manifestation of our time*, the great possibility of constructing a liberated personality with each person as the starting point—in a word, the *decolonization of culture*."[24] This last line is particularly important with regard to *Zombi candidat* because, although Solanas

Five. *Zombi candidat à la présidence*

and Getino were writing about the 1960s decolonization process, Haiti, as much of the world, is experiencing a resurgence of the colonial project. In fact, it seems to be what Victor had in mind when he wrote the character of Zéphirin. On one hand he is iconographic as the zombi because of the figure's historical and cultural resonance, both nationally and internationally. However, he diverges significantly from other zombis. Not only is he portrayed in the film as "everyman"; someone with whom "the people" can relate, but he has a personality. In this sense Zéphirin is contradictory because, not only does he see and witness, but he can dance, he continues to love, and he rejects his exploitation. His "liberated personality" thus represents the decolonized culture of the Haitian underclass that resists appropriation and exploitation by the Haitian elite in league with international forces.

Kyle Bishop's discussion of Gayatri Spivak's essay, "Can the Subaltern Speak?" in his essay, "The Sub-Subaltern Monster" (2008) also offers a useful lens through which to read Antonin's zombi. According to Spivak the subaltern are silent in terms of politics and culture. However, Antonin subverts this view by having the zombi, Zéphirin, be sought after by politicians who ostensibly want to center him in the political process by having him run for president. At the same time it is clear that he is only viable as a candidate once he is zombified, which will allow the politicians to control him. In fact, other potential candidates are rejected because they are seen as not being malleable enough. As one of the politicians says, speaking about one of the potential candidates, Pedro Achille, "Once he is in power he will manipulate everything in his favor." The politicians' fear is not even that Achille will work for the country, but that he will take the spoils of the position for himself.

Intellectualism is an undesirable characteristic for a puppet president. Therefore, if Zéphirin were to be president he would be silenced by politics even while being in the center of it; silenced precisely because of his central position. He would be unable to speak out against the corruption that put him in the position in the first place or on behalf of the masses for whom he was presumably elected. This is essentially what the bourgeois men tell him when they explain that they "will take care of everything" after he accepts their invitation to run. Even though after Zéphirin agrees to run, the politicians shout, "Voice of the people!" they have the exact opposite plan for the subaltern/silenced masses. Nonetheless, from the beginning of the film it is clear that no one can control Zéphirin's voice. In fact, while several forces, Zèl Loray, the politicians, and Baron Samedi, fight for control of him, Zéphirin manages to subvert each of them, choosing to speak for himself *and* being heard, at least, by the audience.

Like the subaltern of Spivak's essay, this "liberated zombi," a contradiction, constitutes a potential threat to the imperialist powers personified in both the politicians who try to recruit him and Baron Samedi who attempts to disempower him by taking away the person for whom he lives, Swamen. Unlike the traditional zombi who has been "thingified," turned into a "beast of burden," "incapable of any real human contact or discourse" Zéphirin asserts his autonomy throughout the film, proclaiming his power for "real human contact"[25] and intimacy. In fact, Zéphirin is the anti-zombi; the opposite of everything that zombis, as they have been traditionally portrayed, represent. In this sense, he is the embodiment of the Haitian masses who are repeatedly recruited by the elite to support their agendas, spoken for by journalists and ethnographers, but who also repeatedly and in a myriad number of ways, claim their subjectivity. Demonstrating that the subaltern can find a voice even when they do not have an audience that is willing to listen, ethnographers and journalists *can* interview them, and document their opinions and ideas[26] as we see in the film.

In opening the film with the disclaimer, "This movie is the expression of unleashed imagination of the authors who probably fed themselves up with salt and rhum. Any resemblance with real personalities is only pure coincidence" Antonin draws the viewer's attention to the zombi that resides in all of us; even those who use their imaginations to comment on reality. While on one hand the authors' released consciousness comes from outside in the form of salt and rum, they imbibe the formula to release their imaginations, signifying a taking of control over their own liberation, represented by the salt and the alcohol. The brief guide to understanding the zombi's actions that is subsequently provided: "The zombi skin color and the swiftness of his reflexes change depending on the quantity of salt that he absorbs, the time between the takes, his emotional condition, his libido and the atmospheric pressure" reflects a self-conscious on the part of the filmmaker about the work that the film is doing. Not only is it entertaining, but it is also meant to provide sociopolitical commentary.

Five. *Zombi candidat à la présidence*

Zombi candidat and Everyman

The linkage between the degraded state of the Haitian masses and the zombi is made in the first street scenes from Port-au-Prince. The camera quickly shifts from traffic congestion, a passenger bus that regularly travels between Haiti and the D.R., a woman selling *kleren* (locally-brewed alcohol) and rum, beds for sale on the street, all backed by a cacophony of sound (car horns, loud music, the voices of street hawkers) before panning to a young man dressed in a cream colored suit, white tie, and white shoes sitting atop a mound of garbage as he listens to a news report about a zombi that has escaped from his master, a *bokor* named Zèl Loray. This linkage is extended during the ensuing press conference being held in the zombi's honor when one of the doctors who accompanies him remarks that it is a huge opportunity to be able to talk with someone who is a testimony to the depth of the sad reality of life in the country. He makes sure that he directs the audience to ask Zéphirin questions with "respect and courtesy" before the reporters charge the table with their tape recorders.

Unlike the zombi who has no will of his own, Zéphirin has the power to not only "look and talk back," but to set the parameters for the conversation. For example, a young man who questions the veracity of his claim that he is a zombi is subjected to a spell that drives him and his skepticism out of the pressroom. As the zombi continues staring forward the second doctor announces, "No impertinent questions, please." When another female journalist questions his authenticity he disappears from public view, but is soon revealed to be making love to the woman almost bringing her to orgasm before being interrupted by a nearby Christian man who exorcizes Zéphirin from her body. Even though his presence is not seen, it is still felt in the most intimate of terms, perhaps as a comment on the hidden faces (and bodies) of poverty that those in power refuse to see, but which are still felt throughout the nation.[27]

The fact that the zombi can answer questions is remarkable in itself. The fact that Zéphirin is afforded courtesy and respect by elite members of the society is also astounding. In life he was only a taptap driver and in death he represents the most disfranchised sector of society. However, once the audience witnesses the zombi's power—superhuman rather than subhuman—it becomes clear how important he is to, not only science, but to the nation, as the second journalist illustrates in his question: "Can zombis contribute to the development of the country and attract tourists?" Of course, the question raises many issues; not the least of which is the connection between foreign tourism and zombification of the poor majority that I discussed in Chapter Three. Not only does it summon the fate of many Caribbean countries as popular tourist destinations, but it recalls Haiti's particular history and contemporary dilemma. As I have argued, when Haiti was a popular tourist destination under the Duvaliers, poor young men and women selling their bodies for money proliferated. More recently, with more recent governments, the clarion call has been "Haiti is open for business." What this means for the masses who have no other viable way of making a living is yet to be seen. Will beaches and cheap hotels again become the "offices" of the young men and women who have nothing more than their bodies to sell?

The next journalist begins with the acknowledgment that Zéphirin was not born a zombi: "No one can be born a zombi." When she asks for the origins of his zombification, his initial response, denoting a slow awakening of his memory, comes out only as a word: "Swamen." When probed further he explains that when he was younger, handsome and strong, Swamen was the first and last woman in his life. The audience then gets a flashback to the source of his zombification when he was taken by fever after Swamen's husband, Syus, caught the two in bed together and then zombified Zéphirin with Zèl Loray's help. As Zéphirin raises his head from his reflection about the past, the camera zooms in and the viewer sees that his eyes have a classic sign of the zombi: eyelids looking as if they have been eaten by acid as anthropologist and writer Zora Neale Hurston witnessed in Haiti and described in *Tell My Horse*. He tells the audience that the only thing he remembers after death came to take him is being awakened by Zèl Loray and his apprentice, Karies, in the cemetery.

Again, while most scholars claim that the zombi has no memory of his past life, in *Le barbare imaginaire* (1988) Laënnec Hurbon writes "*les zombis recontent tout ce qu'ils avaient vécu. Car ils n'étaient pas morts pour de vrai*" (zombi remember everything they've lived through because they were not really dead).[28] As such, Zéphirin is able to remember the job he held, how he and Swamen met, how he died, his zombification, his time with Zèl Loray, and his eventual escape. When the journalist whom he later entrusts with his story in exchange for helping him find Swamen,

Nicole, asks Zéphirin what kind of work he did while he was zombified, the filmmaker provides a flashback of the kind of people who commission Zèl Loray's services. The first is a mulatto man who suspects his wife of cheating on him. However, when Zèl Loray sends Zéphirin to watch the woman, he ends up sleeping with her. Zéphirin's laughing after telling the story establishes his humanity even as he is zombified and reinforces his connection to the spiritual realm of the Ghedes and their domain of death and sex.

In a second example, Roger Julmé, a presidential candidate, seeks out Zèl Loray to help him win the upcoming presidential election. Although Zèl Loray instructs Zéphirin to act as Ogou, the god of war and justice, and give Julmé the answer he wants, again, reflecting the mischief of the Ghedes as well as Zéphirin's willfulness, when the time comes he strays from the script and tells Julmé to storm the presidential palace. At the press conference, it is revealed that, acting on "Ogou's orders," Julmé had indeed, tried to stage a coup d'état immediately following the election and was subsequently imprisoned.

La politique de doublure, Puppet Presidencies and the Zombi

When Zéphirin's story becomes well-known, several members of the elite class seek him out to run for president in a practice that is known as *la politique de doublure*. Originating in the nineteenth century, *la politique de doublure* was a policy whereby "controllable, preferably elderly and illiterate black generals were made president of the republic to create the illusion that the government was in fact a reflection of the Haitian people and in league with their interest."[29] While in the past the pliant puppet would be chosen from amongst the "heroes of the wars of independence and popularly perceived as heads of state,"[30] today in a country where "everyone is a zombi" as one character from the film comments, a zombi president would be the best puppet. The installation of President Phillipe Sudré Dartiguenave by the U.S. government in 1917 may be considered an example of *la politique de doublure* as well. Several scholars have suggested that former President Michel Martelly is another example. As Patrick Sylvain characterizes Martelly, whose installation was overseen by MINUS-

TAH, the international military force, "the political emergence of a popular singer known for his superficial and sexually explicit lyrics, is more than anything, akin to a stage comedy, a momentous farce."[31] This continuation of *la politique de doublure* in the twenty-first century seems to be as effective as it was in the nineteenth and early twentieth century at mollifying "the overwhelmingly black population while perpetuating elite control" as "an example of the fact that the history of Haitian politics is largely a study in smoke and mirrors,"[32] according to Bellegarde-Smith.

La politique de doublure as an effective political strategy is introduced in the film in a scene in which the group of powerful men who later recruit Zéphirin sit around drinking in one of their opulently decorated homes mulling over potential presidential candidates. After Pedro is rejected, one of the men advances the idea of Zéphirin, the zombi as a presidential candidate. When it is suggested that he cannot run because he is a zombi, another of the men asks, "But what is the problem? This is a country of dead people, a country where everyone is a zombi. A zombi president wouldn't be a president." Another talks about how in his neighborhood all the children imitate the zombi. In a scene that comments on the historical practice of gaining "control of the state apparatus through control of the presidency"[33] and its spoils, when one of the men poses the question of whether the zombi will agree to run, another man responds with the question, "Which Haitian would refuse to be a candidate?" When one of the men tries to make a distinction between the zombi as a Haitian and as a dead person, he is rebuffed with the assertion, "He is a Haitian dead person." In other words, there is no distinction to be made between the two. They are, in fact, one in the same. Anyone who does not believe that, according to another character in the film, is HGM (Genetically Modified Haitian), corrupted and not "authentically" Haitian. Distinguishing him as a "Haitian dead person" also implies that there are other nations that harbor the walking dead, although perhaps different types; a point that George Romero made with his zombie movies.

When Zéphirin meets the delegation made up of three of the members of the elite group, they pitch the presidency to him. In trying to convince him to run, one member, Lucien Atié, comes up with a phrase that recalls that which François Duvalier devised when he declared himself President-for-Life: "Vox populi, vox Dei! The voice of the people, the voice of God! You are the people's voice!" Levi then comes up with the slogan:

Five. *Zombi candidat à la présidence*

"Vox zombi, vox populi! (the voice of the zombi, the voice of the people)." He continues, "Down with the living. There is a slogan that will work. All those who don't work, all the poor are dead people. All those enjoying life are alive." However, in declaring the voice of the zombi the voice of the people, they also declare its silence, as not only is the zombi not supposed to speak, but also, in the system of *la politique de doublure*, the president is a puppet who contributes to the silencing of the population.

When Zéphirin asks the group if when he becomes president, he will be a puppet, Levi avoids the question telling him that to say that he will be a puppet does not make sense. He is already president. The men will merely act as his team to help him manage his office; to help direct him, so that together, they will be "masters" of the country. Finally, Nicole's father tries to convince Zéphirin that he will be giving the country a chance, telling him that it is God's will that a zombi save the country. While on one hand they declare themselves "masters" of the country, signifying despotism rather than democracy, they speak of giving the country a chance as if the people's voice will decide policy; contradictions that are the very basis for *la politique de doublure*. Momentarily convinced that he is doing the right thing, Zéphirin agrees and the stage is set for the zombi to "run" Haiti.

The effectiveness of the men's campaign becomes immediately apparent when a montage of the population depicts support for the zombi's candidacy. These include a group of students being interviewed by a reporter in front of the electoral council office. To the reporter's question of what they think of the zombi's candidacy, one student responds, "The zombi is a resurrection angel. Also, he's come back to life to save this country. Down with the living, down with all those who haven't yet died." Bringing in the gendered aspect of the zombi, a young woman asks, "Are there only male zombis? Are there no female zombis?" after which all of the students cheer, "Down with the living. Long live the zombi!" In a scene that illustrates the appropriation of *The Bible* for political purposes, a minister is shown declaring that, "A modern reading of the scriptures allows us to understand how in the interest of the poorest, God's word can come out of a dead person's mouth. Therefore, we believe that the zombi is heaven-sent. Jesus brought Lazarus back to life and it is Jesus who brought Zéphirin back to life, in the interest of all of God's children living in Haiti."[34] He is followed by a teenager on the street who, while hitting his chest like a gangsta rapper, declares, "Zombis came out of the entrails of the Haitian people. He knows all the misery and suffering that the people endure. So, zombi, president or death! Down with all those who ignore the suffering. Long live the zombi. He is one of us!" A *mambo* with a purple scarf on her head, the color of Baron and Brigitte (Baron's companion), an *ason* (sacred rattle) in her hand, and passion in her voice follows him and intones, "With the zombi as president, it is the country's culture that will live again! It is the country's culture that reinforces itself so the country can move forward!"

The zombi's lone detractor is a middle-aged man in a shirt and tie who says, "We will never accept that Satan's child becomes president. "No, by the power of Jesus Christ this plot will not see the light of day. His rejection of "Satan's child," however, is undermined by a street vendor who follows him saying, "We are tired of these people who suck our blood. I will vote for the zombi with the bald head. Down with all the living because they are the big eaters. All the zombi needs is a little salt." Her declaration links the zombi to former President Martelly whose nickname is *Tèt Kale* (bald head).[35] It is also significant that while she makes her remarks, a UN peacekeeper is seen in the background; one of the "big eaters" as many poor Haitians have come to view them, calling them "tourist-a."[36] Somewhat prophetically perhaps, the scene then shifts to an aerial view of Port-au-Prince with the presidential palace at its center, drawing a connection between the bald-headed zombi and Martelly.

Women and the Nation Redux

In this final section I discuss the ways that *Zombi candidat's* conflation of women and the nation is a useful lens through which to view the unequal and exploitative relationship that persists between the Haitian elite and the poor majority. The gendering of the nation can be found from the time of Haiti's inception, when as Mimi Sheller argues in *Citizenship from Below: Erotic Agency and Caribbean Freedom* (2012), citizens were defined as men and their worth determined by their ability to be good fathers, sons, and husbands.[37] The conflation of women and the nation is one consequence of that. It also speaks to the history of repeated military invasions that the country has endured (the latest of which is still

Five. *Zombi candidat à la présidence*

in progress), which conjures the desire to protect and defend the nation as one would defend one's mother, wife, sister, or daughter.[38]

This conflation of women and the nation has profound historical significance, for as Joan Dayan notes in *Haiti, History and the Gods* (1998), following the founder of the nation, Jean-Jacques Dessalines' death, his wife, Défilée, "became the embodiment of the Haitian nation: crazed and lost, but then redeemed through the body of the savior."[39] In *Zombi candidat*, Swamen stands in for the nation in peril. However, she/it is potentially saved by an unlikely hero: the zombi. And while it would seem that *Zombi candidat* is pessimistic about the fate of the Haitian nation in having Swamen die at the end, the audience learns that all hope is not lost when Swamen is seen alive and well at the film's "real" ending.

If Zéphirin represents everyman—the disfranchised masses—then Swamen represents the nation that is being fought over both in the political and spiritual realms. This connection is made early in the film when, following the press conference, Zephirin and Nicole go in search of Swamen. After learning that her husband has died and Swamen has gone to live in Port-au-Prince, Zéphirin begins to cry, proclaiming that he will not be able to live without Swamen: "I will become a dead person with no soul, a zombi with no hope." Ironically, this is what he is supposed to be already. In response to Nicole's asking him not to cry he says, "I'm not a human being. I am a dead person with no soul." His response points to the love that he has from Swamen as the source of his life. She *is* his soul. But, again, if we think of Swamen as the nation, then Zéphirin is also talking about Haiti when he says that if he cannot find her he will lose his soul. She is, in effect, lost to him at this point. However, their reuniting means hope for the country. The fact that he later finds her as a born-again Christian seems to point to at least one threat to their reunification—the Protestant Church.

The need to protect women as representative of the nation is explored when, at a dance club, Zéphirin, dressed in a white suit with white shoes that visually connects him and the man who sat atop the garbage heap in the beginning of the film, confronts Julmé who holds Nicole hostage to get Zéphirin to give himself up. In the scene, Zéphirin appears, not as himself, but as Ogou on horseback as he did in Zèl Loray's *houmfort*. The dialogue is confusing as neither the audience nor Julmé is sure if he is talking with the zombi or with Ogou who tells Julmé that his coup d'état did not succeed because he did not believe in him. Then, invoking the country's revolutionary history, he declares, "We did not chase the white men from the country in order to treat women violently"[40] before directing Julmé to follow him to the cemetery where they find the Ghedes playing with a skull while Baron Samedi watches a soccer match on television.

When the soccer match is interrupted by Swamen who appears on TV to tell Zéphirin that she is now a Christian, it is not Zéphirin who reacts violently, but Baron. Yelling "Treason!" he takes Julmé's gun, puts it to his head and asks, "Why keep on living?" Again, making the connection between Protestantism, a religion that is intolerant of Vodou and demands forsaking the *loas* for Jesus, Baron exclaims, "She dared say that Jesus is her man!" It is also here that life and death collide as, though they stand in Baron's domain, the cemetery—in his own house, as it were—Zéphirin has the audacity to tell Baron that once Swamen sees him and she remembers their orgasms, she will forget Jesus. In this exchange, the sacred is made secular with Jesus being able to take a human lover and enter into a dispute over a woman. However, the real fight is between Zéphirin and his deity, Baron, evidenced by one of the Ghedes cutting in and admonishing him for talking that way about the woman that Baron loves: "They must have given you some sugar," the Ghede chastises, implying that Zéphirin has lost his mind for speaking about taking Baron's woman away from him. Baron has claimed Swamen for himself. As such, she cannot belong to Zéphirin; something that Zéphirin, as a child of Haiti should know. But as a double affront, Swamen has also forsaken her spiritual heritage in choosing "the religion of the white man" over him. As Zéphirin tells Baron in trying to get him to reveal where Swamen is, "white men are manipulating her."

After Zéphirin finds Swamen and the two make love, she leaves the church to follow Zéphirin, declaring that if her heart beats again for Zéphirin it is God who wants it so. The audience is left to wonder, is it their love or the memory of their orgasms—a vice of the flesh according to Christian doctrine—that turns Swamen away from the church and into Zéphirin's arms? Or is their passionate lovemaking representative of the passionate life they are meant to live for each other and for the health of the nation as sanctioned by God and their belief system?

Finally, Swamen, beautiful, but poor, represents the fate of many such women when she tells Nicole the story of how her family was near starvation after her father sold his last plot of land. Syus wanted her from the time that she was ten years old and claimed her when she had barely reached puberty. She was essentially sold to Syus by her father, driven as he was by poverty; a sad commentary, not only on the degraded status of girls in the society, but also on the state of agriculture and the peasantry of Haiti which several scholars have discussed extensively.[41] While he was not mean to her—he fed and clothed her—she did not have feelings for him. According to her, Zéphirin gave her a ride one day in his taptap and from that day she loved him. After he died she slept with many men because she was looking for Zéphirin in them. Her story addresses, not only the devalued state of women, but also the devalued state of the land that no longer yields as it should, leaving farmers to be exploited by large landowners and the global economy that they have been shut out of.

But, while Zéphirin resists and overcomes his zombification, Swamen, equally disfranchised by her poverty, is also disfranchised because of her gender. Although indeed, Zéphirin's liberation is tied to his being reunited with Swamen, he actively seeks her out, with the connection between the personal and political being made clear and explicit. According to Nira Yuval-Davis and Floya Anthias, women are involved in national and ethnic processes as well as "economic, political and military struggles."[42] Although Swamen is clearly involved in these processes and struggles, the element of agency is missing from her character. She, like Madeline from *White Zombie*, is rather, a passive figure throughout the film, in need of rescue from the abusive men in her life: her father, her husband Syus, Baron Samedi, Jesus, and finally, her kidnappers. I suggest that Swamen's exclusion from the picture of the liberated zombi that Antonin paints, denotes for me, only half of the formula for a liberated nation. As such, the awakening of the zombified masses that Antonin proposes with the film is only half possible.

The Fight for the Nation: The Political and the Spiritual

The showdown between Zéphirin and Baron Samedi that takes place at a gathering at an upscale hotel held by the men behind Zéphirin's candidacy brings together the fight over the nation both in the political and in the spiritual realms. Antonin portrays another aspect of Haitian political corruption when he shows one of Zéphirin's supporters slipping a monetary contribution directly into his hand. Shortly thereafter Baron and his Ghedes crash the party and Baron accuses Zéphirin of betraying him because, rather than turn Swamen over to Baron, he kept her for himself. In the spiritual realm, Zéphirin is being accused of handing the nation over to the men who will, again, abuse and mishandle her. He sells the nation to the highest bidder as Swamen's father sold her, and turns his back on her (the nation) in favor of "mulattoes with hair like corn silk, perfumed bourgeois, the cream of the diaspora who speak English like true American girls, those who come from France and speak like guitar notes" whom Atié says will be at Zéphirin's feet once he is president.

The scene also reflects a sad state of affairs when the only job that the zombi is qualified to do is ostensibly the highest post in the nation as Atié makes clear when Zéphirin protests his suggestion that he let Baron have Swamen. He asks Zéphirin the all-important question: "If you are not president what will you be? … In Haiti you can only be president. You will not find a job! Not even in a factory! You are only a zombi! A zombi!" The most degraded position in the country (zombi) is also the most exalted position in the land (president), a contradiction, but again, also a commentary on *la politique de doublure* and the depth of corruption that makes such a statement possible. Before leaving the party, Baron warns Zéphirin that if he does not return Swamen to him he can forget about the presidency. Reading Swamen as the nation, Baron is, in fact, demanding that the corrupt politicians that have ruined the country and with whom Zéphirin aligns himself, return the country to him.

A Stolen Nation Returned?

Swamen is kidnapped following Zéphirin's later refusal to run for president. In the ensuing rescue scene, Baron and Zéphirin combine forces to save her. Though Baron gets knocked out, Zéphirin, his spiritual child, continues until he finds Swamen, unties her and they kiss. He then turns to the camera and in another scene of artistic self-consciousness by the filmmaker, says, "Just like in the movies." He and Swamen defeat one of the henchmen who has come in and the two escape. However, Swamen is

Five. *Zombi candidat à la présidence*

shot by another of the henchmen and presumably killed. The film ends with Zéphirin and Baron, both distraught, calling out her name over and over, signifying that the nation is lost to them.

However, it seems all is not lost when a scene follows in which Zéphirin is shown in his bedroom, in the throes of a nightmare and calling Swamen's name over and over while Nicole, his wife is in her home office putting the finishing touches on her novel, *Les amours d'un zombi*. Zéphirin later drives to work and spots a young woman who resembles Swamen walking across the parking lot as he pulls into it. When he calls out her name questioningly, the young woman turns around smiling, the picture of beauty and health. Zéphirin drops his briefcase and among the contents is a saltshaker. The camera focuses in on the saltshaker as a jazz composition called *La Dessalinienne*, a reference to Jean-Jacques Dessalines, Haiti's first leader, and Haiti's revolutionary history, plays.

The Promise of Release

As I have argued in this chapter, *Zombi candidat* turns inward to an examination of the meaning of the zombi in a national context, both politically and spiritually. Unlike earlier zombi/zombie films, which feature the white woman as representative of the foreign imperialist nation, the mulatto woman embodying transgression or the black man, emasculated, vilified, or silenced, in *Zombi candidat* a Haitian man is the unlikely hero. Reflecting Degoul's rereading of the zombi that is conceived through the lens of Third Cinema, *Zombi candidat* turns the common perception of the zombi on its head, portraying it as a site of resistance rather than an object of fear or pity. The zombi, as a form of internalized and interiorized Haitian collective identity, therefore, is an empowered subject, reflecting Haitian history and Haitian people's never-ending struggle to continue to "taste salt"; in other words, keep their consciousness awake so that they may one day, finally realize the dream of liberty that their revolutionary forefather, Emperor Dessalines, had for his children. However, as I have argued, without an equally revolutionary consideration of women in relation to the nation, the disfranchised masses' liberation will remain incomplete.

Conclusion: Tasting Salt

Despite its seemingly disempowered state, the zombi/zombie figure has continued to hold sway within the historical and cultural traditions from whence it emerged in Haiti as well as internationally. Furthermore, despite, or perhaps, because of its liminal state, neither dead nor alive, both alive and dead, it has managed to change and evolve over the years, providing profound sociopolitical, economic, and ecological commentary. As scholars like Kyle Bishop have argued, the rise and fall and rise of the zombie is a reflection of societal anxieties that get projected onto these "monsters." In many ways they are reflections of the monsters within all of us. As I have argued throughout this text, a reading of many of the zombie films from the early twentieth, and even late twentieth century, provide insight into white anxieties around the Other taking over, whether it was through the threat that the mulatto posed as evidence of sexual transgression and the potential extermination of whiteness and its privileges as in *The Love Wanga*, or white male anxieties around white female sexuality let loose in the Caribbean in general, and Haiti in particular as in *White Zombie* and *I Walked with a Zombie*. This latter fear was an extension of their anxiety over their loss of control over white women during World Wars I and II when they entered the workforce en masse. The other side of that anxiety, of course, is around still unresolved questions of white masculinity versus black masculinity and that thus, continue to be played out in many ways, including the propagation of stereotypes that shift over time as we see in *The Serpent and the Rainbow*.

In an effort to quell white American male fears, Hollywood has been enlisted time and again. This quelling takes on different guises in different historical contexts and at different historical moments. As I have discussed, different pivotal moments in Haitian history have inspired differ-

Tasting Salt

ent depictions and treatments of zombis/zombies and their masters since they first hit the Hollywood screen in 1932.

In Haiti, out of which the creature made its way onto the international stage vis-à-vis William Seabrook's travelogue, the socio-economic and political conditions of the country that made such a project viable have changed. But the more they have changed the more they have stayed the same. While during Seabrook's tenure the country was occupied by the U.S. military, since 2004, following President Jean-Bertrand Aristide's overthrow and exile, it has been occupied by a multinational military force called MINUSTAH. Several political activists and scholars have labeled MINUSTAH's presence an occupation.[1] One similarity that has been noted between the first and this most recent invasion is the pattern of human rights abuses that were reported at the time of the first occupation and those that have emerged during this latest invasion.

The earthquake that struck the country in 2010 has only served to make the zombi/zombie more prescient as, seen from within the Haitian cultural tradition, many of the souls who were lost in the 35 seconds that the earth shook have not been properly honored. It has also sparked a resurgence of the cogency of the zombi as people try to come to terms with this recent crisis and its aftermath. Many have begun to question if MINUSTAH has done more harm than good after one contingent of the troops inadvertently introduced cholera, which has killed over 7,000 people and mutated into several resistant strains.

As Bishop surmises, the zombie exists in real world form and has ties to science and biology.[2] Moreover, from within the Haitian cultural system, rather than a creature to be feared, the zombi is a creature to be pitied. Relatedly, the possibility of becoming one of the living dead constitutes the greatest fear. According to Bishop, "[B]eing forced to work as a virtually mindless slave represents a fate worse than death itself."[3] The reality of the fear of zombification was brought into relief immediately following the earthquake when news reports surfaced of residents in various areas of Haiti murdering people from their communities (mostly *houngans*) who they believed had spread cholera in order to zombify them.[4] Thus, while the zombi/zombie comments and reflects on disempowerment, disfranchisement, voicelessness, and exploitation that accompany these sociopolitical, economic, and militarized conditions with which the poor masses live every day, it also has very real consequences in everyday life in Haiti.

Conclusion

At the same time, it speaks of resistance, warning of a time when the underclass will rise up and revolt against the military, political, and corporate "masters." This is one of the messages in *Zombi candidat* in the thinking, speaking zombi who remembers his past and is an agent in, not only his individual future, but also that of the nation.

Finally, as I have argued, it is important to look beyond the most obvious (i.e., physiological) manifestations of the zombi/zombie to think about its meaning ideologically. In such an expanded view of the trope of the zombi/zombie and zombification, which reexamines the figure and the process through the lens of capitalism and consumption, we see that its importance to sociopolitical and economic critique is alive and well. As such, we can consider how the ingestion of the Other is still taking place, although in different ways. An examination of international tourism in the Caribbean as it is explored in such feature films as *Heading South* as I have done here, illuminates the continued exploitative relationship between the Global North and the Global South. And as people in the Global South's socio-economic conditions continue to deteriorate, opportunities for them to be commodified and consumed have and will continue to increase. In Haiti, the stage is set for the consumption of the bodies of the Duvalier era to resume in the twenty-first century as the former president announced at every possible opportunity that, "Haiti is open for business." While this would mean a financial boon for the very small minority elite class and international businesspeople, for the masses, "being open for business" would mean something very different.

We should also remember that there is always another side to these conditions. Workers as mere "cogs in the wheel," a condition that has plagued the northern consciousness from the time of the world wars, has given rise to a consumerism that compels workers who are unhappy with their own lives to seek relief outside of themselves. While these tourists are agents in the subjugation of others, they are also victims, zombified themselves, lured by the trappings of consumerism as rewards for their unfulfilling lives "back home." Their suffering makes the suffering of others inevitable.

As *Zombi candidat* suggests, there is hope, at least for the male zombi. The hope is that the creative potential that the creature also embodies will be released.[5] As has happened at several junctures in Haitian history, the so-called zombified masses have proven that they were never completely zombified. They have rather, throughout history, ingested minuscule grains of salt that eventually, inevitably manifest in a fully awakened consciousness that unequivocally rejects subjugation and disfranchisement. We find it in the revolution which resulted in the first black republic in the Western hemisphere, during the first American Occupation when peasants staged armed guerrilla attacks on the invading forces, yet again in 1986 when a popular uprising forced Jean-Claude Duvalier into exile, and then in electing Jean-Bertrand Aristide, a liberation theologist in 1990 and then again in 2000.[6] We can expect to see it again, once they get enough "salt" to spark the reawakening of spirit that perhaps *seems* dormant at the moment.

In fact, there is hope for us as citizens of the Global North to wake up from the nightmare of our own consumption by the capitalist patriarchal machine, and recognize our complicity in others' suffering. This can be achieved by people changing their relationship with themselves, with their communities, and with the rest of the world, which, until now has been driven by endless consumption of physical labor, sexual labor and services, natural and human resources, and manufactured goods. Only when we also "taste salt" will the crises and upheavals such as war, famine, economic collapses, the fear of bio-warfare and deadly food-borne illnesses that were unheard of just a few years ago to name a few and that give rise to the repeated reemergence of the zombie à la Romero and beyond, end and the creature finally be laid to rest.

Chapter Notes

A Note on Spelling

1. Christopher M. Moreman and Cory James Rushton, *Race, Oppression and the Zombie*, p. 2.
2. Ibid.

Introduction

1. Alfred Métraux, *Voodoo in Haiti*, 11.
2. Price-Mars also founded Haiti's Indigenist Movement, which called for Haitians to embrace their spiritual heritage and culture, especially their folklore.
3. Schmidt in Mintz, "Introduction," Métraux, *Voodoo in Haiti*, 23.
4. One of the highest titles someone can take in Haitian Vodou.
5. Patrick Bellegarde-Smith, "The Spirit of the Thing: Religious Thought and Social/Historical Memory," 53. Throughout this text I make a distinction between "enslaved" as a condition to which people are subjected as opposed to a "slave" as a condition that someone internalizes or becomes.
6. Mary Renda, *Taking Haiti*, 13.
7. Laënnec Hurbon, "American Fantasy and Haitian Vodou," 183.
8. Franck Degoul, "'We are the mirror of your fears,'"26.
9. See Laurent Dubois' *Haiti: The Aftershocks of History* for this discussion, pp. 207–208, 314–315.
10. Degoul, "'We are the mirror of your fears,'" 26.
11. Charles Najman, *Haïti, Dieu seul me voit*, 251.
12. Degoul, "'We are the mirror of your fears,'" 29.
13. Referred to as *Zombi candidat* hereafter.
14. The threat is both internal in terms of the repressive Haitian government and external in the American tourist in collaboration with the American government.
15. Najman, *Haïti, Dieu seul me voit*, 251.
16. Several scholars have also written about this etymology, usually drawing heavily on Ackerman and Gauthier's article. See Bishop, *American Zombie Gothic*, Moreman and Rushton, *Race, Oppression and the Zombie*, and Davis, *The Serpent and the Rainbow*.
17. The word has also been traced to *jumbie*, the West Indian term for "ghost."
18. Garraway, *The Libertine Colony*, 179.
19. See Ackerman and Gauthier, 475, who attribute the rationale to Max Beauvoir in Wade Davis' *The Serpent and the Rainbow* (1988) and *Passage of Darkness* (1985). A similar explanation has been offered by Laënnec Hurbon in *Le barbare imaginaire* (1988): 191.
20. Hurbon, *Voodoo*, 192–193; Métraux, *Voodoo in Haiti*, 282.
21. Hurston, *Tell My Horse*, 62.
22. Ibid.; Hurston also claims that zombis/zombies do not have the power of speech unless given salt (183).
23. Hurbon, *Le Barbare imaginaire*, 193. Translation mine.
24. Mbembe, "Necropolitics," *Public Culture*, 21.
25. Ibid.
26. Ibid.
27. Karen McCarthy Brown, *Tracing the Spirit*, 25.
28. Joan Dayan, *Haiti, History and the Gods*, 37.
29. Quoted in Carolyn Fick, *The Making of Haiti: The Saint Domingue Revolution from Below*, 31.
30. René Depestre, "Change," 20.
31. See Bishop's discussion of this in *American Zombie Gothic*, 52.

Notes—Introduction

32. MINUSTAH stands for the United States Stabilization Mission in Haiti. It is an international military operation that has been functioning in the country since 2004.

33. See, for example, Haiti Grassroots Watch's discussion of what this invitation to foreign businesses and vacationers means to the poor in "Haiti—Open for Business."

34. Kaiama Glover, *Haiti Unbound*, 59.

35. Hurbon, *Le Barbare imaginaire*, 192.

36. Her description is based on a story that she heard while conducting field research. I am aware of the scholarship that has interrogated Hurston's relationship with her work in the Caribbean. As Gwendolyn Mikell notes in "When Horses Talk: Reflections on Zora Neale Hurston's Haitian Anthropology" (1982), "Hurston's Haitian ethnography…is a delicate balance between the calm insider's and the agitated outsider's perspectives" (222) and while the Caribbean required more explanation than her work from the U.S. "Haiti required more: explanation and justification" (224). Finally, some of the judgments that she passes about Haitian society mark her as a product of her time. She was, according to Mikell, the embodiment of all the contradictions inherent in a racist society, and as such, she instinctively reacted to many aspects of Caribbean society" (229). Ifeoma Kiddoe Nwankwo reads Hurston more critically in "Insider and Outsider, Black and American: Rethinking Zora Neale Hurston's Caribbean Ethnography" (2003), arguing that while Hurston was accused of primitivization of blacks in *Mules and Men*, her "negative approach is magnified when she encounters Caribbean blacks." Her treatment of the Caribbean results from and reflects "both the exoticization of the other inherent in the anthropological gaze, the U.S. imperialist gaze, and…the binaristic black weltanschauung" (73).

37. Hurston, *Tell My Horse*, 183.

38. While there was sex tourism before this time, the chapter in which I discuss the phenomenon focuses on late twentieth century trends and the encroachment of female sex tourists.

39. See Faustin E. Wirkus and Tanner Dudley, *The White King of La Gonâve* (1931). Interestingly, it was republished in February 2015 by Ishi Press, indicating renewed interest in this period of history.

40. Chris Vials, "The Origin of the Zombie in American Radio and Film," 44.

41. *Ibid.*, 42.

42. *Ibid.*

43. Lizabeth Paravisini-Gebert, "The Representation of Woman as Zombie," 43.

44. Todd K. Platts, "Locating Zombies in the Sociology of Popular Culture," 547.

45. Vials, "The Origin of the Zombie in American Radio and Film," 46.

46. I detail the U.S. expansionist project in Chapter One.

47. Michael Richardson, *Otherness in Hollywood Cinema*, 122.

48. Hans Schmidt, *The United States Occupation of Haiti, 1915–1934*, 66.

49. See Schmidt, *The United States Occupation of Haiti*; Bellegarde-Smith, *Haiti: The Breached Citadel*; Renda, *Taking Haiti: Military Occupation and the Culture of U.S. Imperialism, 1915–1940*; Ramsey, *The Spirits and the Law: Vodou and Power in Haiti*; Dubois, *Haiti: The Aftershocks of History*.

50. Beauvoir hosted Wade Davis when he conducted his ethnographic research for *The Serpent and the Rainbow*.

51. Personal interview, Mariani, Port-au-Prince, Summer 2011.

52. Gwenda Young, "The Cinema of Difference," 102.

53. As Todd K. Platts remarks, Romero's *Night of the Living Dead* (1968) "was a game changer for films concerning the living dead," 550.

54. Kevin Alexander Boon, "Ontological Anxiety Made Flesh," 34.

55. The Indemnity Treaty that Boyer signed with France granted Haiti recognition as an independent country in return for the 150 million francs that was supposed to be paid within five years. This sum was reduced to 90 million francs in 1838.

56. I take this idea from Robyn Longhurst in her article, "Viewpoint: The Body and Geography," 97–106.

57. The black female body would be even more monstrous; perhaps too monstrous for early filmmakers to imagine.

58. Mimi Sheller, *Consuming the Caribbean*, 135.

59. Vials, "The Origin of the Zombie in American Radio and Film," 47.

60. Michele Faith Wallace, "The Good Lynching and the Birth of a Nation," 98.

61. *Ibid.*, 99.
62. Sheller, *Consuming the Caribbean*, 139.
63. According to Phillips, Legendre is simultaneously identified with decaying with (Eastern) European aristocracy and "the natives," Gyllian Phillips, "*White Zombie* and the Creole," 29.
64. *Ibid.*
65. Paravisini-Gebert, "The Representation of Woman as Zombie," 46.
66. See Sheller, *Consuming the Caribbean*.
67. Dendle, "The Zombie as Barometer of Cultural Anxiety," 45.
68. Vials, "The Origin of the Zombie in American Radio and Film," 51.
69. *Ibid.*, 52.
70. Quoted in Marcia England, "Breached Bodies and Home Invasions," 354. England takes the quote from Tim Cresswell and Deborah Dixon, "Introduction: Engaging film" in Tim Cresswell & Deborah Dixon, Eds., *Engaging Film: Geographies of mobility and Identity* (Lanham, MD: Rowman & Littlefield, 2002), 4.

Chapter One

1. See for example, Jennifer Fay's "Dead Subjectivity: White Zombie, Black Baghdad, Gyllian Phillips' "*White Zombie* and the Creole: William Seabrook's *The Magic Island* and American Imperialism in Haiti," Gary D. Rhodes' *White Zombie: Anatomy of a Horror Film*, Kyle Bishop's "The Sub-Subaltern Monster: Imperialist Hegemony and the Cinematic Voodoo Zombie" and *American Zombie Gothic: The Rise and Fall (and Rise) of the Walking Dead in Popular Culture*, as well as essays in the edited volumes, *Generation Zombie: Essays on the Living Dead in Modern Culture* and *Race, Oppression and the Zombie: Essays on Cross-Cultural Appropriations of the Caribbean Tradition*, to name a few.
2. Ann Kordas also makes this argument in her discussion of white southern anxiety around the loss of free African American labor following the abolition of slavery and *White Zombie*. See her essay "New South, New Immigrants, New Women, New Zombies: The Historical Development of the Zombie in American Popular Culture," in Moreman and Rushton, 18–21.
3. Rhodes, *White Zombie*, 74–81; Bishop traces the zombi/zombie in written and theatrical form prior to this time in *American Zombie Gothic*, 60–62. Ann Kordas also traces the zombi/zombie in its various iterations before it appeared in Seabrook's text in "New South, New Immigrants, New Women, New Zombies," 16–17.
4. Degoul, "'We are the mirror of your fears,'" 29.
5. *Ibid.*
6. Bishop, *American Zombie Gothic*, 37.
7. *Ibid.*
8. There was a stage play that preceded *White Zombie* called simply *Zombie*. Written by Kenneth Webb, the play also clearly shows the influence of *The Magic Island*.
9. While Bishop asserts that Saint Sebastien is an analogue for Haiti (*American Zombie Gothic*, 84), for me it specifically recalls colonial Saint-Domingue, and with it, the slave system that, as I argue the white male longed for a return to.
10. The film is loosely based on Emily Bronte's *Jane Eyre*.
11. Laurent Dubois, *Haiti: The Aftershocks of History*, 19.
12. *Ibid.*
13. *Ibid.*
14. Carolyn E. Fick, *The Making of Haiti*, 31–2.
15. *Ibid.*
16. Men and women of African descent who were not enslaved. See Dubois, *Haiti*, 19.
17. Enslaved people who were born on the island.
18. See John K. Thornton's excellent essay, "African Soldiers in the Revolution," on the military prowess of Congo warriors who were imported to the island shortly before the revolution and credited with contributing greatly to the success of the revolution.
19. Dubois, *Haiti*, 16.
20. *Ibid.*
21. Alyssa Goldstein Sepinwall, "The Specter of Saint-Domingue: American and French Reactions to the Haitian Revolution" 317.
22. Tim Matthewson, "Jefferson and the Nonrecognition of Haiti," 37.
23. Quoted in Noam Chomsky, *Year 501: The Conquest Continues*, 201.
24. Sepinwall, "The Specter of Saint-Domingue," 317.
25. Métraux, *Voodoo in Haiti*, 283.

Notes—Chapter One

26. See, for example, Althéa de Peuch Parham's *My Odyssey: Experiences of a Young Refugee from Two Revolutions, by a Creole of Saint Domingue* (1959) and accounts related in Jeremy D. Popkin's *Facing Racial Revolution: Eyewitness Accounts of the Haitian Insurrection* (2007).
27. See Fleurimond W. Kern's essay "The Haitian Flag—Birth of a Symbol" for a discussion of American's and German's disrespectful treatment of the Haitian flag.
28. Also called an indemnity tax, in an agreement with then-President Jean-Pierre Boyer in 1825, France demanded 150,000,000 gold francs (later reduced to 90 million in 1838). See Kate Ramsey, *The Spirits and the Law*, 63–64.
29. Simón Bolívar, whom Haiti had helped extricate Colombia from Spanish rule, later denounced the nation saying that it fomented "racial conflict." See Chomsky, *Year 501*, 200.
30. Bishop, *American Zombie Gothic*, 66.
31. Jennifer Fay, "Dead Subjectivity: White Zombie, Black Baghdad," 93.
32. Laënnec Hurbon, "American Fantasy and Haitian Vodou."
33. Quoted in Chomsky, *Year 501*, 200.
34. *Ibid.*
35. *Ibid.*, 200–201.
36. Sheller "Natural Hedonism," 171.
37. *Ibid.*, 175. Sheller provides specific examples in her article.
38. *Ibid.*, 172.
39. Between the years 1911 and 1915 a series of political assassinations and forced exiles meant that the Haitian presidency changed hands six times. Under such political instability the U.S. could not hope to attract U.S. businesses and turn it into another source of revenue that Cuba was at the time.
40. Lola Young, *Fear of the Dark: Race, Gender and Sexuality in the Cinema*, 74.
41. Sheller, *Consuming the Caribbean*, 146.
42. Chera Kee, "'They are not men...they are dead bodies!': From Cannibal to Zombie and Back Again," 9.
43. Rhodes, *White Zombie*, 77.
44. Young, "The Cinema of Difference," 102.
45. *Ibid.*
46. Wallace, "The Good Lynching and The Birth of a Nation," 88.
47. Rhodes, *White Zombie*, 48.
48. Bishop also remarks on this in regard to the racial dichotomy that the film presents with all of the white characters being depicted as redemptive and the black characters being portrayed as villainous (*American Zombie Gothic*, 78).
49. *White Zombie* as well as *The Love Wanga* were the first of the films produced about voodoo that were set in Haiti (Rhodes, *White Zombie*, 46).
50. Bishop, "The Sub-Subaltern Monster," 150.
51. *Ibid.*
52. Rhodes, *White Zombie*, 48.
53. *Ibid.*, 46.
54. *Ibid.*, 39.
55. Norma Manatu, *African American Women and Sexuality in the Cinema*, 52.
56. *Ibid.*
57. *Ibid.*
58. Young, "The Cinema of Difference," 105.
59. *Ibid.*
60. *Ibid.*
61. Patrick Bellegarde-Smith, *Haiti: The Breached Citadel*, 24.
62. Leslie Desmangles, *The Faces of the Gods*, 92.
63. *Ibid.*
64. *Ibid.*
65. *Ibid.*, 93.
66. McCarthy Brown, "Serving the Spirits," 206.
67. A mystical world that recalls Africa and the ancestors.
68. Desmangles, *The Faces of the Gods*, 117.
69. *Ibid.*
70. Maya Deren, *Divine Horsemen*, 112.
71. *Ibid.*
72. Ramsey, *The Spirits and the Law*, 126.
73. Fay, "Dead Subjectivity," 88.
74. The *bokor* or priestess as hypnotist comes up again in *The Love Wanga* when Cleeli is able to hypnotize Susie and make her agree to help her kill Eve. According to Bishop, hypnotism is used because it was not yet known how zombies were made.
75. See Bishop's *American Zombie Gothic*, 74, and Fay's "Dead Subjectivity," 84.
76. When Betsy and Jessica attend a voodoo ceremony immediately after meeting Carrefour at the crossroads, those in attendance are singing a song for Papa Legba, thus making a connection between the two *loas*.
77. Deren, *Divine Horsemen*, 101.

Notes—Chapter One

78. *Ibid.*
79. *Ibid.*
80. *Ibid.*
81. *Vèvè* are symbols that are used to call the *loas* during ceremonies and rituals.
82. Quoted in Fay, "Dead Subjectivity," 91; and Bishop, *American Zombie Gothic*, 49.
83. Bryan Senn, *Drums of Terror*, 52.
84. Hurbon, "American Fantasy and Haitian Vodou," 59.
85. Desmangles, *The Faces of the Gods*, 131.
86. *Ibid.*, 132.
87. *Ibid.*
88. Vials, "The Origin of the Zombie in American Radio and Film," 42.
89. Dayan, *Haiti, History, and the Gods*, 58.
90. *Ibid.*
91. Fay, "Dead Subjectivity," 86.
92. She says that the mill is the primal scene of the occupation economy. "Once financed by German money, HASCO became by virtue of the occupation the largest American interest in Haiti and one of the few economically prosperous ventures during the occupation. The company's profit margin was predicated on attracting locals to the steady unrelenting work at unimaginably low wages." Fay, "Dead Subjectivity," 87. According to Hans Schmidt, Haitians earned 20 cents for every 12 hours of work making Haiti the cheapest labor market in the Americas (170).
93. Dubois, *Haiti: The Aftershocks of History*, 19.
94. *Ibid.*, 20.
95. *Ibid.*
96. Young, "The Cinema of Difference," 111.
97. Richardson, *Othering in Hollywood Cinema*, 126.
98. Polly Pattullo, *Last Resorts*, 142.
99. Senn, *Drums of Terror*, 54.
100. Young, "The Cinema of Difference," 113.
101. Rhodes comments that regardless of its factual shortcomings, St. John's text was well known to academics and popular audiences. "Few questioned its accounts of voodooism, probably because of St. John's apparent believability," 72–73.
102. St. Sebastian is a Christian martyr. According to Christian legend, during Diocletian's third century persecution of the Christians, St. Sebastian was charged as a Christian, tied to a tree, shot with arrows and left for dead. He survived, recovered and returned to preach to Diocletian. The emperor then had him beaten to death with a club (England 2006: 362n).
103. Phillips, "*White Zombie* and the Creole," 29.
104. According to Article 12 of the Haitian Constitution, "No white, irrespective of his country, can land in this territory as a master and property owner and not in the future be permitted to acquire any property" (cited in Bellegarde-Smith, *Haiti: The Breached Citadel*, 65). The U.S. removed the foreign landowning clause from the Constitution by dissolving the National Assembly, which refused to concur with their plans. Peasant landowners became peons and the independent land tenure system was replaced by foreign-dominated plantations.
105. As already noted, the Marines and personnel were coming from the United States where Jim Crow laws were stringently enforced and imbibed by those who benefitted from them.
106. Phillips, "*White Zombie* and the Creole," 38: 9n.
107. Renda, *Taking Haiti*, 226; Jennifer Fay pushes the insinuation in this scene even further. She reads the moment when Beaumont reaches over to touch Legendre's hand as the two holding hands across the table gazing into each other's eyes (96) and comments that "If Beaumont is to become the next white zombie, then we may presume that he too will be dressed for bed according to his master's wishes" (*ibid.*).
108. Rhodes, *White Zombie*, 38.
109. Tony Williams (1993) would disagree, suggesting that the gown resembles a funeral shroud.
110. Richardson, *Otherness in Hollywood Cinema*, 126.
111. *Ibid.*
112. Harold Courlander, *The Drum and the Hoe*, 137.
113. Young, "The Cinema of Difference," 112.
114. Fay, "Dead Subjectivity," 96.
115. *Ibid.*, 96–97.
116. Sir Spenser St. John, *Hayti: Or, The Black Republic* 188.
117. Rhodes, *White Zombie*, 35.

118. Using the writer Lord Bryon as a model, his physician, John Polidori created a character named Lord Ruthven, a cruel, world-traveling aristocrat who preyed on innocent young women, luring them to his lair and feeding on their blood. The key to their desirability was their innocence. The stretch to the Vampyre from the zombie is not far at all as Dracula was a very popular character by the time *White Zombie* was filmed. The lead character played by Bela Lugosi, had also played in *Dracula* whose set was used for *White Zombie*.

119. This war for souls has been taken up contemporarily by Protestantism, which violently denounces Vodou, and has stepped up their campaign since the 2010 earthquake.

120. It was actually Article 246. As Ramsey notes, the word, "zombie" was inserted strategically into the translated text (172).

121. Kordas, "New South, New Immigrants, New Women, New Zombie," 26.

122. *Ibid.* While Jessica is clearly guilty of sexual transgression in trying to run away with her husband's brother, Madeline of *White Zombie*, however, is portrayed as an "innocent" who, like a "white slave" who was lured into a life of prostitution as a result of her ignorance and naiveté, is not responsible for her zombification (Kordas, 27).

123. Renda, *Taking Haiti*, 223.
124. *Ibid.*
125. *Ibid.*
126. Paravisini-Gebert, "The Representation of Woman as Zombie," 45.
127. Tony Williams, "White Zombie: Haitian Horror."
128. Fay, "Dead Subjectivity," 96.
129. See also Bellegarde-Smith, *The Breached Citadel*. In it, Bellegarde-Smith says, "The struggle for economic hegemony among the United States, France, Germany, and Great Britain in Haitian national life had shifted the major problem in Haiti away from questions of the distribution of wealth and power among the elite and peasants to a situation in which there was little wealth and power to distribute (97). Also, since foreign whites could not own property in Haiti many Germans married Haitian women in order to circumvent the law and own businesses.
130. Rhodes, *White Zombie*, 39.
131. Sheller, "Natural Hedonism," 173.

Chapter Two

1. Fay, "Dead Subjectivity," 86.
2. Phillips, "*White Zombie* and the Creole," 29.
3. Bishop, *American Zombie Gothic*, 80.
4. Phillips, "*White Zombie* and the Creole," 29.
5. While it may appear that I equivocate on the issue of Adam's race, at some points suggesting that he is white and other times black, my discussion of him actually highlights his racial ambiguity that, as I argue, was a source of anxiety for white American society.
6. Phillips, "*White Zombie* and the Creole," 29.
7. See Laurent Dubois' *Avengers of the New World: The Story of the Haitian Revolution* (Cambridge, MA: Harvard University Press, 2004) for a discussion of this history.
8. A brilliant satirical novel, *Black No More*, by George S. Schuyler, originally published in 1931, is about this very dilemma.
9. Black, "Looking White, Acting Black," 27.
10. As Mark H. Harris writes, "The moral of the story is, of course, 'Stick to your own kind!' Luckily *Ouanga* was hardly seen in the U.S., allowing miscegenation to go unchecked...." in http://www.blackhorrormovies.com/ouanga.htm.
11. Senn, *Drums of Terror*.
12. In the film there are three kinds of *wangas*: one for protection, one for love, and one for death.
13. I have written about this in another context in "Workings of the Spirit: The Goddess Ezili in *The Love Wanga* (1935)" in *God in Every Woman: Gender and Power in Haitian Vodou*, Eds. Claudine Michel and Patrick Bellegarde-Smith (forthcoming).
14. Blackhorrormovies.com.
15. Vials, "The Origin of the Zombie in American Radio and Film," 46.
16. *Ibid.*
17. Dayan, *Haiti, History, and the Gods*, 56.
18. Quoted in Dayan, *Haiti, History, and the Gods*, 56. I discuss Cleeli as possessed by several manifestations of the goddess of love, Erzulie in "Workings of the Spirit: The Goddess Ezili in *The Love Wanga* (1935)" (forthcoming).
19. *The Chicago Defender* (National Edition) (1921–1967). Chicago: January 19, 1935.

Notes—Chapter Three

20. Boon, "Ontological Anxiety Made Flesh," 34.
21. K. Sue Jewell, *From Mammy to Miss America and Beyond*, 46.
22. We have in recent years seen such debates resurface on a large scale around questions of President Obama's acceptability as president of the United States.
23. Kamala Kempadoo, "Theorizing Sexual Relations in the Caribbean: Prostitution and the Problem of the 'Exotic,'" 428.
24. *Ibid.*, 430.
25. There is a considerable amount of scholarship on this subject as well as literature from within the African American tradition that explores the advantages and toll that such a decision takes on those who practiced it and their families. See Nella Larsen's *Passing*, for example, and James Weldon Johnson's *Autobiography of an Ex-Colored Man*.
26. Quoted in Dubois, *Haiti: The Aftershocks of History*, 127.
27. Colby M. Chester, "Haiti: A Degenerating Island: The Story of Its Past Grandeur and Present Decay," 200.
28. *Ibid.*, 214.
29. *Ibid.*, 209.
30. *Ibid.*, 214.
31. Catherine Lutz and Jane Lou Collins, *Reading National Geographic*, 5.
32. *Ibid.*
33. Renda, *Taking Haiti*, 13.
34. Colby, "Haiti: A Degenerating Island," 217.
35. *Ibid.*, 214.
36. *Ibid.*, 215.
37. *Ibid.*, 216.
38. Lutz and Collins, *Reading National Geographic*, 5.
39. *Ibid.*, 6.
40. Colby, "Haiti: A Degenerating Island," 216.
41. *Ibid.*, 217.
42. In fact, a very conservative estimate of the number of Haitians who lost their lives during the first seven years of the occupation is 2500 while the number of Marines who died during their tour, not all because of Haitian aggression, is 16. See Schmidt, *The United States Occupation of Haiti*, 103.
43. Harry Johnson, "Haiti and Its Regeneration by the United States," 147.
44. *Ibid.*, 151.
45. Bishop, *American Zombie Gothic*, 44.

46. See Renda's (*Taking Haiti*) and Ramsey's (*The Spirits and the Law*) discussion of the reinstatement of the *corvée* system in this regard.
47. Capitalization in the original.
48. *The Love Wanga* is actually part of a series entitled "Something Weird Video."
49. See anthropologist Michel-Rolph Trouillot's much cited work on the "unthinkability" of Haiti in *Silencing the Past: Power and the Production of History* (1995).
50. Kordas, "New South, New Immigrants, New Women, New Zombies," 19.
51. *Ibid.*
52. Dubois, *Haiti*, 208.
53. *Ibid.*
54. According to Senn the British publicity exploited the theme of hero worship when it emphasized the fact that, "the exterior of the house shown throughout the film is that of [Lord Admiral] Nelson's old home, now occupied by the Governor General of Jamaica" (40).
55. Dubois, *Haiti*, 208.
56. See, for example Rashmee Roshan Lall, "Haiti's Seeds of Change? With Agricultural Output Down the Island is Turning to Textiles."
57. See *The Negro Family: The Case for National Action* (known as the Moynihan Report, 1965).
58. See my discussion of the "Catchline" in Chapter One.
59. Desmangles, *The Faces of the Gods*, 125.
60. Courlander, *The Drum and the Hoe*, 20.
61. Deren, *Divine Horsemen*, 115.
62. Kordas, "New South, New Immigrants, New Women, New Zombies," 29.
63. Vials, "The Origin of the Zombie in American Radio and Film," 47.
64. Deren, *Divine Horsemen*, 115.
65. I am invoking here the image of "the breached citadel," the title of Patrick Bellegarde-Smith's groundbreaking work on Haitian history. In the text he implies the meaning of breached citadel by defining an unbreached citadel as "a people's imagery, myths, beliefs, and history as parts of an internally coherent worldview" (24).

Chapter Three

1. I would like to thank Dean Makuluni for first bringing this film to my attention.

Notes—Chapter Three

2. For the lyrics to the song, refer to their album, *The Royal Scam* (1976).

3. I refer here to the poem, "Strange Fruit," penned by Abel Meeropol in 1937 and made famous by blues singer, Billie Holiday about lynchings in the Jim Crow south. Many black men were lynched for alleged relations with white women. The fruit also refers to the mulatto who was the result of black and white unions, uncontainable evidence of sexually transgressive behavior between mostly white men and black women, but in the case of Dobs, it is a white woman with a black man and in a different geographical location.

4. The novel was translated as *Heading South* in 2010.

5. Moreman and Rushton, "Introduction," *Race, Oppression and the Zombie*, 7.

6. Jen Webb and Sam Byrnand, "Some Kind of Virus," 90.

7. *Ibid.*, 93.

8. I use the term, "taking of Haiti" to riff off of Mary Renda's historical text about the U.S. Marine Occupation of Haiti and the country's entry into the popular American imagination.

9. Although North American men were still very much a presence on the Haitian landscape, I focus here on female tourists who came to Haiti in search of Haitian boys and men called "beach boys." Much work has been done on male tourists to the Caribbean (see Sheller, *Consuming the Carribbean*, "Natural Hedonism"); (Urry, *The Tourist Gaze*); (Pattullo, *Last Resorts*). By focusing on female tourists I do not mean to ignore or discount the other side of the story.

10. Kempadoo, "Theorizing Sexual Relations in the Caribbean," 433.

11. The 1990s was not the first time that Haiti had been accused of spreading disease. In the 1500s Ruy Diaz de Isla published *Trabado Sobre el Mal Serpentino que Vulgarmente en España se Llama Buvas* (1539) in which he drew a connection between travel, sex, and disease. In the text he claims that Columbus and his crew had contracted the disease of syphilis in Hispaniola and brought it back to Barcelona. Five hundred years later Haiti (⅓ of the island of Hispaniola) was accused of being the source of HIV/AIDS; another, at the time, deadly sexually transmitted disease. Just as syphilis was marked as "an import from faraway lands and different peoples—it was the classic disease of "the Other"—so too was HIV/AIDS associated with "the Other"; in this case, the inheritors of the land that was occupied by the original "Other": the native population. (See Simon Carter and Stephen Clift, "Tourism, International Travel and Sex," 8).

12. Paul Farmer, *AIDS and Accusation*, 145.

13. The Tonton Macoutes were formed and mobilized under François Duvalier and continued under his son. They were extremely violent, committing acts of rape, torture and murder en masse, sending much of the middle and intellectual class into exile.

14. Farmer, *AIDS and Accusation*, 146.

15. Carter and Clift, "Tourism, International Travel and Sex," 8.

16. Farmer, *AIDS and Accusation*, 146.

17. Carter and Clift, "Tourism, International Travel and Sex," 8. The sex industry infrastructure has been studied extensively in countries like Bangkok and Thailand, Jamaica and the Dominican Republic, all of which are still favorite destinations for sex tourists.

18. Farmer, *AIDS and Accusation*, 146.

19. Edward Herold, Rafael Garcia, and Tony DeMoya, "Female Tourists and Beach Boys," 982.

20. Klaus de Albuquerque, "In Search of the Big Bamboo," 84.

21. *Ibid.*

22. *Ibid.*, emphasis added.

23. Jacqueline Sánchez Taylor, "Tourism and 'Embodied' Commodities," 45.

24. Although in 2012 the minimum wage was raised to $7.00 for an eight-hour day, many people make much less than that.

25. Kempadoo, "Theorizing Sexual Relations in the Caribbean," 434.

26. See *Narrative of the Life of Frederick Douglass, an American Slave.*

27. Wes Craven's *The Serpent and the Rainbow* refers to Duvaliers' practice of disappearing people. It is also something about which the Haitian filmmaker, Raoul Peck has talked, remarking that after he finished making the film, *L'Homme sur le quais* (1991) he realized that much of it stemmed from his own memory of "henchmen…storm[ing] into government offices and remov[ing] workers simply for not being vocal supporters of Mr. Duvalier" (Pierre-Pierre *NYT* C6).

28. Under both Duvaliers, spies were reputedly everywhere so citizens had to be ex-

Notes—Chapter Three

tremely careful about who they talked to and what they said.

29. Quoted in Marr, "Interview with Derek Walcott."
30. Gavan Titley, "All Sights Reserved," 205; 210.
31. *Ibid.*, 208.
32. Carter and Clift, "Tourism, International Travel and Sex," 10.
33. Kempadoo, "Theorizing Sexual Relations in the Caribbean," 427.
34. Beckles, *Natural Rebels*, 68–69.
35. Frank Fonda Taylor, *To Hell with Paradise*, 175.
36. Ian Gregory Strachan, *Paradise and Plantation*, 9.
37. *Ibid.*, 2.
38. *Ibid.*, 31–32.
39. Depestre and Dayan, *A Rainbow for the Christian West*, 59. I discuss Legba's traits in further detail in my forthcoming book, *Istwa*.
40. Elizabeth McAlister "Love, Sex, and Gender Embodied," 129.
41. Depestre and Dayan, *Rainbow for the Christian West*, 60.
42. See Depestre and Dayan's *Rainbow for the Christian West*, 60 and Deren's *Divine Horsemen*, 99 for this description.
43. Eddy is about 15 years old, the same age as Legba when Brenda first had sex with him.
44. Strachan, *Paradise and Plantation*, 30–31.
45. Carter and Clift, "Tourism, International Travel and Sex," 9.
46. Cynthia Enloe, *Bananas, Beaches and Bases*, 31.
47. I am aware that not all sexual relationships were physically forced during these different eras, but I refer to the unequal power relations that circumscribe all sexual relationships between the colonized and the colonizer.
48. I refer here to my earlier discussion of the Caribbean offering itself to be consumed by the American tourist.
49. Brenda later steps outside of that space and is traumatized because of it.
50. Kordas, "New South, New Immigrants, New Women, New Zombies," 16.
51. See my discussion of the differences of opinion around the zombi's/zombie's memory in the Introduction.
52. She is referring presumably to Sir Peter Paul Rubens, a 17th century Flemish Baroque painter.
53. Pattullo, *Last Resorts*, 88–90.
54. Albuquerque, "In Search of the Big Bamboo," 84.
55. In Laferrière's text Brenda is fifty-five years old. Ellen never gives her age.
56. Strachan, *Paradise and Plantation*, 1.
57. Phillips, "*White Zombie* and the Creole," 38: 26 n.
58. Deborah Root, *Cannibal Culture*, 62.
59. I briefly discuss the system in Chapters One and Two.
60. Sheller, "Natural Hedonism," 179.
61. Sánchez Taylor, "Tourism and 'Embodied' Commodities," 42.
62. Quoted in Sheller, "Natural Hedonism," 179.
63. *Ibid.* Brenda later dances suggestively with Eddy on the beach and doesn't seem to understand why the others disapprove.
64. This subtitle is a play on Dany Laferrière's novel, *How to Make Love to a Negro Without Getting Tired* (2010).
65. Albuquerque, "In Search of the Big Bamboo," 83; The phrase, "The Big Bamboo" comes from a song by the same name by the Calypso group, The Mighty Skipper in the 1950s. It has come to be one of the stereotypes associated with Caribbean men.
66. Sheller, *Consuming the Caribbean*, 161.
67. *Ibid.*
68. Julia O'Connell Davidson, "Sex Tourism and Child Prostitution," 9.
69. The film is about how, under Baby Doc, all of the creole pigs of Haiti were killed by the U.S. government as a preventive measure against the spread of swine flu to the U.S. pig population. None of the pigs that were eventually tested in Haiti were infected, but thousands of American pigs were sold to Haitian farmers with disastrous results.
70. Two examples are *Sankie Pankie* (2007) from the Dominican Republic and *Born in Brothels: Calcutta's Red Light Kids* (2004) from India.
71. Titley, "All Sights Reserved," 216.
72. Stephen Harper talks about this sense from consumers in relation to George Romero's *Dawn of the Dead*.
73. Bishop, "The Idle Proletariat," 234.
74. Steve Briodowski, "*Dawn of the Dead*: A Retrospective."
75. Stephen Harper "Zombies, Malls, and the Consumerism Debate."
76. Stephen Harper makes this observation

about Morris' position in his article, "Zombies, Malls, and the Consumerism Debate."
77. *Ibid.*
78. Sánchez Taylor, "Tourism and 'Embodied' Commodities," 48.
79. This is a reference of the 1930s U.S. workforce that Renda and Bishop discuss in relation to *White Zombie*.
80. bell hooks, *Black Looks*, 23.
81. Gary Younge, "No Refuge from Reality," 2.
82. Titley, "All Sights Reserved," 208.
83. He was not the first president of Haiti to make this declaration as Nancy Dorsinville says in "Goudo Goudou," the phrase was a resounding mantra in the weeks prior to the earthquake during René Préval's administration.
84. Haiti Grassroots Watch, "Open for Business."
85. *Ibid.*
86. Ramon Sahmkow, "Haiti Is a Future Tourist Destination, Says President."
87. Sheller, *Consuming the Caribbean*, 201.

Chapter Four

1. Degoul, "'We are the mirror of your fears,'" 26.
2. Anna Fahraeus, "Historicising Racialised Objects of Horror," 89.
3. *Ibid.*, 93.
4. Senn, *Drums of Terror*, 216–217.
5. Robert Lawless, *Haiti's Bad Press*, 24. Bob Corbett also wrote of Davis' "Indiana Jones Bravado" (1990).
6. J. Michael Dash, *Haiti and the United States*, 141.
7. *Ibid.*, 142.
8. *Ibid.*, 143.
9. Broderick, *Now a Terrifying Motion Picture!*, 176.
10. David Inglis does an excellent job of evaluating the book in relation to the film in "Putting the Undead to Work."
11. *Ibid.*, 57.
12. *Ibid.*, 55.
13. See "Pat Robertson Says Haiti Paying for Pact to the Devil."
14. Ker Than, "Haiti Earthquake and Voodoo: Myths, Ritual, and Robertson."
15. Vials, "The Origin of the Zombie in American Radio and Film," 51.

16. Ironically, Dargent's first name means "of money." Dennis at one point offers to make him rich, but he declines the offer, presumably because he is already wealthy from his corrupt machinations.
17. "*Blanc*" literally means "white," but it is used to refer to foreigners regardless of their skin color.
18. Degoul, "'We are the mirror of your fears,'"32.
19. *Ibid.*
20. *Ibid.*,34.
21. *Ibid.*, 35.
22. *Ibid.*, 36.
23. *Ibid.*
24. *Ibid.*
25. Originally built by the French when Saint-Domingue was its colony, Fort Dimanche was used as a military facility during the American Occupation in the 1920s. Under Papa Doc, it was where detractors from his government were brought to die, as Patrick Lemoine relates in *Fort Dimanche: Dungeon of Death* (1999). Baby Doc continued with the tradition when he became president.
26. Dubois, *Haiti: The Aftershocks of History*, 357.
27. Martin-Luc Bannardot and Gilles Danroe, eds., *La chute de la maison Duvalier*, 63.
28. Dubois, *Haiti: The Aftershocks of History*, 357–358.
29. Elizabeth Abbott, *Haiti: An Insider's History of the Rise and Fall of the Duvaliers*, 299.
30. Dayan, *Haiti, History, and the Gods*, 56.
31. See several articles in Mark Schuller and Pablo Morales' edited volume, *Tectonic Shifts*, for discussions of U.S. interference in Haitian politics, including Jean-Yves Blot, "The November 28, 2010 Elections: Another Catastrophe for Haiti," Roland Belizaire's "Foreign Domination: When Will We See a Rupture?" and Patrick Sylvain's "Martelly's Election: Shades of Populism and Authoritarian Rule."
32. Again, in the filmmaker's imagination.
33. Degoul, "'We are the mirror of your fears,'" 28.
34. Morris, "I Walked With a Zombie," 52.
35. See Amy Wilentz, "In Haiti, Waiting for the Grand Bayakou."
36. Such calls have been made explicitly, especially in the years following the earthquake with one of the most recent coming

Notes—Chapter Five

from Haiti's first Roman Catholic cardinal, Chibly Langlois, who is quoted as saying that voodoo is a "'big social problem' for his desperately poor country, arguing that the religion offers 'magic' but no real solutions to a population deprived of justice and a political voice." See "Voodoo Won't Save Haiti Says Cardinal."

37. The story can be found in Bishop's *American Zombie Gothic*, 50.
38. Boluk and Lenz, *Generation Zombie*, 5.
39. Morris, "I Walked With a Zombie," 55.
40. *Ibid.*
41. Emphasis added.
42. See my discussion of this debate in the Introduction.
43. Degoul, "'We are the mirror of your fears,'" 36.
44. For example, in the afterword to Évelyne Trouillot's novel, *Memory at Bay* (2010), Jason Herbeck quotes Edwidge Danticat who wrote that, "Books that might seem innocent…could easily betray [those who had them in their possession]. Novels with the wrong titles. Treatises with the right titles and intentions. Strings of words that, uttered, written, or read, could cause a person's death" (134).
45. Degoul, "'We are the mirror of your fears,'" 32.
46. *Ibid.*, 28.
47. *Ibid.*, 35.

Chapter Five

1. Referred to as *Zombi candidat* hereafter.
2. See Newitz ("War and Social Upheaval Cause Spikes in Zombie Movie Production"); Toppe ("Reversing the Gospel of Jesus"); and Platts ("Locating Zombies in the Sociology of Popular Culture").
3. Taptaps are brightly colored reconstituted pick-up trucks that serve as public transportation in Port-au-Prince and several larger cities and provinces.
4. Degoul, "'We are the mirror of your fears,'" 25.
5. Quoted in J.P. Jardel, "Représentation des cultes afro-caribéens et des pratiques magico-religieuse aux Antilles. Une approche du préjugé racial dans la littérature para-anthropologue," 459.
6. Degoul, "'We are the mirror of your fears,'" 28.
7. The city of Léogâne is significant in the story because it was the site of original resistance to the American Occupation in 1915. See Pressley-Sanon's article, "Haitian (Pre)Occupations: Ideological and Discursive Repetitions: 1915–1934 and 2004 to Present" for a discussion of its historical significance; Degoul, "'We are the mirror of your fears,'"29.
8. Degoul, "'We are the mirror of your fears,'" 31.
9. The inextricable link between the elite class and the political class can be found in Haitians' use of the word *leta* to refer to both the government and the economic elite. See Smith, *When the Hands are Many*, 21.
10. Deren, *Divine Horsemen*, 112.
11. *Ibid.*, 113.
12. McCarthy Brown, "Systematic Remembering, Systematic Forgetting," 84.
13. *Ibid.*, 85.
14. *Ibid.*
15. Daraine Luton, "Haiti's Rate of Fertility Tripled-Report."
16. I am by no means discounting the well-documented fact that women and girls have been subjected to numerous brutal sexual assaults since the earthquake. I am simply attempting to consider other aspects of life post-earthquake that are not accounted for in the reporting of statistics and the news.
17. "Living Vodou: Unedited Interview." "On Being with Krista Tippett." *NPR*.
18. Deren, *Divine Horsemen*, 102.
19. Vials, "The Origin of the Zombie in American Radio and Film," 47.
20. *Ibid.*
21. Fatimah Tobing Rony, *The Third Eye*, 4.
22. *Ibid.*
23. *Ibid.*, 213.
24. Fernando Solanas and Octavio Getino, "Toward a Third Cinema," emphasis in original.
25. Aimé Césaire, *Discourse on Colonialism*, 42.
26. Bishop, "The Sub-Subaltern Monster," 146.
27. A poignant example of the bourgeoisie being forced to see the face of poverty is in one of the stories in the anthology, *Haiti Noir* (2011), edited by Edwidge Danticat. The story, "Rosanna" by Josaphat-Robert Large, is about

a young bourgeois girl who is kidnapped and murdered. Her body is left atop a pile of burning garbage that her family only notices when one of their own is part of it. However, the author makes It clear that the same pile of what until then, was assumed to be "just garbage," for years, had existed.

28. Hurbon, *Le barbare imaginaire*, 193.

29. Bellegarde-Smith, *The Breached Citadel*, 96.

30. *Ibid.*

31. Patrick Sylvain, "Martelly's Election: Shades of Populism and Authoritarian Rule" in *Tectonic Shifts*, 205.

32. Bellegrade-Smith, *The Breached Citadel*, 97.

33. Charles Arthur and Michael Dash, eds., *Libète: A Haiti Anthology*, 47.

34. Taking the story of messengers of God coming back to life farther, Kevin Boon says, "we might rightly refer to the stories of Lazarus and Jesus as zombie tales," a point that always makes him "titter" every time he passes a "church with a sign outside that reads, "He is Risen" (see Boon, "Ontological Anxiety Made Flesh," 36–37). The zombi as he is envisioned by Antonin is, in fact, in line with a biblical reading of the revived dead. Unlike the traditional zombi who has no soul, or the popular zombi who does not return from the dead with a sense of identity or an intact body, Zéphirin has both of these. As he is also driven by love, he embodies Jesus' message.

35. Whether the connection is deliberate or not is not clear.

36. Jean-Yves Blot, "The November 28, 2010 Elections: Another Catastrophe for Haiti" in *Tectonic Shifts*, 195.

37. Sheller, *Citizenship From Below*,148.

38. In their introduction to *Woman, Nation, State* (1989), the editors of the collection of essays, Nira Yuval-Davis and Floya Anthias, suggest that there are five major ways in which women are involved in national and ethnic processes:

1. As biological reproducers of members of ethnic collectivities;
2. As reproducers of the boundaries of ethnic/national groups;
3. As participating centrally in the ideological reproduction of the collectivity and as transmitters of its culture;
4. As signifiers of ethnic/national differences—as a focus and symbol in ideological discourses used in the construction, reproduction and transformation of ethnic/national categories;
5. As participants in national, economic, political and military struggles.

39. Dayan, *Haiti, History and the Gods*, 40.

40. Ogou is believed to have ensured the revolution's success as a guiding spirit.

41. See Trouillot (*Haiti, State Against Nation*); Farmer (*AIDS and Accusation*); Ramsey (*The Spirits and the Law*).

42. See their "Introduction" to *Woman, State, Nation* (1989).

Conclusion

1. See Schuller and Morales, *Tectonic Shifts*; Ezili Dantò, "Haiti: Jan 1, 2013: Another Independence Day Under Occupation."

2. Bishop, *American Zombie Gothic*, 37.

3. *Ibid.*, 52.

4. See Joseph Guyler Delva, "Haiti Urged to Halt Cholera Anti-Voodoo Lynchings" and Jean A. Valme, "Officials: 45 People Lynched in Haiti Amid Cholera Fears."

5. Kaiama Glover makes this suggestion in *Haiti Unbound: A Spiralist Challenge to the Postcolonial Canon*.

6. Both Duvalier and Aristide returned to the country in 2011 after the earthquake.

Works Cited

Abbott, Elizabeth. *Haiti: An Insider's History of the Rise and Fall of the Duvaliers*. New York: Simon & Schuster, 1988.

Aizenberg, Edna. "'I Walked with a Zombie': The Pleasures and Perils of Postcolonial Hybridity." *World Literature Today* 73.3 (Summer 1999): 461–466. Print.

Albuquerque, Klaus de. "In Search of the Big Bamboo: How Caribbean Beach Boys Sell Fun in the Sun." *The Utne Reader* (Jan–Feb. 2000): 82–86. Print.

Arthur, Charles, and J. Michael Dash. "The Status Quo: Elites, Soldiers and Dictators,." In Charles Arthur and J. Michael Dash, eds. *Libète: A Haiti Anthology*. Kingston: Ian Randle Publishers, 1999: 45–51. Print.

Bannardot, Martin-Luc, and Gilles Danroe, eds. *La Chute De La Maison Duvalier: textes pour l'histoire*. Paris: Karthala, 1989. Print.

Beckles, Hilary. *Natural Rebels: A Social History of Enslaved Black Women in Barbados*. Kingston: Ian Randle Publishers, 1989. Print.

Bellegarde-Smith, Patrick. *Haiti: The Breached Citadel*. Boulder: Westview Press, 1990. Print.

_____. "The Spirit of the Thing: Religious Thought and Social/Historical Memory." In Patrick Bellegarde-Smith, ed. *Fragments of Bone: Neo-African Religions in a New World*. Chicago: University of Illinois Press, 2005: 52–70. Print.

Bishop, Kyle. *American Zombie Gothic: The Rise and Fall (and Rise) of the Walking Dead in Popular Culture*. Jefferson, NC: McFarland, 2010. Print.

_____. "The Idle Proletariat: Dawn of the Dead, Consumer Ideology, and the Loss of Productive Labor." *The Journal of Popular Culture* 43. 3 (2010): 234–248. Web. 20 December 2015.

_____. "The Sub-Subaltern Monster: Imperialist Hegemony and the Cinematic Voodoo Zombie." *The Journal of American Culture* 31.2 (2008): 141–152. Web. 20 December 2015.

Black, Cheryl. "Looking White, Acting Black: Cast(e)ing Fredi Washington." *Theatre Survey* Null.1 (May 2004): 19–40. Web. 20 December 2015.

Boluk, Stephanie, and Wylie Lenz. "Introduction: Generation Z, the Age of Apocalypse." In Stephanie Boluk and Wylie Lenz, eds. *Generation Zombie: Essays on the Living Dead in Modern Culture*. Jefferson, NC: McFarland, 2011: 1–17. Print.

Boon, Kevin Alexander. "Ontological Anxiety Made Flesh: The Zombie in Literature, Film and Culture." In Niall Scott, ed. *Monsters and the Monstrous: Myths and Metaphors of Enduring Evil*, 38. New York: Rodopi, 2007: 33–43.

Briodowski, Steve. "*Dawn of the Dead*: A Retrospective." *Cinefantastique Online*. October 7, 2007. Web. 4 September 2013.

Broderick, James F. *Now a Terrifying Motion Picture! Twenty-Five Classic Works of Horror Adapted from Book to Film*. Jefferson, NC: McFarland, 2012. Print.

Carroll, Noel. "The Future of Allusion: Hollywood in the Seventies (And Beyond)." October 20 (1982): 51–81. Web. 12 December 2015.

Carter, Simon, and Stephen Clift. "Tourism, International Travel and Sex." In Stephen Clift and Simon Carter, eds. *Tourism and*

Works Cited

Sex: Culture, Commerce and Coercion. New York: Pinter, 2000: 1–19. Print.

Césaire, Aimé. *Discourse on Colonialism*. Trans. Joan Pinkham. New York: Monthly Review Press, 2000. Print.

Chester, Colby M. "Haiti: A Degenerating Island: The Story of Its Past Grandeur and Present Decay." *National Geographic* 19.3 (March 1908). Print.

Chomsky, Noam. *Year 501: The Conquest Continues*. London: Short Run Press, Ltd., 2002. Print.

Clifford, James. *Routes: Travel and Translation in the Late Twentieth Century*. Cambridge: Harvard University Press, 1997. Print.

Courlander, Harold. *The Drum and the Hoe: Life and Lore of the Haitian People*. Berkeley: University of California Press, 1966. Print.

Creed, Barbara. *The Monstrous Feminine: Film, Feminism, Psychoanalysis*. London: Routledge, 1993. Print.

Cripps, Thomas. *Slow Fade to Black: The Negro in American Film, 1900–1942*. New York: Oxford University Press, 1993. Print.

Dantò, Ezili. "Haiti: Jan 1, 2013: Another Independence Day Under Occupation." *Men Anpil, Chay Pa Lou*. Web. 15 August 2013.

Dash, J. Michael. *Haiti and the United States: National Stereotypes and the Literary Imagination*. New York: St. Martin's Press, 2nd Edition, 1988. Print.

Dawn of the Dead. Dir. George Romero. 1978.

Dayan, Joan. *Haiti, History and the Gods*. Berkeley: University of California Press, 1998. Print.

Degoul, Franck. "'We are the mirror of your fears': Haitian Identity and Zombification." In Deborah Christie and Sarah Juliet Lauro, eds. Translated by Elisabeth M. Lore. *Better Off Dead: The Evolution of the Zombie as Post-Human*. New York: Fordham University Press, 2011: 24–38. Print.

Delva, Joseph Guyler. "Haiti Urged to Halt Cholera Anti-Voodoo Lynchings." *Reuters*. Web. 12 December 2015.

Dendle, Peter. "The Zombie as Barometer of Cultural Anxiety." In Niall Scott, ed. *Monsters and the Monstrous: Myths and Metaphors of Enduring Evil*. New York: Rodopi, 2007:45–57. Print.

Depestre, René. "Change." *Violence* 11, No. 9. Paris: Seuil, 1971.

_____. *A Rainbow for the Christian West*. Translated with an Introduction by Joan Dayan. Amherst: University of Massachusetts Press, 1977. Print.

de Peuch Parham, Althéa. Editor and translator. *My Odyssey: Experiences of a Young Refugee from Two Revolutions, by a Creole of Saint Domingue*. Baton Rouge: Louisiana State University Press, 1959. Print.

Deren, Maya. *Divine Horsemen: The Living Gods of Haiti*. New York: McPherson and Company, 1970. Print.

Desmangles, Leslie. *The Faces of the Gods: Vodou and Roman Catholicism in Haiti*. Chapel Hill: University of North Carolina Press, 1992.

Diawara, Manthia. Ed. *Black American Cinema*. New York: Routledge, 1993. Print.

Dorsinville, Nancy. "Goudou Goudou." In Paul Farmer, ed. *Haiti After the Earthquake*. New York: Public Affairs, 2011: 273–281. Print.

Draper, Arthur. "Uncle Tom Will Never Die!." Lindsay Patterson, ed. *Black Films and Film-Makers: A Comprehensive Anthology from Stereotype to Superhero*. New York: Dodd, Mead and Company, 1975: 30–35. Print.

Dubois, Laurent. *Haiti: The Aftershocks of History*. New York: Metropolitan Books, 2012. Print.

England, Marcia. "Breached Bodies and Home Invasions: Horrific Representations of the Feminized Body and Home." *Gender, Place and Culture* 13. 4 (2006): 353–363. Web. 9 September 2013.

Enloe, Cynthia. *Bananas, Beaches and Bases: Making Feminist Sense of International Politics*. London: Pandora, 1989. Print.

Fahraeus, Anna. "Historicising Racialised Objects of Horror: The Black Renaissance Villain." In Dana Lori Chalmers, ed., *Villains, Heroes or Victims?* Oxford:

Works Cited

United Kingdom: Inter-Disciplinary Press, 2010: 89–93. Print.

Farmer, Paul. *AIDS and Accusation: Haiti and the Geography of Blame.* Berkeley: University of California Press, 1992. Print.

———. "An Anthropology of Structural Violence." *Current Anthropology* 45. 3 (June 2004): 305–325. Web. 9 September 2013.

Fay, Jennifer. "Dead Subjectivity: *White Zombie*, Black Baghdad." *CR: The New Centennial Review* 8.1(2008): 81–101. Web. 9 September 2015.

Fick, Carolyn E. *The Making of Haiti: The Saint Domingue Revolution from Below.* Knoxville: University of Tennessee Press, 1990. Print.

Garraway, Doris L. *The Libertine Colony: Creolization in the Early French Carribean.* Durham: Duke University Press, 2005.

Glover, Kaiama. *Haiti Unbound: A Spiralist Challenge to the Postcolonial Canon.* Liverpool: Liverpool University Press, 2010. Print.

Haiti Grassroots Watch. "Haiti—Open for Business." Web. 4 May 2013.

Harper, Stephen. "Zombies, Malls, and the Consumerism Debate: George Romero's Dawn of the Dead." *Americana: The Journal of American Popular Culture 1900 to Present.* Web. 4 September 2013.

Heading South, Dir., Laurent Cantet, 2005

Herold, Edward, Rafael Garcia and Tony DeMoya. "Female Tourists and Beach Boys: Romance or Sex Tourism?" *Annals of Tourism Research* 28. 4 (2001): 978–997. Web. 12 December 2015.

hooks, bell. *Black Looks: Race and Representation.* Boston: South End Press, 1992. Print.

Hurbon, Laënnec. "American Fantasy and Haitian Vodou." In Donald Cosentino ed. *Sacred Arts of Haitian Vodou.* Los Angeles: UCLA Fowler Museum, 1995: 181–197. Print.

———. *Le Barbare imaginaire.* Paris: Cerf, 1988. Print.

Hurston, Zora Neale. *Tell My Horse: Voodoo and Life in Haiti and Jamaica.* New York: Perennial Library, 1990.

I Walked with a Zombie. Dir. Jacques Tourneur. 1943.

Inglis, David. "Putting the Undead to Work: Wade Davis, Haitian Vodou and the Social Uses of the Zombie." In Christopher M. Moreman and Cory James Rushton, eds. *Race, Oppression and the Zombie: Essays on Cross-Cultural Appropriations of the Caribbean Tradition.* Jefferson, NC: McFarland, 2011: 42–59. Print.

Jardel, Jean-Pierre. "Représentation des cultes afro-caribéens et des pratiques magico-religieuse aux antilles. une approche du préjugé racial dans la littérature para-anthropologue." In Jean Barnabé, Jean-Luc Bonniol, Raphaël Confiant, Gerry L'Etang. eds. *Au visiteur lumineux: Des îles creoles aux sociétés plurielles.* Petit-Bourg: Ibis Rouge Editions, 2000. Web. 10 December 2015.

Jewell, K. Sue. *From Mammy to Miss America and Beyond: Cultural Images and the Shaping of U.S. Social Policy.* New York: Routledge, 1993. Print.

Johnson, Harry. "Haiti and Its Regeneration by the United States." *National Geographic Magazine* 38.6 (1920). Print.

Johnson, James Weldon. *Autobiography of an Ex-Colored Man.* New York: Dover Publications, 1995. Print.

Kee, Chera. "'They are not men ... they are dead bodies!': From Cannibal to Zombie and Back Again." In Deborah Christie and Sarah Juliet Lauro, eds. *Better Off Dead: The Evolution of the Zombie as Post-Human.* New York: Fordham University Press, 2011: 9–23. Print.

Kempadoo, Kamala. "Theorizing Sexual Relations in the Caribbean: Prostitution and the Problem of the 'Exotic.'" In Yanique Hume and Aaron Kamugisha, eds. *Caribbean Cultural Thought: From Plantation of Diaspora.* Kingston: Ian Randle Publishers, 2013: 425–443. Print.

Keresztesi, Rita. "Hurston in Haiti: Neocolonialism and Zombification." In Christopher M. Moreman and Cory James Rushton, eds. *Race, Oppression and the Zombie: Essays on Cross-Cultural Appropriations of the Caribbean Tradition.* Jefferson, NC: McFarland, 2011: 31–41. Print.

Kern, Fleurimond W. "The Haitian Flag—

Works Cited

Birth of a Symbol." In Pat Chin, Greg Dunkel, Sara Flounders, and Kim Ives, eds. Translated by Greg Dunkel. *Haiti: A Slave Revolution: 200 Years After 1804*. New York: International Action Group, 2004: 97–102. Print.

Kordas, Ann. "New South, New Immigrants, New Women, New Zombies: The Historical Development of the Zombie in American Popular Culture." In Christopher M. Moreman and Cory James Rushton, eds. *Race, Oppression and the Zombie: Essays on Cross-Cultural Appropriations of the Caribbean Tradition*. Jefferson, NC: McFarland, 2011: 15–30. Print.

Kovin, Mikel J. "The Folklore of the Zombie Film." In Shawn McIntosh and Marc Leverette, eds. *Zombie Culture: Autopsies of the Living Dead*. Lanham, MD: Scarecrow, 2008: 19–34. Print.

Laferrière, Dany. *Heading South*. Trans. Wayne Grady. Vancouver: Douglas and McIntyre, 2009. Print.

Lall, Rashmee Roshan. "Haiti's Seeds of Change? With Agricultural Output Down the Island is Turning to Textiles." *Canada Haiti Action Network*. August 21, 2013. Web 28 August 2013.

_____. "Voodoo Won't Save Haiti Says Cardinal." *The Guardian*. July 13, 2014. Web. 7 December 2015.

Larson, Nella. *Quicksand and Passing*. Deborah E. McDowell, ed. New Brunswick: Rutgers University Press, 1986. Print.

Lawless, Robert. *Haiti's Bad Press*. Rochester, VT: Schenkman Press, 1992. Print.

Leab, Daniel J. *From Sambo to Superspade: The Black Experience in Motion Pictures*. Boston: Houghton Mifflin Company, 1975. Print.

"Living Vodou: Unedited Interview." "On Being with Krista Tippett." *NPR*. Web. 1 September 2013.

Longhurst, Robyn. "Viewpoint: The Body and Geography." *Gender, Place, and Culture: A Journal of Feminist Geography* 2.1 (1995): 97–106. Web. 2 September 2013.

Luton, Daraine. "Haiti's Rate of Fertility Tripled-Report." *The Gleaner*. October 22, 2010. Web. 8 January 2012.

Manatu, Norma. *African American Women and Sexuality in the Cinema*. Jefferson, NC: McFarland, 2003. Print.

Mapp, Edward. *Blacks in American Films: Today and Yesterday*. Metuchen: Scarecrow, 1972. Print.

Marr, Andrew. "Interview with Derek Walcott." *The Observer Escape*. April 27, 1999. Web. 9 September 2015.

Matthewson, Tim. "Jefferson and the Nonrecognition of Haiti." *Proceedings of the American Philosophical Society* 140.1 (March 1996): 22–48. Web. 10 December 2015.

Mbembe, Achille. "Necropolitics." Libby Meintjes, trans. *Public Culture* 15.1 (2003): 11–40. Web. 29 March 2016.

McAlister, Elizabeth. "Love, Sex, and Gender Embodied: The Spirits of Haitian Vodou." In Joseph Runzo and Nancy M. Martin, eds. *Love, Sex and Gender in the World Religions*, vol. 2. Oxford: Oneworld, 2000: 128–145. Print.

McCarthy Brown, Karen. "Serving the Spirits: The Ritual Economy of Haitian Vodou." In Donald Cosentino, ed. *Sacred Arts of Haitian Vodou*. Los Angeles: UCLA Fowler Museum of Cultural History, 1995: 205–223. Print.

_____. "Systematic Remembering, Systematic Forgetting." In Sandra T. Barnes, ed. *Ogun: Old World and New*. Bloomington: Indiana University Press, 1997: 65–89. Print.

_____. *Tracing the Spirit: Ethnographic Essays on Haitian Art, from the Collection of the Davenport Museum of Art*. Seattle: University of Washington Press, 1995. Print.

_____. "Voodoo." In Arthur C. Lehmann and James E. Myers, eds. *Magic, Witchcraft and Religion: An Anthropological Study of the Supernatural*, 2nd edition. Palo Alto, CA: Mayfield, 1989: 321–326. Print.

McIntosh, Shawn. "The Evolution of the Zombie: The Monster That Keeps Coming Back." In Shawn McIntosh and Marc Leverette, eds. *Zombie Culture: Autopsies of the Living Dead*. Lanham, MD: Scarecrow, 2008:1–17. Print.

Meisch, L. "Gringas and Otavelenos:

Works Cited

Changing Tourist Relations." *Annals of Tourism Research* 22 (2): 441–462. Web. 2 September 2013.

Mercier, Paul. "The Fon of Dahomey." In Daryll Forde, ed. *African Worlds: Studies in the Cosmological Ideas and Social Values of African Peoples*. New York: Oxford University Press, 1954, 210–234. Print.

Métraux, Alfred. *Le Vaudou Haïtien*. Paris: Editions Gallimard, 1958. Print.

_____. *Voodoo in Haiti* (1959). Trans. Charteris, Hugo; Introduction by Sidney W. Mintz. New York: Schocken Books, 1972. Print.

Modleski, Tania. *Feminism Without Women: Culture and Criticism in a "Postfeminist." Age*. New York: Routledge, 1991. Print.

Moreman, Christopher M., and Cory James Rushton. "Introduction." In Christopher M. Moreman and Cory James Rushton, eds. *Race, Oppression and the Zombie: Essays on Cross-Cultural Appropriations of the Caribbean Tradition*. Jefferson, NC: McFarland, 2011: 1–12. Print.

Morris, Hamilton. "I Walked with a Zombie: Travels Among the Undead." *Harper's Magazine* (November 2011): 52–61. Web 9 September 2013.

Morris, Meaghan. "Things to Do with Shopping Centres." In Simon During, ed. *The Cultural Studies Reader*. London: Routledge, 1995: 391–409. Print.

Morrisey, Marietta. *Slave Women in the New World: Gender Stratification in the Caribbean*. Lawrence: University Press of Kansas, 1989. Print.

Najman, Charles. *Haïti, Dieu seul me voit*. Paris: Balland, 1985. Print.

Newitz, Annalee. "War and Social Upheaval Cause Spikes in Zombie Movie Production." *I09: We Come from the Future*. Web 27 August 2013.

Noble, Peter. *The Negro in Films*. New York: Arno Press and the New York Times, 1970. Print.

O'Connell Davidson, Julia. "Sex Tourism and Child Prostitution." In Stephen Clift and Simon Carter, eds. *Tourism and Sex: Culture, Commerce and Coercion*. New York: Pinter, 2000: 54–73. Print.

Paravisini-Gebert, Lizabeth. "The Representation of Woman as Zombie." In Margarite Fernández Olmos and Lizabeth Paravisini-Gebert, eds. *Sacred Possessions: Vodou, Santería, Obeah, and the Caribbean*. New Brunswick: Rutgers University Press, 1997: 37–58. Print.

"Pat Robertson Says Haiti Paying for Pact to the Devil." *CNN*. January 13,2010. Web. 28 August 2013.

Pattullo, Polly. *Last Resorts: The Cost of Tourism in the Caribbean*. London: Cassell, 1996. Print.

Phillips, Gyllian. "*White Zombie* and the Creole: William Seabrook's *The Magic Island* and American Imperialism in Haiti." In Stephanie Boluk and Wylie Lenz, eds. *Generation Zombie: Essays on the Living Dead in Modern Culture*. Jefferson, NC: McFarland, 2011: 27–40. Print.

Pierre-Pierre, Garry. "Exporting Haitian Culture to the World." *New York Times*. May 12, 1996: C6. Print.

A Pig's Tale. Written and Narrated by Maggie O'Kane. New York: Crowing Rooster, 1998.

Pines, Jim. *Blacks in Films: A Survey of Racial Themes and Images in the American Film*. London: Studio Vista, 1975. Print.

Platts, Todd K. "Locating Zombies in the Sociology of Popular Culture." *Sociology Compass* 7.7(2013): 547–560. Web. 5 September 2015.

Popkin, Jeremy D. *Facing Racial Revolution: Eyewitness Accounts of the Haitian Insurrection*. Chicago: University of Chicago Press, 2007. Print.

Pressley-Sanon, Toni. "Haitian (Pre)Occupations: Ideological and Discursive Repetitions: 1915–1934 and 2004 to Present." *Caribbean Studies Journal* 42: 2 (July–December 2014): 115–153. Web. 15 October 2015.

_____. *Istwa across the water: Haitian History, Memory, and the Cultural Imagination* (forthcoming).

_____. "Workings of the Spirit: The Goddess Ezili in *The Love Wanga* (1935)." In Claudine Michel and Patrick Bellegarde-Smith, eds. *God in Every Woman: Gender and Power in Haitian Vodou* (forthcoming).

Works Cited

Pruitt, D., and S. Lafont. "For Love and Money: Romance Tourism in Jamaica." *Annals of Tourism Research* 22.2 (1995): 442–440. Web. 15 January 2016.

Ramsey, Kate. *The Spirits and the Law: Vodou and Power in Haiti*. Chicago: University of Chicago Press, 2011. Print.

Regester, Charlene. *African American Actresses: The Struggle for Visibility, 1900–1960*. Bloomington: Indiana University Press, 2010. Print.

Renda, Mary. *Taking Haiti: Military Occupation and the Culture of U.S. Imperialism, 1915-1940*. Chapel Hill: University of North Carolina Press, 2001. Print.

Rhodes, Gary. D. *White Zombie: Anatomy of a Horror Film*. Jefferson, NC: McFarland, 2001. Print.

Richardson, Michael. *Otherness in Hollywood Cinema*. Continuum: New York, 2010. Print.

Rony, Fatimah Tobing. *The Third Eye: Race, Cinema, and Ethnographic Spectacle*. Durham: Duke University Press, 1996. Print.

Root, Deborah. *Cannibal Culture: Art, Appropriation and the Commodification of Difference*. Boulder: Westview Press, 1996. Print.

Sahmkow, Ramon. "Haiti Is a Future Tourist Destination, Says President." AFP. December 5, 2011. Web. 15 August 2013.

St. John, Sir Spencer. *Hayti: Or, The Black Republic* (1884). London: Frank Cass and Company, 1971. Print.

Sánchez Taylor, Jacqueline. "Tourism and 'Embodied' Commodities: Sex Tourism in the Caribbean." In Stephen Clift and Simon Carter, eds. *Tourism and Sex: Culture, Commerce and Coercion*. New York: Pinter, 2000: 41–53. Print.

Schmidt, Hans. 1995. *The United States Occupation of Haiti, 1915-1934*. New Brunswick: Rutgers University Press. Print.

Schuller, Mark, and Pablo Morales, eds. *Tectonic Shifts: Haiti Since the Earthquake*. Sterling, VA: Kumarian Press, 2012. Print.

Schuyler, George S. *Black No More: A Novel*. New York: Modern Library, 1999. Print.

Seabrook, William. *The Magic Island*. New York: Harcourt, Brace and Company, 1929. Print.

Senn, Bryan. *Drums of Terror: Voodoo in the Cinema*. Baltimore: Midnight Marquee Press, 1998. Print.

Sepinwall, Alyssa Goldstein. "The Specter of Saint-Domingue: American and French Reactions to the Haitian Revolution." In David Patrick Geggus and Norman Fiering, eds. *The World and the Haitian Revolution*. Bloomington: Indiana University Press, 2009: 317–338. Print.

The Serpent and the Rainbow. Dir. Wes Craven. Universal Studios, 1987.

Sheller, Mimi. *Citizenship from Below: Erotic Agency and Caribbean Freedom*. Durham: Duke University Press, 2012. Print.

———. *Consuming the Caribbean: From Arawaks to Zombies*. New York: Routledge, 2003. Print.

———. "Natural Hedonism: The Invention of Caribbean Islands as Tropical Playgrounds." In Sandra Courtman, ed. *Beyond the Blood, the Beach and the Banana: New Perspectives in Caribbean Studies*. Kingston: Ian Rand Publishers, 2004: 170–185. Print.

Solanas, Fernando, and Octavio Getino. "Toward a Third Cinema." *Cinéaste* 4.3 (Winter 1970–71): 1–10. Print.

Smith, Jennie M. *When the Hands Are Many: Community Organization and Social Change in Rural Haiti*. Ithaca: Cornell University Press, 2001. Print.

Strachan, Ian Gregory. *Paradise and Plantation: Tourism and Culture in the Anglophone Caribbean*. Charlottesville: University of Virginia Press, 2002. Print.

Sylvain, Patrick. "Martelly's Election: Shades of Populism and Authoritarian Rule." In Mark Schuller and Pablo Morales, eds. *Tectonic Shifts: Haiti Since the Earthquake*. Sterling, VA: Kumarian Press, 2012: 204–207. Print.

Taylor, Frank Fonda. *To Hell with Paradise*. Pittsburgh: University of Pittsburgh Press, 1993. Print.

Works Cited

Than, Ker. "Haiti Earthquake and Voodoo: Myths, Ritual, and Robertson." *National Geographic News*. January 27, 2010. Web. 6 December 2015.

Thornton, John K. "African Soldiers in the Haitian Revolution." *Journal of Caribbean History* 25 (1991): 58–80. Print.

Titley, Gavan. "All Sights Reserved: All-Inclusive Resorts and the Imagined Caribbean." In Sandra Courtman, ed. *Beyond the Blood, the Beach and the Banana: New Perspectives in Caribbean Studies*. Kingston: Ian Rand Publishers, 2004: 205–220. Print.

Toppe, Jana. "Reversing the Gospel of Jesus: How the Zombie Theme Satirizes the Resurrection of the Body and the Eucharist." In Regina Hansen, ed. *Roman Catholicism in Fantastic Film: Essays on Belief, Spectacle, Ritual and Imagery*. Jefferson, NC: McFarland, 2011: 169–182. Print.

Trouillot, Michel-Rolph. "The Caribbean Region: An Open Frontier in Anthropological Theory." *Annual Review of Anthropology* Vol. 21 (1992): 19–42. Web. 10 October 2013.

_____.*Haiti, State Against Nation: The Origins and Legacy of Duvalierism*. New York: Monthly Review Press, 1990. Print.

Urry, John. *The Tourist Gaze: Leisure and Travel in Contemporary Societies*. London: Sage, 1990.

Valme, Jean A. "Officials: 45 People Lynched in Haiti Amid Cholera Fears." *CNN*. Web. 12 December 2015.

Vials, Chris. "The Origin of the Zombie in American Radio and Film: B-Horror, U.S. Empire, and the Politics of Disavowal." In Stephanie Boluk and Wylie Lenz, eds. *Generation Zombie: Essays on the Living Dead in Modern Culture*. Jefferson, NC: McFarland, 2011:41–53. Print.

Wallace, Michele Faith. "The Good Lynching and the Birth of a Nation: Discourse and Aesthetics of Jim Crow." *Cinema Journal* 43, No. 1 (Fall 2003): 85–104. Web. 12 December 2015.

"Wards of the United States: Notes on What Our Country Is Doing for Santo Domingo, Nicaragua, and Haiti." *National Geographic Magazine* 30.1 (August 1916). Print.

Webb, Jenn, and Sam Byrnand. "Some Kind of Virus: The Zombie as Body and Trope." *Body & Society* 14.2 (2008): 83–98.

White Zombie. Dir. Victor Halpern. 2005.

Wilentz, Amy. "Waiting for the Grand Bayakou." *New York Times*. November 25, 2010: A37. Web. April 5 2013.

Williams, Tony. "*White Zombie* Haitian Horror." *Jump Cut: A Review of Contemporary Media* 28 (April 1983): 18–20. Web. 20 December 2015.

Wirkus, Faustin E., and Tanner Dudley. *The White King of La Gonâve: The True Story of the Sargent of Marines Who Was Crowned King on a Voodoo Island*. Garden City, NY: Doubleday, Doran & Company, 1931. Print.

Young, Gwenda. "The Cinema of Difference: Jacques Tourneur, Race and "I Walked with a Zombie" (1943). *Irish Journal of American Studies* 7 (1998): 101–119. Web. 9 September 2013.

Young, Lola. *Fear of the Dark: Race, Gender and Sexuality in the Cinema*. New York: Routledge, 1986. Print.

Younge, Gary. "No Refuge from Reality: Gated Communities Will Not Isolate Rich from the Chaos." *The Guardian*. December 2, 2002. Web. 6 April 2013.

Yuval-Davis, Nira, and Floya Anthias, eds. *Woman, Nation, State*. Hampshire: Macmillan, 1989. Print.

Zombi candidat à la présidence ... ou les amours d'un zombi. Dir, Arnold Antonin. 2009.

Index

affranchi 65, 66
African-American 4, 33, 35, 43, 65, 68, 70, 72, 78, 106, 169n2, 170n55, 173n25
Antonin, Arnold 4, 12, 18, 24, 141, 148, 149, 150, 159, 160, 178n34
Aristide, Jean-Bertrand 3, 163, 165, 178n6

beach boy 18, 22, 90, 91, 93, 94, 101, 102, 103, 105, 115, 117, 174n9
beach resort 13, 22, 57, 85, 91, 93, 96, 97, 101, 102, 105, 108, 111, 112, 115, 116, 117
Beauvoir, Max 18, 127, 133, 167n19, 168n50
Beavers, Louise 33
Bellegarde-Smith, Patrick 7, 35, 146, 154, 167n5, 168n49, 170n61, 171n104, 172ch1n129, 172ch2n13, 172n65, 178n29
Birth of a Nation 20, 168n60, 170n88
Bishop, Kyle 4, 5, 26, 30, 34, 38, 64, 75, 112, 149, 162, 163, 167n16, 167n32, 169n1, 169n3, 169n6, 169n9, 170n30, 170n48, 170n50, 170n74, 170n75, 171n82, 172n3, 173n45, 175n73, 176n79, 177ch4n37, 177ch5n26, 178n2
black *see* African-American
Bois Caïman Ceremony 27, 111
bokor 11, 13, 17, 32, 37, 38, 124, 133, 135, 136, 142, 151, 170n74
Boon, Kevin 3, 18, 19, 70, 168n54, 173n20, 178n34
Boyer, Jean-Pierre 19, 168n55, 170n28

cannibalism 8, 9, 23, 31, 32, 47, 56, 74, 113, 114
Cantet, Laurent 1, 10, 22, 90, 91, 99, 100, 103, 105, 113
capitalism 90, 94, 100, 164
Carib 32
ceremony 27, 47, 58, 81, 86, 138, 170n76
Chavannes, Jean-Baptiste 65
Chester, Colby M. 73, 173n27, 174n40
cholera 24, 163
Chomsky, Noam 29, 169n23, 170n29, 170n33
Christianity 8, 38, 49, 56, 57, 59, 62, 74, 75, 86, 122, 123, 146, 151, 157, 158, 171n102

Christophe, King Henri 8, 129
Citadelle Laferrière 129
cog in the wheel 114, 164
colonialism/neocolonialism/postcolonialism 7, 11, 12, 13, 14, 16, 22, 23, 25, 26, 27, 28, 30, 35, 42, 43, 44, 45, 50, 54, 56, 62, 64, 65, 79, 82, 83, 89, 98, 99, 100, 101, 106, 118, 132, 143, 149, 169n9
Columbus, Christopher 32, 89, 141, 174n11
concubine 45, 71, 95, 115
consumer (consumerism) 112, 113, 114, 117, 123, 164, 175n72
corruption (corruptive) 14, 17, 21, 32, 36, 38, 39, 43, 44, 51, 54, 55, 56, 57, 58, 59, 60, 61, 62, 63, 66, 68, 69, 73, 77, 80, 82, 86, 87, 90, 115, 119, 120, 132, 133, 137, 138, 145, 147, 149, 154, 160, 176n16
corvée 37, 106, 173n46
Craven, Wes 23, 119, 121, 122, 123, 125, 128, 131, 132, 133, 136, 140, 174n27
Cuba 10, 11, 27, 28, 30, 45, 75, 170n39

Dahomey 99
dance 47, 78, 79, 99, 122, 133, 149, 157, 170n76, 175n53
Dartiguenave, Philippe Sudré 76, 153
Davis, Wade 14, 23, 119, 120, 121, 122, 123, 124, 125, 129, 131, 132, 133, 167n16, 167n19, 168n50, 176n5
Dayan, Joan 12, 43, 69, 128, 157, 167n28, 171n89, 172n17, 172n18, 175n39, 175n41, 175n42, 176n30, 178n39
Defilée 157
Degoul, Franck 8, 9, 25, 119, 123, 124, 125, 133, 135, 136, 141, 142, 143, 144, 161, 168n8, 168n10, 168n12, 169n4, 176n1, 176n18, 176n33, 177ch4n43, 177ch4n45, 177ch5n4, 177n6, 177n7, 177n8
Dendle, Peter 3, 18, 35, 61, 169n67
Depestre, René 12, 13, 167n30, 175n39, 175n41, 175n42
Deren, Maya 36, 37, 39, 40, 42, 144, 145, 146, 170n70, 170n77, 173n61, 173n64, 175n42, 177n10, 177n18

Index

de St. Méry, Moreau 69
Dessalines, Emperor Jean-Jacques 27, 50, 72, 73, 157, 161
Desmangles, Leslie 35, 37, 42, 170n62, 170n68, 171n85, 173n59
double consciousness 147
drum (drumming) 20, 47, 54, 55, 58, 59, 67, 76, 80, 83, 85, 87, 133
Dubois, Laurent 27, 28, 45, 78, 79, 127, 167n9, 168n49, 169n11, 169n16, 169n19, 171n93, 172n7, 173n26, 173n52, 173n55, 176n26
Dubois, W.E.B. 147
Dutty, Boukman 27
Duvalier, François (Duvalierism) 9, 23, 92, 95, 97, 105, 117, 121, 123, 125, 127, 130, 132, 134, 135, 139, 152, 154, 164, 174n13, 174n27, 174n28
Duvalier, Jean-Claude 9, 89, 115, 125, 127, 128, 130, 132, 134, 135, 139, 152, 164, 165, 174n28, 178n6

economy 30, 55, 74, 92, 129, 159, 171n92
elite class 66, 71, 72, 144, 149, 150, 151, 153, 154, 156, 164, 172n129, 177n9
exploitation 9, 10, 11, 13, 14, 22, 30, 34, 47, 80, 83, 89, 91, 100, 101, 105, 109, 112, 113, 117, 118, 144, 145, 149, 156, 159, 163, 164, 173n54

Farmer, Paul 92, 93, 94, 174n12, 174n14, 174n16, 174n18, 178n41
Fatiman, Cécile 27
fear 8, 9, 10, 16, 19, 20, 21, 23, 26, 28, 38, 39, 41, 42, 43, 47, 50, 51, 52, 55, 56, 59, 60, 64, 67, 68, 77, 78, 80, 88, 89, 123, 124, 127, 135, 138, 142, 149, 161, 162, 163, 165
feminine (womanhood) 26, 34, 35, 42, 53, 61, 68, 71, 82, 86, 98
Fetchit, Stepin 33
Fick, Carolyn 27, 167n29, 169n14
France 7, 8, 19, 27, 29, 30, 62, 129, 160, 168n55, 170n28, 172n129

Garden of Eden 46, 82
gaze 69, 89, 101, 102, 104, 110, 147, 148, 168n36
gender 4, 20, 32, 45, 61, 77, 85, 98, 101, 114, 155, 156, 159
Ginen 36

Halpern, Edward 22, 25, 26, 32, 33, 39, 52
Halpern, Victor 22, 25, 26, 32, 33, 39, 52
Hayti, or the Black Republic (St. John) 7, 48, 171n116
hegemony 26, 65, 172n129
Hollywood 1, 5, 16, 18, 30, 32, 33, 41, 70, 78, 121, 122, 136, 162, 163

hooks, bell 109, 114, 176n80
horror 17, 21, 22, 23, 50, 64, 73, 75, 77, 89, 119, 131
houmfort 14, 40, 55, 57, 58, 157
houngan 18, 27, 32, 40, 55, 57, 58, 111, 124, 127, 129, 133, 143, 144, 163
Hurbon, Laënnec 8, 11, 13, 14, 41, 134, 152, 167n7, 167n19, 167n20, 167n23, 168n35, 170n32, 171n84, 178n28
Hurston, Zora Neale 11, 14, 152, 167n21, 167n22, 168n36, 168n37

Imitation of Life 70, 72
imperialism 4, 15, 16, 23, 25, 26, 29, 30, 32, 41, 44, 62, 74, 76, 79, 85, 98, 99, 123, 124, 129, 132, 138, 148, 150, 161, 168n36
indemnity tax 19, 168n55, 170n28
innocence 34, 39, 53, 56, 59, 61, 63, 68, 109, 172n118, 172n122, 177n44

Jamaica 27, 28, 45, 67, 174n17
Jefferson, Thomas 7
Jennings, Brent 135
Jezebel 70
Jones, Indiana 120, 121, 122, 136, 137, 176n5

Kordas, Ann 59, 78, 169n2, 169n3, 172n121, 172n122, 173n50, 173n62, 175n50

Laferrière, Dany 90, 91, 175n55, 175n64
Legba (character) 10, 91, 95, 97, 99, 100, 102, 103, 104, 105, 107, 108, 109, 110, 112, 114, 115, 116, 175n43
Legendre, Murder 21, 26, 33, 34, 37, 38, 39, 41, 43, 45, 50, 51, 52, 56, 57, 62, 64, 65, 117, 169n63, 171n107
Leonard, Sheldon 67, 73
liberation 7, 24, 150, 159, 161, 165
liminal 5, 11, 70, 71, 96, 97, 100, 105, 115, 130, 162
loas (*lwas*) 1, 10, 24, 25, 32, 35, 36, 39, 40, 42, 47, 58, 76, 81, 82, 86, 91, 99, 103, 120, 126, 127, 128, 129, 137, 142, 144, 145, 147, 158, 170n76, 171n81
Lugosi, Bela 20, 26, 172n118

MacDonald, J.P. 31, 78
The Magic Island 8, 9, 15, 25, 119
mambo 21, 22, 27, 125, 130, 156
Mammy 173n21
Manatu, Norma 34, 69, 170n55
Martelly, Michel 13, 17, 117, 153, 156
masculine (manhood) 42, 52, 71, 81, 98, 101, 138
matriarch 26, 80, 81
Mbembe, Achille 12, 13, 167n28

Index

McCarthy Brown, Karen 12, 13, 36, 167n27, 170n66, 177n12
McDaniel, Hattie 33
McQueen, Butterfly 33
memory 3, 5, 11, 12, 14, 16, 17, 27, 37, 49, 102, 108, 128, 132, 134, 135, 152, 158, 174n27, 175n51
Métraux, Alfred 7, 13, 29, 167n1, 167n3, 167n20, 169n25
miscegenation 20, 21, 22, 50, 64, 65, 86, 172n10
missionary 26, 34, 55, 56, 57
Mokae, Zakes 135
monster (monstrous) 4, 17, 18, 19, 20, 21, 23, 32, 66, 70, 71, 77, 87, 88, 162, 168n57
mulatto (mixed-race) 17, 19, 20, 21, 22, 35, 43, 50, 51, 64, 65, 66, 67, 68, 69, 70, 71, 72, 73, 77, 80, 83, 84, 85, 88, 89, 90, 98, 129, 139, 147, 153, 160, 161, 162, 174n3
Muse, Clarence 33

The National Geographic 73, 74, 75, 123
native 14, 16, 17, 26, 43, 50, 54, 55, 57, 58, 59, 62, 64, 67, 82, 88, 89, 91, 101, 106, 114, 117, 119, 120, 135, 137, 147, 169n63, 174n11
New Woman 54, 59, 67

occupation: American 8, 9, 15, 16, 25, 30, 31, 37, 44, 55, 64, 74, 76, 78, 79, 80, 101, 106, 110, 111, 120, 124, 142, 143, 144, 163, 165, 171n92, 173n42, 174n8, 176n25, 177n7; MINUSTAH 13, 24, 91, 163
Ogé, Vincent 65
Other 15, 18, 20, 23, 33, 35, 42, 48, 68, 76, 80, 97, 98, 112, 113, 114, 118, 119, 120, 122, 123, 124, 125, 130, 131, 148, 162, 164, 174n11

paradise 31, 46, 48, 66, 73, 80, 82, 86, 87, 89, 92, 96, 98, 103, 104, 109, 115, 116, 117
Paravisini-Gebert, Lizabeth 15, 22, 61, 168n43, 169n65, 172n126
paternalism 8, 16, 17, 74, 80
Péralte, Charlemagne 39, 111
Pétion, Alexander 50, 72
Pierre, André 111
plantation 8, 11, 12, 22, 26, 27, 31, 37, 45, 47, 50, 54, 64, 66, 67, 68, 72, 78, 79, 83, 85, 97, 98, 171n104
Platts, Todd K. 16, 168n44, 168n58, 177n2
La politique de doublure 9, 141, 153, 154, 155, 160
possession 12, 14, 44, 48, 51, 53, 55, 57, 58, 59, 61, 71, 74, 76, 83, 84, 85, 86, 87, 104, 120, 123, 126, 129, 133, 134, 136, 137, 138, 140, 145, 172n18, 177n44
power (disempower) 7, 9, 16, 18, 22, 28, 30, 32, 34, 35, 37, 38, 40, 41, 42, 44, 47, 50, 51, 52, 53, 54, 55, 56, 57, 58, 61, 62, 64, 65, 67, 68, 73, 74, 78, 81, 85, 89, 91, 97, 98, 99, 101, 104, 107, 108, 109, 110, 114, 119, 123, 124, 125, 126, 127, 129, 133, 134, 136, 138, 139, 141, 143, 144, 147, 149, 150, 151, 154, 156, 161, 162, 163, 167n22, 172n129, 175n47
Préval, René 13, 176n83
Price-Mars, Jean 7, 143, 167n2
prostitution 93, 97, 109, 172n122
Protestantism 157, 158, 172n119
puppet 37, 76, 142, 144, 149, 153, 155
purity (impurity) 18, 21, 34, 35, 50, 56, 60, 65, 68, 70, 71

racism 17, 18, 33, 34, 66, 70, 106, 108
Ramsey, Kate 168n49, 170n28, 170n72, 172n120, 173n46, 178n41
Renda, Mary 8, 15, 51, 60, 62, 74, 85, 167n6, 168n49, 171n107, 172n123, 173n33, 173n46, 174n8, 175n79
resistance 7, 17, 31, 37, 44, 79, 83, 110, 133, 140, 143, 149, 159, 161, 163, 164, 177n7
revolution 7, 8, 9, 12, 16, 17, 19, 23, 25, 27, 28, 29, 31, 32, 39, 42, 50, 65, 72, 105, 110, 111, 115, 119, 121, 122, 123, 125, 127, 129, 131, 133, 134, 135, 137, 139, 140, 143, 148, 158, 161, 165, 169n18, 178n40
Rhodes, Gary D. 31, 33, 34, 51, 56, 61, 75, 169n1, 169n3, 170n43, 170n47, 170n49, 170n52, 171n101, 171n108, 171n117, 171n130
Robertson, Pat 122, 123, 176n13
Romero, George 4, 18, 112, 113, 154, 165, 168n53, 175n72

Saint-Domingue 12, 13, 19, 27, 28, 29, 41, 43, 45, 65, 69, 79, 122, 169n9, 169n21, 169n24, 176n25
St. John, Spenser 7, 8, 31, 48, 56, 171n101, 171n116
salt 5, 39, 52, 77, 100, 105, 112, 114, 115, 148, 150, 156, 161, 162, 165, 167n22
Sans Souci 129
satire 24, 113, 141, 145, 172n8
Sau d'Eau 129, 137
Schmidt, Hans 17, 30, 167n3, 168n48, 168n49, 171n92, 173n42
Seabrook, William 8, 10, 15, 16, 25, 31, 40, 48, 57, 68, 119, 132, 147, 163, 169n1, 169n3
Senn, Bryan 40, 41, 47, 67, 121, 171n83, 171n99, 172n11, 173n54, 176n4
serviteur 36, 39, 40, 42, 58, 82
Sheller, Mimi 19, 31, 32, 61, 106, 109, 118, 156, 168n58, 169n62, 169n66, 170n36, 170n37, 170n41, 172n131, 174n9, 175n60, 175n62, 175n66, 175n87, 178n37
silence 10, 22, 58, 80, 90, 95, 97, 102, 104, 105, 110, 111, 148, 149, 155, 161

Index

skin-lightening 72
slave (slavery) 3, 7, 8, 9, 10, 11, 12, 13, 14, 16, 19, 22, 25, 26, 27, 28, 29, 32, 34, 37, 38, 42, 44, 45, 46, 47, 49, 65, 69, 71, 72, 75, 78, 79, 81, 83, 84, 85, 94, 98, 99, 106, 118, 122, 128, 129, 132, 142, 143, 163, 167n5, 169n2, 169n9, 169n16, 169n17, 172n122, 174n26
south (southern) 5, 17, 25, 28, 50, 62, 75, 78, 88, 111, 118, 135, 164, 169n2, 174n3
Spirit (spiritual) 1, 7, 10, 11, 12, 13, 14, 16, 28, 32, 35, 38, 41, 42, 43, 46, 47, 51, 58, 59, 68, 83, 86, 100, 105, 113, 121, 126, 127, 128, 129, 130, 132, 133, 134, 135, 137, 143, 144, 145, 153, 157, 158, 159, 160, 161, 165, 167n2, 167n5, 167n27, 168n49, 170n28, 170n66, 170n72, 172n13, 172n18, 173n46, 178n40, 178n41
Spirits: Baron Samedi 32, 36, 37, 51, 120, 126, 127, 128, 130, 142, 144, 145, 150, 158, 159; Brigitte 156; Carrefour 21, 36, 39, 40, 41, 42, 55, 60, 61, 99, 170n76; Damballah 47, 58, 66, 81, 82, 86; Erzulie 36, 42, 43, 128, 129, 137, 172n18; The Ghedes (Gedes) 120, 127, 128, 130, 144, 145, 146, 147, 153, 158, 160; Legba 36, 39, 99, 100, 103, 105, 170n76, 175n39; Ogou 153, 157, 178n40
Spivak, Gayatri and the subaltern 149, 150
sugar 8, 27, 37, 44, 45, 47, 50, 79, 98, 143, 158

taptap 3, 142, 151, 159, 177n3
Tell My Horse: Voodoo and Life in Haiti and Jamaica (Hurston) 11, 152, 167n21, 168n37
Terwilliger, George 22, 64, 67, 68, 72, 77
Third Cinema 148, 161, 177n24

Tonton Macoute 92, 95, 96, 115, 123, 126, 127, 130, 131, 135, 138, 174n13
tourism 4, 5, 8, 9, 10, 14, 16, 17, 19, 21, 22, 23, 31, 46, 48, 76, 89, 90, 91, 92, 93, 94, 95, 96, 97, 98, 100, 101, 103, 104, 106, 107, 109, 111, 113, 114, 116, 117, 118, 129, 133, 148, 152, 156, 164, 167n14, 168n38, 173n42, 174n9, 174n17, 175n48
Tourneur, Jacques 2, 22, 25, 26, 32, 35, 39, 40, 41, 43, 48, 59
Trouillot, Michel-Rolph 19, 173n49, 177n44, 178n41
Tyson, Cathy 135

Uncle Tom 33

vèvè 40, 171n81
Vials, Chris 4, 15, 16, 17, 20, 23, 43, 68, 83, 122, 147, 168n40, 168n45, 168n59, 169n68, 171n88, 172n15, 173n63, 176n15, 177n19

Walcott, Derek 96, 98, 175n29
Wallace, Michele 20, 33, 168n60, 170n46
wanga (*ouanga*) 66, 67, 76, 77, 79, 81, 82, 85, 86, 87, 172n12
Washington, Fredi 66, 69, 70
Wilson, Woodrow 31
Winfield, Raul 135

Yorùbá 10, 99

zombi astral 11
zombi cadaver 11
zombify 10, 24, 34, 38, 51, 52, 95, 112, 125, 139, 144, 163

www.ingramcontent.com/pod-product-compliance
Ingram Content Group UK Ltd.
Pitfield, Milton Keynes, MK11 3LW, UK
UKHW042012140426
5217IPUK00015B/1122